MITCH WINSTON

KID LIGHTNING AND THE WAVE OF PEACE

(RIGHT BACK)

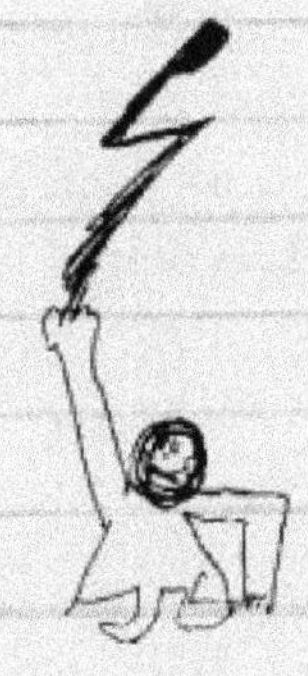

KID LIGHTNING AND THE WAVE OF PEACE

MitchWinston.com

Author can be contacted at:
NaturalSelection33@Yahoo.com

ISBN#: 978-0-578-14321-7

Cover designed by Fredda Jo Malena.
Edited by Steven D. Litvintchouk.

Warning: This work contains adult language and sexual situations and is intended for adults only.

I want to thank my family, friends and all the good people I have met in my life for your support. I also thank everyone who reads this. May you all, for as long as possible, "Stay vertical!" And if you can't, then as my dad told me and showed me in so many ways, "Keep that gleam in your eye."

This book covers my first thirty years alive. It has two aspects.

1. Original, chronological writings, either scanned in directly, or re-typed on a gray background. I deleted certain things and disguised some names and places. I did not change the plot, nor the essence of the content.

2. Present-day narrations. As someone who *has* inhaled, I may have mis-remembered a few things relating to sequence, quantity, size and culpability. Any resemblance to real people, living or dead, is coincidental.

To the unresolved…

Chapter 1

Natural Selection

"A tough little Jew!"

AN INCIDENT on the ice cream line rattled me. The kid ahead of me spilled chocolate syrup on my shirt. I asked him to apologize, but he gave me a bloody nose instead. Then *I* froze up. The pain from the punch didn't last, but the regret that I didn't retaliate did. I soon rose to the top-ten-percent in strength and toughness at my all-Jewish summer camp, but this reputation did not follow me back to sixth grade, where a real world top-ten-percenter had been targeting me all week. I had to stand up to him, or he wouldn't stop. I shadowboxed in front of my bathroom mirror Thursday night to prepare for the battle.

On Friday afternoon, I was kneeling by my locker when he kicked my books, scattering them. I popped up and punched him in the face, and then the stomach. This stunned him for a few seconds—but I had no more moves planned. The (now smiling) top-ten-percenter rained punches to my face and head. I could only attempt to hold down his arms and plead for mercy, "It's over, it's over, stop! Please stop!" Luckily, a teacher intervened and rescued me. The top-ten-percenter never bothered me again.

Age fourteen, Middle School newspaper

Our reporters interviewed Mitchell Winston, the recently-elected President of the H.C. Crittenden Student Council. Here is a summary of his response:

Q: Why did you run for President?

A: I ran because I saw a lot of things the school needed, and I thought I could get them.

Q: Do you like being President?

A: Yes, because I know what's going on and I, myself, can try to change things.

Q: Before the election, did you think you would win?

A: I had good competition, but I had a feeling I would win.

Q: Out of all the other people who ran, would you say you were the best; and if so, why?

A: Yes, otherwise, I would not have run at all.

My confidence in this interview was inspired by my new hero, lead singer Eddie Wilson, from the movie I had just seen, *Eddie and the Cruisers*. Eddie had said, "If you can't be great, then there's no reason to ever play music again." My dad also told me to try to be great and keep "that gleam" in my eye. I didn't know I had "that gleam," but if I did, I got it from him. He was the most enthusiastic and witty person I ever knew, eager to expose my sister and me to things he enjoyed, like his favorite sports teams, old records, black and white movies, and wheat pennies. One morning, he dragged me out of bed at 4 a.m. and drove me to a nearby beach to see Halley's Comet, visible to the naked eye once every 75 years. He said this would be "our only chance to see it together." We thought we saw it, and then went to the diner for fried egg sandwiches, *his* dad's favorite.

Around this time I became consumed with the idea of seeing a real dead body. When an acquaintance of my dad's passed away, I accompanied him to the viewing. We approached the casket, and the man looked at peace—*I* was quite the opposite. Panic set in while I tried to hold back nervous laughter, a growing concern for me those days. I needed to exit the situation, fast. On our way out, the deceased's daughter was greeting people at the door. Instead of telling her what my dad had coached me to say—"I'm so sorry for your loss"—I said, "Congratulations!" The girl looked through me deadpan, didn't answer, and I scurried to my dad's car in agony. (I must have confused the moment with a Bar Mitzvah receiving line.) This mistake haunted me for more than a year, until I allowed my father to convince me that the girl was in a daze and hadn't registered what I said. That moment became a staple on my dad's list of "Funniest Winston Moments," which he shared often, for years to come.

"Behind the Antlers," Freshman year, Byram Hills High School newspaper

In your last issue of The Oracle, an article, "Behind the Bow," was written about sport hunting. Even though the author did not take a definite position for/against this very debatable topic, I found it hard not to recognize how glorious the hunt was depicted to be. When survival is not the matter, killing cannot be justified…

The main argument used by the hunter is that the overpopulation of deer justifies hunting, a practice which will "even out the population." A man by the name of Charles Darwin suggested the theory of natural selection, that is, the "survival of the fittest." A bullet or an arrow by no means decides if the animal is fit to survive in the population, as the most-fit animal may be killed while the weakest may be left alive. In addition, if overpopulation justifies killing, then I can easily point out a severe contradiction involving the human race: because there is an overpopulation of people, which causes starvation in India, Africa, Asia, and North and South America, should we kill the "extra" people to solve this problem?

Hunting is by no means glorious. In the future, when confronted by the ever-present debate on hunting, do not sympathize with the men "behind the bow," but think of the defenseless creatures "behind the antlers."

There was a new kid in my high school, Josh Metternich, with Tom Cruise looks and his *Top Gun* brashness. He was getting close to my long-standing friends, including Tommy Shenhipper and Jeff Culhaney, whom I had known since elementary school. (Maybe I was a bit territorial.) Josh, sitting at the desk behind me in European History class, was blowing paper dots, the kind that come from hole-punchers, into my hair. I turned around and said, "Josh, stop." He did it again and again, while he and Tommy giggled. I turned around again and said, "Seriously Josh, stop, or I'm gonna do something." A minute later, of course, he did it again, and I jumped out of my chair like a crazy person, wheeled around and yelled at him, "WHAT THE FUCK ARE YOU DOING?!" The class went silent, everyone staring at us. We were kicked out of class and told to wait in the teacher's office. While we were waiting, Josh apologized to me. And when the teacher arrived, he took full responsibility again. As often happens after fights, we became best friends.

Some months later, we were hanging out at Josh's house with two girls. Josh was inside with one, and I was by the pool kissing the other. I was getting hit by tiny pebbles, of origins unknown, and faint laughter emanated from behind the bushes. This time, the mischievous perpetrator was Andy Metternich, Josh's younger brother by two years. If Josh was Tom Cruise from *Top Gun*, then Andy was Matt Dillon from *The Outsiders*. We became best friends too. My friendship with each Metternich was spawned by unrelated, unauthorized incidents of spherical objects catapulted my way. I was closer with each than they were with each other. They often quarreled, and I played the role of the perfect buffer.

Around the time we became friends, Josh and Andy's father took the wrong path and made some bad mistakes. The casualty of his behavior was the Metternich family structure, including divorce and loss of assets. The successful business that had been started by Josh and Andy's grandfather and its valuable building in Manhattan would have been theirs someday. Now both were gone. Rumors of the Metternich family's dynastic rise and fall permeated Armonk, New York, a small town, and each Metternich boy suffered in his own way, each in his own heart. But while different in personality, the two brothers shared a unique charm. Perhaps it was "the gleam" that my dad talked about. I sometimes felt guilty around Josh that my dad was so amazing. Other times I felt like a father figure to Andy.

I had a nightmare during my junior year of high school: While peeing in the urinal of the school bathroom, I was picked up from behind and dragged into the hallway, my pants down in front of everybody, including my childhood crushes Lauren Bernstein and Sarah Kipnes. I froze up (again) and did not retaliate. The guy who grabbed me was the great Matt Muller, the Hero of Byram Hills, the toughest guy in the school and Armonk's best athlete in years. (And when I woke up there was pee in my garbage can.) Josh found the dream hilarious, but it shook me up. It sent me back into training camp, shadowboxing in front of my bathroom mirror. I was fantasizing about incidents in which I would be wronged—and *would* fight back.

My real opportunity came soon: At a party one night, a large, drunk, and misinformed football player was bothering Jeff Culhaney. The football player insisted, with growing intensity, that Jeff apologize to a certain scorned damsel who was crying nearby. Her tears had nothing to do with the football player, so I asked him, "Please leave my friend alone." He asked me if I always "handled my friend's business," and I replied, "Yeah, I actually do." He pushed me backward, with force, onto the car I was leaning against.

I rebounded off the car and threw a straight right to his face, exactly as rehearsed, which knocked him down, cut his lips, bloodied his nose, and gave him two instant black eyes. He was unable to fight more, but kept screaming—like in the movie *My Bodyguard*—"YOU BROKE MY NOSE! YOU BROKE MY NOSE! I'M GONNA FUCKING KILL YOU!! ARE YOU FUCKING CRAZY?" More large, drunk and misinformed football players rushed to the scene, ready to fight, including Matt Muller and the real-world top-ten-percenter. A chaotic skirmish ensued, but various cross-alliances prevented things from escalating. I looked down at my hands—my knuckles were covered in blood, each finger cut when they hit my victim's teeth. I felt like Rocky Balboa after the famous meat punching scene.

My "victim" that night was not a bad guy. He was only bad that night, in both disposition and fighting ability, an early testament to the power of alcohol. He called me at home the next day and apologized. He admitted that I "got the better of" him and said our conflict was 100% over. I apologized too and felt strong guilt for hitting him. This gesture gave me instant respect for him, and also relief, since he had a lot of devoted football teammates, who would have loved to get even. A few days later, I was walking to my car after soccer practice, and Stratigakis approached me. He was the *biggest* guy in the school, and also a football player. My conflict with his teammate was resolved, but I wondered if Stratigakis didn't get the message, or didn't care, and was coming to destroy me. I knew my one-punch strategy would not work on this giant. He grabbed both my shoulders and shook me—I remembered how it felt to freeze up with fear. But then he let go, smiled, and bellowed with respect, "You're one tough little Jew!" I was reminded of this moment years later, sadly, when I learned that Stratigakis had died as a young man.

"Presidential Views," Senior Year, Byram Hills High School Newspaper

...We have ordered one-liter plastic Bobcat drinking cups, Bobcat locker mirrors, and Bobcat kazoos. Hopefully, when these arrive, people will become more aware that we are not only students but also members of a club that is capable of having fun. That may sound *Brady Bunch*-ish, but it is really true. At the upcoming student council meeting, dress-up days will be planned as well as other school spirit raising events. With homecoming approaching and most teams off to a good start, hopefully sports will be another instrument to raise spirit.

I hope you have been well informed of what is going on. Please speak to me if you have any ideas, criticisms, or compliments. Student council is a representative of the majority of the students in our school. Apathy is our worst enemy. Indifferent people are our biggest weakness. Hopefully, with that in mind, we can all have a successful year.

Mitchell Winston, President

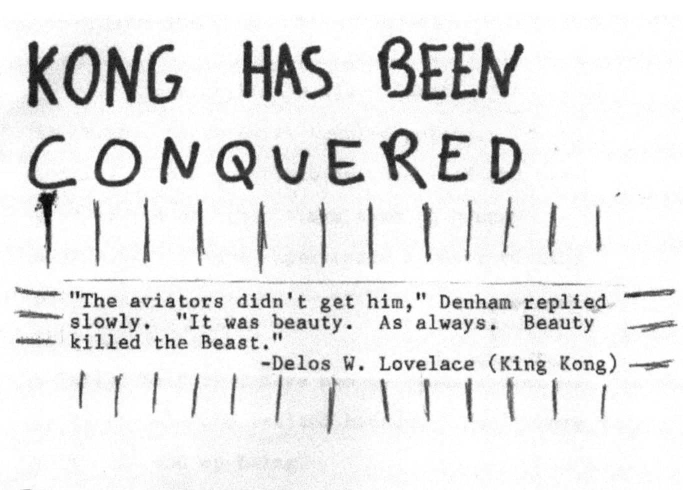

"Turning Points," Senior Year, Mr. Pryor's English Class

...I still talk to her on the phone every night, but I know for a fact she has no interest in me. I've tried giving up on our friendship to alleviate some of the pain I feel around her, but that makes me feel even more lonely. She treats me like crap sometimes, but I can't get mad at her. I see her walking in the halls and she is the most beautiful thing I have ever seen.

I am not the joker I have always been. I am much more serious and set back. I am honestly making attempts to change back to my old self. Maybe I am attempting to reverse the irreversible.

It is often that I fall into a daydream and think about the distant future. I wonder where I'll be in 15 years, who I'll be with, and if I'll be enjoying my life. I like to think that my wife will be beautiful, we'll live a comfortable life, and have a great family. Of course, Sarah somehow ends up in my dream. Will I know her then? Will she still make me miserable? Sadly, with all that I have just explained, I honestly hope she will.

Sarah's brother was the one who wrote "Behind the Bow," but he and I got along. I also got along with her artistic parents, who exposed me to some great Bob Dylan songs, like "Quinn the Eskimo," and of course "Sarah"—the only one in the family I couldn't conquer. My dad appreciated my *King Kong* analogy, "Beauty killed the beast... I am Kong" He enjoyed good analogies.

Chapter 2

Pulling a Vickers

"Let's Go!"

IN MY FIRST TWO YEARS playing high school soccer, I broke my nose twice, requiring surgery both times. After the second surgery, a hole appeared in my septum which caused me to snore, and a bump formed on the ridge of my nose. The doctor said that he could take some extra ear cartilage and fill the hole in my nose, and while he was at it get rid of the bump. I didn't know I had "extra" ear cartilage, but it seemed like a good idea. He got rid of the bump, but the ear cartilage exited my nose after my first sneeze. My dad lamented that I would never be able to "smell how things sounded," or "hear how they smelled."

I didn't want to break my nose again. I still played soccer, but not with "reckless abandon," which is how my dad described my formerly aggressive style. I tried to avoid collisions with man and ball, and I would subtly allow my hard-headed co-defensemen Blaney and Henderson to field pop-ups and 50-50 balls. But as the left fullback, I never lost focus on my defensive assignment, our opponent's right wing, usually their fastest guy. In three seasons of varsity soccer, I never let anyone score on me, and I achieved Westchester County honors and the co-captainship. Still, I knew my dad was right: I would have been a much better player if I had retained my reckless abandon. Regardless, my dad came to every game and videotaped each one, focusing on me. I edited my best moments into a personal highlight reel, "Eye of the Tiger" playing in the background as I graced the field with a white turtleneck under my soccer jersey.

My heart was set on going to an Ivy League college, so I applied to all eight. I sent my soccer highlight reel to each school's coach. I was least interested in the University of Pennsylvania, but after I received rejections from the other seven, UPenn shot to the top of my list. The UPenn soccer coach had given me a "starred application," which went into a different selection pile than those given to the general public and probably helped get me in. I thought I had a good chance to make the team. The coach told me to come to school a week early, ready to play, and recommended that I jump rope fifteen minutes a day all summer. He said that most freshmen came to college out of shape, and jumping rope would give me an advantage.

I did not jump rope once. My dad thought this was from laziness; I tried to explain that I "just couldn't get started." He reminded me that I had received the same advice a few years earlier from my private *tennis* coach and had ignored it too. She had said jumping rope daily would improve my footwork, which was what I was missing to develop into a Division I college player. I never rose above the third singles rank on my high school tennis team, while a harder working, less talented athlete (at least in my mind) achieved the number one singles ranking and became a Division I player.

I arrived at UPenn a week early, subtly out of shape, but I held my own in defensive drills with the varsity players, focusing on my defensive assignment and never letting him score. On the day of formal tryouts, many unrecruited freshmen showed up for the first time. The coach divided everyone into two teams, the current varsity and his heaviest recruits against his apparent *mild interests*. To my surprise, I was placed with the mild interests, and the two sides were pitted in a competitive scrimmage. After twenty minutes, the coach stopped the game, called my team over, thanked us for coming and sent us home. My fifteen-year soccer career had ended abruptly, and I was upset as I left the field. Two other mild interests introduced themselves as Jeremy Cage and Lee Deerman. They were from California—friendly, laid-back and jovial—and they didn't take the news as harshly. We walked back to the dorms together.

During my ill-fated soccer week, I had missed some crucial freshman social opportunities, and I felt lonely. I decided to pledge a Jewish fraternity, one that had a reputation for being cool. I assumed they would pick me, based on my usual top ten percent stature in all-Jewish circles. On selection night they were supposed to come knocking on my door to deliver my bid and take me to a party to meet the brothers and new pledges. I lay in my bed awake all night. I heard knocking down the hall, more than once, but it never reached my door. I was rejected by a *Jewish* fraternity for not being cool enough! (I presumed that they thought, based on my words, that I would make the soccer team; and when I didn't, my stock plummeted.)

As a safety measure, I had also attended a recruiting event for another Jewish fraternity, AEPi, with a reputation for being uncool, but whose brothers were more friendly and welcoming. They had a group of five relatively cool upperclassmen, whom I dubbed "The Elderly Five," who were passionate about turning around AEPi's reputation. They didn't care that I didn't make the soccer team; they were glad to have someone cool enough to try out! They said that if I accepted their offer to pledge AEPi, they *really would* come knocking that night. I didn't have to lie in bed for long. When we got to the AEPi house, everyone was celebrating, but I was skeptical, trying to size up the coolness in the room. Then I saw Jeremy Cage and Lee Deerman! They had decided to join AEPi too, which sealed the deal for me.

Like The Elderly Five before us, my pledge class also cared about becoming a cool fraternity and turning around our reputation. But AEPi's uncool had staying power, and our intentions were mocked and doubted by the other Jewish fraternities. Then Sammy Vickers came knocking on *our* front door: He was a real-world-tough Jewish guy, built like Mike Tyson, and the former backup quarterback at the University of Pittsburgh. He was also an AEPi brother at Pittsburgh, and had just transferred to UPenn. Since he didn't know anyone at UPenn, his first stop had been our fraternity house. (We knew he would never have chosen AEPi if he had started at UPenn, but we didn't care, and never let him leave.) At inter-fraternity competitions and parties, when scuffles and near-fights would occur, Sammy Vickers never backed down to anyone. Then he chose the hottest girl at UPenn and made her his girl. His swagger gave us the edge we needed to hold our ground against the other fraternities in toughness *and* coolness.

When we competed against the other fraternities in football, Vickers' role as quarterback provided another shot of coolness. With a flick of the wrist, he zipped rifle-like passes forty yards downfield, one after the other, into our hands—throws so perfect we were *forced* to hold on—and we were beating the cooler fraternities. When things got chippy on the field, Vickers' modus operandi was to confront the enemy head-on and ask if there was a problem. His question was usually (wisely) answered with a no, and peace would prevail. He had credibility, an obvious willingness to fight, which caused most violence to be avoided. I called this method, "Pulling a Vickers." And I applied it myself more than once, re-cementing *my own* top ten percent reputation for coolness and toughness—in Jewish circles only.

Josh Metternich was attending New York University, and I told him about our new hero. He asked me who would win in a fight, Sammy Vickers or the great Matt Muller. I envisioned this hypothetical clash of the titans, an epic war I would have paid to see, and predicted Muller as the would-be victor in a close battle. It was difficult to picture Muller falling to anyone—but I couldn't say for sure—a testament to Sammy Vickers' toughness and credibility in *all* circles.

I shared a special bond with Jeremy Cage and Lee Deerman. The three of us became best of friends. I think they had "the gleam" too. Jeremy, stocky and pigeon toed with short curly hair, had a somewhat sheltered viewpoint on life, labeling certain "non-Penn" people as *random*, but his naïveté was combined with a great deal of likability and charm. When he was upset that his bedroom ceiling was too low, someone convinced him to go to the hardware store and get a "ceiling jack" to raise it, and he was out the door to get it—until I stopped him. On another occasion, after drinking too much and panicking that he was going to die, Lee and I took him to the Emergency Room. Jeremy promised the doctor that his parents were rich, and if he saved him, he would "help him out in the future." Lee Deerman was tall and thin, with longish wavy hair, athletic and full of energy. He never sat down during UPenn football games, urging others to follow suit. He received care packages from his parents every week, filled with food and funny clothes—even full outfits—including a green corduroy suit and five of the same Hawaiian shirts in five different color schemes. All three of us had great relationships with our parents. Our fathers were each of our best friends.

Lee and Jeremy often joked about my impulsivity, how quickly I would succumb to temptation and change my mind, like falling in love with a different girl every day, or ordering ridiculous products from television infomercials. Late one night, a Red Lobster commercial featured an endless shrimp platter next to a basket of buttery biscuits. Five minutes later the three of us were driving through the mean streets of Philly to the only Red Lobster in town. It didn't matter that we had a midterm paper due at 10 a.m. the next day, assigned to us a month in advance, which none of us had started. When we got assignments such as these, Lee would generally hole up in his room all afternoon the day before it was due, and finish late that night. Jeremy was a worse procrastinator, and would start that night, finishing around 4 a.m. But I still "couldn't get started"—I would set my alarm for 5 a.m. the next day and pop out of bed, full of adrenaline, intending to start and finish before class. And when things went wrong with our *best laid* plans, we were masters at great excuses with passionate deliveries.

I was a freshman when the New York Giants made the Super Bowl. On Super Bowl Sunday, I was planning to drive from Philadelphia to Armonk to watch the game with my dad. Watching the Giants together was our most sacred father-and-son ritual, and to miss watching the Super Bowl with him was inconceivable. My car was being repaired that week, scheduled for completion on Sunday morning when I would pick it up and drive to Armonk. When I got to the gas station, the mechanic told me the car would not be ready until Monday. So I decided to stay in Philadelphia for the Super Bowl. When I called my dad to tell him, he said he "knew" I was kidding and was looking out the window to see if I was already in the driveway. But I wasn't there, and wouldn't be. He said he understood, and to enjoy the game; but sounded deflated and sad.

About four hours before kickoff, I envisioned my dad, alone, watching our New York Giants in the Super Bowl. I must have showed a somber countenance because Lee Deerman asked me what was wrong. After I explained, he said two words: "LET'S GO!" And our journey began: We jogged fifteen blocks to the Philadelphia Amtrak station on 30th and Market, me laboring, out of breath, The Deerman running gracefully, his feet silent as they hit the pavement. When we arrived at the station, we learned that the only feasible train to New York was *Reservations Only* and *Sold Out*. We wandered to the platform anyway, where the ticket-taker left his post and entered the train a few minutes before departure. We snuck on behind him and headed for the bathroom, where we remained for the entire ride, playing chess on a travel board that Lee had grabbed on his way out the door. As the train headed to New York City, various passengers in search of relief knocked on the bathroom door. Lee and I took turns answering, sounding as sick and nauseous as possible: "Sorry sir, I'm so sorry. I'm feeling very sick. Can you please use the restroom in the next car?"

Our train arrived at New York City's Penn Station with the Super Bowl starting in an hour, and I called our ride, Melissa G., to provide our travel update. We had one more train to catch, which left from Grand Central Station. We sprinted the mile across Manhattan—but missed the perfect train by two minutes. The next was a full hour away. We accepted our fate that we would miss the first half of the game and trudged to the platform to rest our legs and kill the hour. To make things worse, the train that we missed was still visible, teasing us as it rolled toward the dark tunnel that exits Grand Central Station. It paused at the end of the platform, presumably held for a minute to let another train exit first. Without words, The Deerman sprang up and dashed down the platform toward the train. I followed. We reached the last car and pried open the sliding door, squeezing ourselves on, in plain view of its surprised human cargo. We headed for the bathroom, stowaways again, and played another game of chess to pass the 33 minute ride. We arrived at the North White Plains train station, 20 minutes before kickoff—and only a 14 minute drive to Armonk.

Melissa G., a devoted friend who still attended Byram Hills, was waiting for us at North White Plains. In the past, she had showered me with gifts and affection, including huge pizza-sized chocolate chip cookies and the *Eddie and the Cruisers* soundtrack on cassette, so I didn't doubt she would be there waiting. She drove The Deerman and me to Armonk and dropped us off at the end of my parents' driveway. We snuck to the front door and rang the bell. My dad answered, his expression changing from confusion to shock to pure joy. I will never forget that look. Lee and I were in exactly the right place at exactly the right time.

During halftime of the Super Bowl, my dad played some of his old records for Lee. One was "The Crepitation Contest," the epic clash in flatulence between Paul Boomer and Lord Windesmear. (Boomer won by forfeiture when Lord Windesmear defecated on his final push.) Then my dad played us a song called "I'm My Own Grandpa," in which the singer proves through an unlikely sequence of marriages, divorces, and births that he has actually become his own grandfather! Lee loved the song, so my dad handwrote the lyrics, and soon we were singing it together: "Now many, many years ago when I was twenty-three, I was married to a widow who was pretty as can be. The widow had a grown-up daughter who had hair of red; my father fell in love with her and soon the two were wed…"

The football game was tightly contested, and tense for my dad, but Lee stayed calm. He asserted that the Giants victory was "preordained" when we gallantly embarked from Philadelphia. I believed him, but my dad wasn't convinced, and we re-focused on The Super Bowl for the second half. On the last play of the game, with the Giants leading by one point, the Buffalo Bills lined up for an all-or-nothing field goal attempt. *After* the kick sailed wide right, my dad bought into Lee's preordainment idea, and we celebrated together.

A year later, back at UPenn, Lee got sick with mononucleosis, which led to pneumonia. Jeremy and I took him to the hospital, where he stayed for a week, and then a second one. His swollen head looked twice its normal size. Lee's parents had already flown in, and the doctor said he would probably have to return to California with them and skip the rest of the semester to recover. My parents drove from Armonk to visit Lee in the hospital too, where he was constantly sleeping. At Lee's bedside, my dad continued their sacred song, "This made my dad my son-in-law, and changed my very life. My daughter was my mother 'cause she was my father's wife…" As my dad sang "I'm My Own Grandpa," which he somehow knew by heart, Lee perked up like a symphony conductor—albeit a drunken one—and moved his right hand and huge head to the beat. He made a strong recovery and did not miss the semester.

March 1992, Management 111 Midterm Exam, last page

ADVICE IN SHORT;
EXPORT TO BRAZIL
EXPAND TO GERMANY
STAY OUT OF INDONESIA.

✓ 7/10

Prof. Surie,
I am sorry I was late to the exam. I tried to be very brief in my answers. Sorry so sloppy as I had to constantly rush to make up for the last 10 minutes-[illegible]

September 1992, Business Management Paper (excerpts)

Taking Candy from a Baby (A Start-up in three acts)

ACT 1: My father, whose business is in the shopping center industry, informed me of a vacant store in a mall close to my hometown. While personally surveying the sight, I noticed its central location and existing cabinetry. I decided that a candy store would be the perfect fit. After negotiating with the mall manager a reduced rent plan, a lease was drawn up. After signing my name to it, The Candy Man was born. In retrospect, this lease signing symbolized the effectual end of the entrepreneurial side of this venture. I now had to build up and run a business, which of course requires a manager.

My initial lack of business experience led me to believe that I would be able to both maintain my full-time internship in New York City at Madison Square Garden Boxing, and run this "low maintenance" business at the same time in a successful manner.

ACT 2: How wrong I was! Countless calls from the mall manager to my office in the city informed me that the store was not open until hours after it was supposed to be. Not only were my employees late, but they also helped themselves to heaping portions of candy each time they would leave the store at night. (The employees were allowed to eat all the candy they wanted for free during their shifts, but had to pay for whatever they took home.) And their cash registers always had less money than actual sales.

The one exception was when my sister Fredda worked. At the end of her shifts the cash register always contained *more* money than sales, which was puzzling until I solved the mystery: She put money in the register every time she ate a piece of candy—even during her shifts—which added up. She felt too guilty to take even one morsel for free. My dad joked that she was not only our best employee, but also our best customer!

ACT 3: As the summer progressed, I became wiser. I called in an experienced management consultant to help me solve my woes: My father. Together we turned the existing mess into a successful business. We had an employee meeting. Late employees were docked pay. The "Winston Profit Incentive Plan" was instituted, allowing workers to make extra money if sales were up. Mall security guards were instructed to keep a watchful eye on employees. We switched to a cheaper candy company and adjusted prices according to sales volume. In short, the help of my father, an experienced manager, completely turned around the business. Profits were realized for the first time. The business was now a smooth running machine. When the summer was over, we sold the business for $16,000, five times my initial investment.

After paying us half, our buyer was diagnosed with cancer, and he and his wife asked for more time to pay their balance. My dad pointed out that we had already made a profit *and* learned a lot, which was *Dayenu*—sufficient for us—taken from his favorite Hebrew Passover song. He suggested we forgive the rest of their debt and grant the stricken couple title to the business, which I grudgingly agreed to.

Daily Pennsylvanian, University of Pennsylvania

I am delighted to have been elected the next President of the UA (Undergraduate Assembly, or Student Government). I am certain that the choice of the UA members will prove to be a wise one. As I look down the list of all the new UA members, I see one common bond. We are all eager to pursue the paramount goal of the Penn Student government: To directly benefit the lives of the student body at Penn.

Students care about sleeping – we should improve dormitories. Students care about eating – we should improve dining service. Students care about social events, going out at night – we should improve non-Greek social events. Students care about not getting killed – we should improve security. These are basic issues that if we can affect and make a little bit better then students will be directly benefited.

All Undergraduate Assembly meetings are open to the public and we encourage a wide participation from all interested students. Remember, apathy is our worst enemy. Let's begin the fight today and prove that the UA surely did not "meet its downfall on 2:00 PM Sunday afternoon," as stated by our outgoing chairperson, but instead has begun its ascent.

Mitchell Winston, President

Written one year after college graduation

I wanted to write down some of the scams I have pulled in my life, because there have been quite a few. I guess most of them started in college. First of all, I was a horrible student. I never came to class, and when I did, I was always at least 15 minutes late for a one-hour class. I once lied to my Management professor when he asked why I always showed up late. I told him I was a very serious golfer, and I met with my pro each morning for 9 holes, and that I did my best to get to class on time. He totally believed me, or at least respected my attempt at a great story.

I almost failed Accounting 1, and I ended up with a D. I hated that bitchy professor, and I hated Accounting. I remember going in to ask if I could somehow get my grade up to a C. She said, "I can offer to re-grade your final, but you were eight points away from an F. If I find more mistakes, you risk an F." I told her I would keep the D, and then asked for a D+. She said those don't exist.

I remember a statistics project. It was due the next day, and my partner and I hadn't started. So we made up this experiment how we had our friends play pinball sober, and again after a few beers, predicting and demonstrating how their scores would go down. It was a joke, but we got an A. I then used the same fake experiment for my next two statistics classes, and got B's, with glee. What a joke.

I also had my Legal Studies episode, when I stayed up all night for the first time in my life, and after drinking ten cups of coffee and taking No-Doze pills, I went to the final, shaking, and could not even read or write one letter. I ended up falling asleep, and getting an F on the final. When I showed up in the professor's office to see if I could catch a break, he told me that I had received the fourth lowest grade in the class on the final, so he could not help me. I remember saying, "I slept through the test!! Who did I beat?"

> Toby Tyler and I were always trying to transfer from UPenn into Wharton, and each semester we were being rejected for low grades, and getting letters from Wharton saying we probably would never be admitted, and urging us to pursue a major at UPenn's College of Arts & Sciences...

If we weren't admitted to Wharton, every Wharton class we took would be considered an elective. By ignoring these warnings and continuing to take only Wharton classes, Toby Tyler and I risked requiring two extra years of college to graduate. My parents, who were paying for my college education, did not know the extent of my risk and its potential financial ramifications. I continued my feverish lobbying of the Wharton admissions advisor, reiterating how bad it would look if the Student Government President needed six years to graduate from a four-year school! He urged me to do whatever it took to achieve a 3.4 GPA in my junior year, or I would never be accepted into Wharton, and there was nothing more he could do for me. Faced with this all-or-nothing crisis, I had no problem "getting started" early and studying hard—for the first time in my life.

> ...The first semester of junior year I got 2 A's, a B, and a D in finance. My finance professor informed me, in a thick German accent, that he would not raise my grade, even after I begged him in his office for two hours. My entire chance of getting into Wharton was about to be over. But I wouldn't leave his office, and he allowed me to change my D to a W, for *Withdraw*. I ended up getting 2 A's and a B (and a W that didn't count)—a 3.7 GPA for that semester, and a 3.1 second semester. This was the 3.4 I needed to slip into Wharton. (Toby Tyler got in too.) I am sure I probably have the lowest GPA of any Wharton transfer ever.

Upon graduation, my preference was to enter the field of management consulting, but I had been rejected by every consulting firm that came to the Wharton campus. The feedback I received was that my grades were not good enough to warrant an interview or that I "rambled on" during the few I had. Nearly everyone at Wharton had their jobs lined up by December of their senior year, but it was late March, with graduation two months away, and I had nothing. The only offer I had received by then was from a pest control company, Terminix, in their management training department. The job seemed decent and a good way to gain corporate experience—until I learned I would have to start in the field, killing cockroaches and rodents at various locations. I knew this wasn't for me, but I had no other leads, and requested more time to consider their offer.

The last management consulting firm scheduled to come to Wharton's campus was Theodore Barry & Associates (TB&A), a firm with a good reputation, based in Manhattan's Rockefeller Plaza. I knew little about TB&A, only their name and prestigious location, but they were my last option. I sent them my letter and resume in advance, according to protocol, but was not granted an interview. So I resubmitted my materials, along with a passionate letter, asking them to "re-review your prior rejection." They granted my request to reconsider—and rejected me again. For my final attempt, I "bid my points," proverbial job search currency given to each Wharton student to demonstrate the candidate's level of interest in a particular company compared to other Wharton students. The top five bidders of points were granted the last five interviews, and I was number five. But it got me into the room, where I beheld Brian Levitt, the messiah of my job hunt, *sent* to Wharton by TB&A to conduct their first round interviews.

Brian was an analyst at TB&A—and an AEPi brother at UPenn—two years older than me. In my interview, we discussed AEPi, not TB&A. (This was fortuitous, because notwithstanding my all-out crusade to *get* the interview, I knew nothing about the company.) Brian was part of AEPi's "Old Guard," the predecessors of

The Elderly Five. He lamented that the friendly, welcoming vibe he once loved about AEPi had vanished in the cool revolution. He said the new brothers were rude and dismissive toward him, and I was one of only a few who treated him with respect and encouraged his continued involvement. He had the power to slip me into the second round of TB&A's interviews, and said this was my payback; but that was all he could do. He also advised me to research the company, because it was obvious to him I had not done so.

I was invited to Rockefeller Plaza the next week for a full day of interviews with TB&A's associates, directors, and partners. I did my research in advance and was armed with smart questions about management consulting for the utility industry. In all seven meetings, I looked my interviewer in the eye and said, "I have never wanted to work for a company as much as I do for Theodore Barry & Associates. If you pick me, I will not let you down." They offered me the job that night.

New York City called.

Chapter 3

Upper West Hostilities for Midwest Utilities

"Great-times-Great!"

I NEEDED AN APARTMENT in Manhattan and a roommate. I decided to room with Toby Tyler. I had been close to Toby during my first two years of college, bonded by our love for the New York Knicks and our desire to transfer into Wharton. (The latter proved more successful.) Back in school, I was intrigued by Toby's quirkiness and bluntness. He viewed touching himself as a homosexual act, since he was a guy, so he masturbated by "bed-fucking"—the friction between he and his mattress providing the Immaculate Conception he desired. Toby didn't like Jeremy Cage, and was vocal about his distaste, which caused some divergence between us. After the emergence of Sammy Vickers, Toby Tyler became his devoted henchman, and we grew apart further. But we were still friends, with jobs in Manhattan, so rooming together was convenient.

We found a nice apartment in a doorman building on 70th and Broadway for $1,450 per month. It had only one bedroom, but we planned to build a wall in the living room to create a second bedroom, a common practice for cash-strapped newcomers to Manhattan. After graduation, I went on a trip to Europe with

Jeremy and Lee. Toby took occupancy of the apartment two weeks before me and supervised the building of the wall. By the time my parents drove me to the city to see the apartment and help me move in, Toby had already occupied the master bedroom. It was twice the size of the newly carved out bedroom, designated for me, whose dimensions Toby had determined when he supervised the wall's construction. Its tininess was disappointing, but I expected a substantial rental discount to ease the pain. Unfortunately, Toby had also *determined* the rental split: 50-50. It wasn't fair. My dad (privately) suggested proposing to Toby that *he* could decide the rental split if *I* could pick the bedroom, or vice versa. Toby wouldn't budge on either. His counteroffer was for me to walk away from the apartment. He was *Pulling a Vickers* by showing a credible willingness to find a new roommate—whom I suspected, ironically, *was* Sammy Vickers! With work starting in a few days, I needed that apartment, so I backed down and accepted his terms. I lost a lot of respect for Toby Tyler from this incident and it never came back.

At Lehigh University for her senior year, my ex-girlfriend Lorena had purchased a newborn Pomeranian named Rex, a few weeks too early in his development—before the breeder should have permitted the adoption. Then one of Lorena's friends dropped Rex, who injured his front right paw and had a seizure. Lorena brought him to the vet, who kept him overnight for tests and observation. The next day, the vet said that Rex was doing better. His leg was not broken, and the seizures were from the fall and would probably not recur. He said she should come pay the $400 bill and pick him up. Lorena first asked the girl who dropped Rex to pay, who refused, claiming she didn't have the money. Instead of finding a way to get the money, Lorena made the cold decision to abandon Rex at the vet's office, using the "potential for recurring seizures" as her excuse for not being a fit owner. She had the ability to turn her emotions on and off like a water faucet, and

Rex's water had stopped flowing. I called the vet's office and asked what they would do with Rex if nobody came for him, and his assistant told me the dog would be put to sleep.

I was in upstate New York on assignment for TB&A. I couldn't believe that Lorena and her friend would abandon Rex. On Friday after work, I drove four hours—from Binghamton, NY to Bethlehem, PA—to pay the vet bill and bail out Rex, and then two hours to my apartment in Manhattan, with little Rex next to me. His life was now in *my* hands. Toby Tyler was not thrilled with our visitor, but Rex's cuteness won him a one-week respite in our apartment until I was scheduled to go back on the road. I sectioned off a small area in our large living room (from which the carving out of my bedroom had barely made a dent), where Rex slowly got stronger. He still limped, but less pronounced. And each time he had to do his business, he dragged himself to the same corner of his little area. I think Rex thought it was his job to keep his space tidy, since he was too weak to go downstairs for real walks. I was sad I couldn't keep him, but I was always on the road and Toby would not have tolerated this. My mom, a dog lover who had been Lorena's biggest fan (until this), considered keeping Rex too. But she already had all the dog she could handle in Frosty, her feisty (and carnivorous) American Eskimo.

When the week ended and no solution presented itself, my sister's friend Rob took Rex to his small Greenwich Village studio apartment to buy time, even though pets were not allowed and he would quickly get caught. Rob and his girlfriend had a love for animals that obliged them to help, as did my mom, who made it her mission to find Rex a permanent home. And she soon did, in a household with five (hopefully) sure-handed kids. A fortunate by-product of this incident was my friendship with Rob. To me, he was "Mr. Greenwich Village," open-minded, cultured and worldly, in love with Paris, and passionate about art and literature. I remember how un-cultured I felt around him. My dad had tried to expose me to classical music, paintings and the opera, which I sometimes resisted and other times enjoyed, but never retained.

Rob and I shared a love for Fredda, my sister. She had recently begun dating a guy named Wendell, whom Rob and I suspected was using zombie drugs—the kind that can turn a person into a zombie. He was nice and friendly, but had no job and no money. Fredda paid for everything, which bothered me. We never understood why Fredda, who was so great, picked Wendell—or similar guys before him. My dad thought it was from lack of self-confidence, which he felt she would outgrow. I thought it was from excessive compassion and a need to take care of lost causes—even at her expense—much harder to outgrow.

At work, I was legally billing *more* than 100% of my time to clients, which made me popular with the partners of TB&A. I quickly got promoted to Senior Analyst. Minutes after my promotion, I was assigned to write a study on the gloves and safety apparel worn by utility field workers in the Midwest. My managing partner congratulated me on my promotion and suggested I compile a quick list of all the Midwestern utility companies, state by state, and meet him in the conference room to discuss which ones I should target. I rushed to my office and called my dad. I needed him to list the Midwestern states for me. He cracked up, asking rhetorically, "You graduated from Wharton, president of everything, and you don't even know the states in the Midwest? What did I pay for?!" Then he listed all twelve, from memory, and I got started. (My lack of retention in literature and the arts was paralleled by basic school subjects like geography and history.) What *did* he pay for?

Before long, the luster and prestige of working for TB&A wore off. I was finding the subject matter dry and contemplating my next step. My dad was also looking for new opportunities. Around this time, New York City's newly elected mayor, Rudy Giuliani, expressed a desire to clean up Times Square. He wanted to eliminate the porn shops and prostitutes and redevelop the rundown theaters that were then showing mostly X-rated content. Giuliani publicly commissioned *The New York State Urban Development Corporation* to accept proposals from groups wishing to lease and occupy those old theaters. We came up with an interesting concept for the Harris Theater. It had opened in Times Square in 1914 and enjoyed an amazing run until the 1930's, but now it was falling apart, both physically and spiritually.

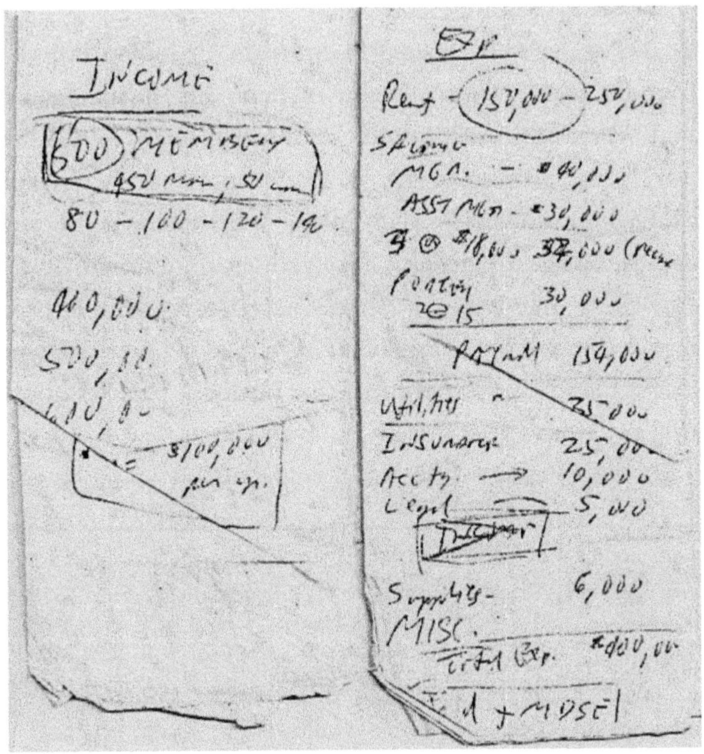

My dad and I *both* liked to think big, and his napkin scribble evolved into our grandiose proposal for the "The Building of Champions." This was to be a state-of-the-art health club and boxing gym, a special events hall, a fine restaurant, and a New York Sports Hall of Fame—all under one roof, open 24 hours a day. Since we would have access to the city's immense talent pool, we planned to manage uniquely gifted entertainers and boxers that we discovered there. Always a big boxing fan, I had gotten a brief taste of the business a few years earlier as a summer intern at Madison Square Garden Boxing. My two-month stint there was more than enough to convince my dad that I was ready to run the Talent Management Division of The Building of Champions. We visited the Harris Theater a few times, and he pointed out where my spacious, windowed office would be. His number one goal, always, was to set me up for huge success.

My dad assembled a management team, including experts from health clubs, gym owners, theater owners, and financiers, and we included everyone's backgrounds in our proposal. He called us the "Dream Team," a play on the 1992 Olympic basketball team with Patrick Ewing, Michael Jordan, Magic Johnson, and others. With the Dream Team in place, we received a commitment of preliminary financing pending the State's acceptance of our proposal, which we worked on every night. We had worked together on many documents in the past, but this business plan was our most extensive and important endeavor—by far.

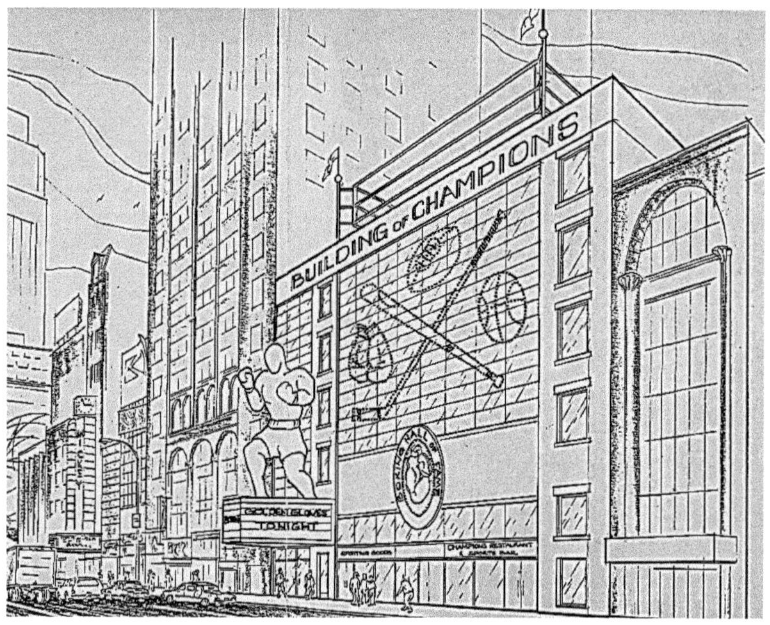

Our writing process consisted of my dad hand-correcting our latest draft with colored pens, arrows, asterisks, and cutouts, and after I edited everything into the computer, it resulted in our next clean draft. The cycle repeated, and repeated, and repeated. I often thought that the document was done, ready to bind and submit—but my dad never agreed. He wanted it to be perfect and insisted on more edits and more drafts. We worked on the document for two months, and the day before it was due we pulled an all-nighter, (my first since my Legal Studies disaster in college). "Take pains, Mitch, take pains," he said, as he marked up yet another draft, while I whined, "Does an extra comma *really* matter in a multimillion-dollar deal? We're fucking done! Let's stop! Please!" On that last night, at around 5 a.m., when even my dad showed signs of fatigue, I implored to him, half-laughing and half-crying, "NO MORE DRAFTS, DAD!! WE'RE DONE!! PLEASE! IT'S FUCKING PERFECT!!" This time he agreed, and we wrapped it up with high hopes and dreams and a sense of joint accomplishment. The camaraderie and laughs we shared always outweighed the difficulty of the work—although this time it was a close call.

Over the next two weeks, we waited to hear whether we were selected by the New York State Urban Development Corporation, confident our lives were about to change. But we received a quick and blunt rejection, learning that our victorious competitor was even bigger and more formidable than the Dream Team: The Walt Disney Company! This was a big defeat, especially for my dad. I tried to cheer him up by telling him that he and I were still the Dream Team, even though we lost to Mickey Mouse. (Walt Disney never redeveloped the Harris Theater. It was demolished years later and replaced by the first branch of *Madame Tussaud's Wax Museum.*)

The rush I had felt while pursuing The Building of Champions cemented the fact that I needed to leave TB&A soon. I wasn't sure what I wanted to do, but I was done with management consulting.

In my eyes, we were hired to help companies publically justify their predetermined strategies—which always included reducing staff levels—without the high-level executives taking the blame. After receiving our reports, the president of a company could issue this type of statement: "Our expert consultants, who have served every major utility in the industry, have recommended we lay off 10,000 people." Our temporary offices at these companies were often right next to the people who would be laid off after we left. This made me feel guilty, and the subject matter was bone-dry.

Things were also dry in my female department, and I almost got back together with Lorena, now at Columbia Law School. Her offer to rekindle, however, came with the ultimatum that we get engaged now or end it forever. I was tempted but unsure. We had dated in college for almost three years and shared some great times, highlighted by passionate fights and equally passionate makeups. There was our trip to London during my sophomore year, when we stayed with my AEPi friend Lovitz (who was studying abroad), from which Lorena made me a fantastic scrapbook. And there was the time we were walking in Greenwich Village, near Astor Place, and I bought a brand-new, in-the-box, stolen video camera from a female drifter on the streets. The drifter asked for $200, and I negotiated her down to $60, which I was proud of. After we completed the transaction, she jumped into a cab and drove away. Then Lorena and I had a serious argument, right on the street, about who should keep the camera. I was the one who had negotiated deftly and laid out the $60, so she grudgingly agreed that I could have it. But by her facial expression, I knew she hoped that *chivalry was alive* and I would hand it over—I didn't. When we got back to the apartment, Lorena sat on the bed and scowled as I removed the outer bubbles from the camera box and then the shrink-wrap. I reached inside the box and felt some newspaper, which was puzzling. Then I reached in further and pulled out a red brick instead of a camera. Lorena burst into laughter, which I had no choice but to join. My only solace was that I had negotiated so well.

I still had feelings for Lorena, and it felt good that she had feelings for me, since we hadn't been together in a while. But I couldn't make up my mind regarding her engagement ultimatum, though I knew not to delay for too long: With faucet-like control over her emotions, this would be the last time her waters would run for me.

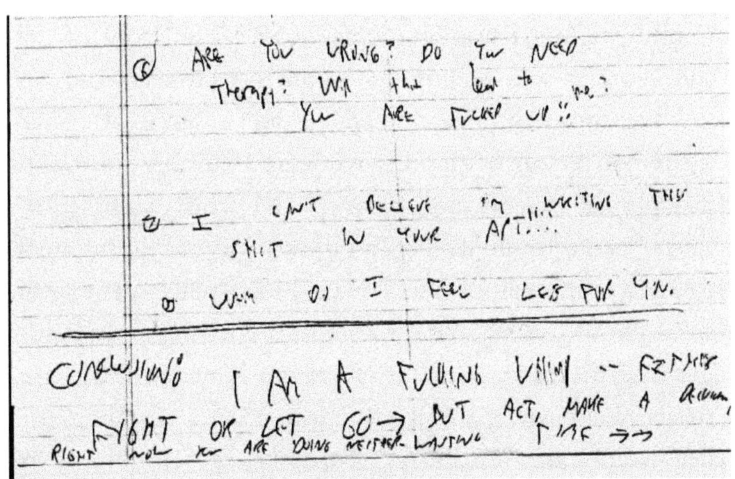

6) ARE YOU WRONG? DO YOU NEED THERAPY? WILL THIS LEAD TO YOU MORE FUCKED UP!!

7) I CAN'T BELIEVE I'M WRITING THIS SHIT IN YOUR APARTMENT!!!!

<u>8) WHY DO I FEEL LESS FOR YOU?</u>
CONCLUSION:
I AM A FUCKING WHIMP--
EITHER FIGHT OR LET GO--
BUT ACT, MAKE A DECISION.
RIGHT NOW YOU ARE DOING NEITHER
WASTING TIME

Through Josh Metternich's recommendation, my dad and I attended a seminar called *The Discovery Program*, run by the Orthodox Jewish Yeshiva, *Aish HaTorah*. In this seminar, through a series of lectures and logic, the *Aish* rabbis had proven to Josh that G-d existed. Each lecture was fascinating and believable, and after attending, my dad and I were also convinced! Also attending the seminar was a naturally beautiful girl with long dirty blonde hair, Hillary Hoffman, who asked great questions of the rabbis. We made eye contact all day; she had "the gleam." I had to get her phone number, but I was embarrassed to ask in front of my dad. But the seminar was ending, so I had no choice—and my dad enjoyed the moment. Hillary handed me a piece of paper—on which she had *already* written her name and number for me—along with the phrase, "Great-times-Great!" Her words summed it up: I had never been as excited about a girl as I was at that moment, and the feeling was mutual. In one day, G-d's existence was proven, my confusion about Lorena was over, and my soul mate was delivered.

The next morning, I was driving from New York City to King of Prussia, Pennsylvania for my latest TB&A assignment. As I travelled south on the Jersey Turnpike, I fell into a trance, overcome with bliss, while looking at the sky. There was a tangible, powerful signal beckoning me. I perceived it as a G-d-like force, inviting me to come closer, and I was happy to oblige.

About an hour later, after exiting the Turnpike, I was driving in the right lane of a two-lane highway, trailing a tow truck that was pulling a sedan. I noticed a cat standing on top of the back seat of the sedan, staring at me. (I thought we were enjoying a special man-feline connection, which I often perceived around Fredda's cats, Kitty and Twinkie, and various other cats I had met in the past. They always seemed to gravitate toward me and climb on me, even though I was allergic to them and could never reciprocate.) *This* cat was now pressing his face against the rear windshield, while I stared back at him. He climbed down and peeked his head out the halfway-down driver's side rear window; then he inched dangerously further out the window. I honked my horn and flashed my lights, to either scare him back inside or signal the tow-truck driver to pull over. Both were in vain. The cat jumped out the window and was transformed into a cloud of fur, blood, and guts by an oblivious vehicle passing in the left lane.

I worshipped Hillary Hoffman, and we became boyfriend and girlfriend. She was only a year older, but more sophisticated and mature. She introduced me to Neil Young's *Harvest Moon*, and "Unknown Legend" and "From Hank to Hendrix" became the background music for our romantic moments, along with the Bonnie Raitt and John Prine duet of "Angel from Montgomery." Hillary enjoyed intellectual environments and witty banter, and both of us were becoming more religious, so we attended a number of Shabbat dinners and Jewish lectures. Afterwards, she would demand authentic justification and rationale for everything questionable I had said during dinner. But due to nerves and a desire to impress, I often found myself rambling nonsensically (talking shit) during these soirees. I would then try to fabricate revisionist justifications to escape Hillary's witness stand. But her "authenticity meter" was too keen to circumvent, even by me, and we argued—while *my* meter for *her* feelings was never as keen.

Hillary was a big fan of the Indigo Girls, and I "took pains" to get us great tickets to their concert at Madison Square Garden one night. In the cab after the show, we were discussing one of her friends, whom I called "a really cool girl." Hillary got offended that I used the word "girl" instead of "woman," claiming it was condescending. (I pointed out that we had just seen the Indigo *Girls,* not the Indigo *Women*, but she wasn't persuaded.) *She* controlled the situation, and I think she sometimes fought because she wanted to be alone. She told the cab driver to drop me at my apartment and then she continued on to hers. I lay in my bed all night, reviewing the incident *ad nauseam*. And I found no answers—nor sleep—to rescue me from my maddening perseveration.

Hillary also controlled the physical situation. She would hold it, allowing only the tip to touch her, in the exact place and way she chose. I was the vibrator, Mr. Great-times-Great—providing pleasure every time, yet always left frustrated and *blue*. I was forced to relieve this painful condition privately, quite often, in Hillary's bathroom, where I wondered how such imbalance could go unnoticed by such a perceptive *woman*. But I was still okay with the arrangement—or any arrangement that involved Hillary and me—yet not the only one with a vote: We drove from Manhattan one night to visit her parents in Toms River, New Jersey. After a nice visit, we got back into my car. I was expecting to go to the movies with her, as we had originally planned. Instead, Hillary said our "chemistry wasn't right" and we "weren't compatible." I pleaded with her to reconsider, but it was in vain, and it was over. She got out of my car and walked back to her parents' house. I headed for the Jersey Turnpike, right back to the city. No blissful trances beckoned.

Chapter 4

Mid-East Tranquility

"Still Mitch"

WHILE I WAS suffering from my breakup with Miss Great-times-Great, Josh Metternich offered me his second *Aish HaTorah* recommendation, The Jerusalem Fellowships: A cheap, co-ed, three-week tour of Israel, supplemented with classes at the *Aish HaTorah* Yeshiva in Jerusalem. I had been to Israel once before, with Josh, five years earlier. That trip was light and fun, and we were immature, but both of us felt a strong connection to the country and our religion. We still wore the gold Stars of David we purchased there.

The Jerusalem Fellowships sounded fun too, but would be more serious and more emotional. Most of the prospective Fellows had attended The Discovery Seminar in their hometowns, where G-d's existence had been proven to them too. This was my chance to explore this further, and the timing was right. I resigned from TB&A, informed Toby Tyler I would not be renewing my lease, and left for Israel.

During the three-week program, I bonded with the rabbis and advanced students, who seemed to show keen interest in my learning experience. I became friends with my *fellow* Fellows, energetic people around my age, and I also received attention from the *female* Fellows, which helped restore my confidence in that area.

One day, we visited the Holocaust Museum, Yad Vashem, where I looked at a photograph of a Nazi cutting off the *payos* (religious sideburns) of a helpless yet prideful elderly Jewish man. As we walked out of the museum, we were handed a pen and paper by our rabbi and asked to write "letters to ourselves" about how we felt.

August 5, 1994

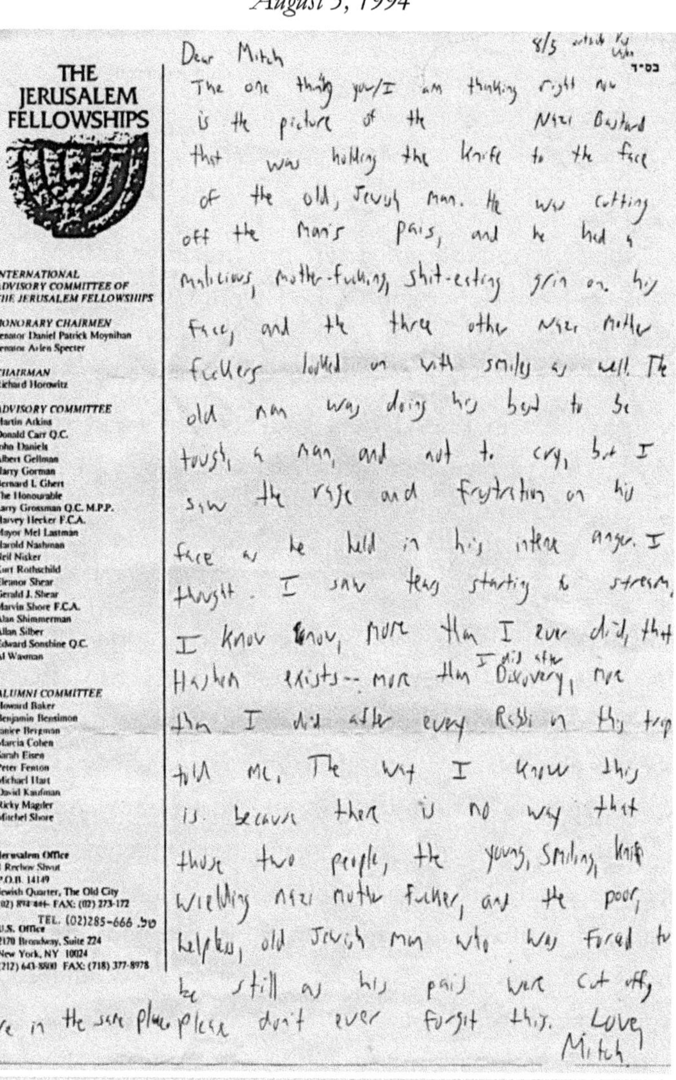

THE JERUSALEM FELLOWSHIPS

INTERNATIONAL ADVISORY COMMITTEE OF THE JERUSALEM FELLOWSHIPS

HONORARY CHAIRMEN
Senator Daniel Patrick Moynihan
Senator Arlen Specter

CHAIRMAN
Richard Horowitz

ADVISORY COMMITTEE
Martin Atkins
Donald Carr Q.C.
John Daniels
Albert Gellman
Harry Gorman
Bernard L Ghert
The Honourable Larry Grossman Q.C. M.P.P.
Harvey Hecker F.C.A.
Mayor Mel Lastman
Harold Nashman
Neil Nisker
Kurt Rothschild
Eleanor Shear
Gerald J. Shear
Marvin Shore F.C.A.
Alan Shimmerman
Allan Silber
Edward Sonshine Q.C.
Al Waxman

ALUMNI COMMITTEE
Howard Baker
Benjamin Bensimon
Janice Bergman
Marcia Cohen
Sarah Eisen
Peter Fenton
Michael Hart
David Kaufman
Ricky Magder
Mitchel Shore

Jerusalem Office
1 Rechov Shvut
P.O.B. 14149
Jewish Quarter, The Old City
(02) 894-441 FAX: (02) 273-172
TEL. (02)285-666 .טל
U.S. Office
2170 Broadway, Suite 224
New York, NY 10024
(212) 643-8800 FAX: (718) 377-8978

בס״ד

Dear Mitch 8/5

The one thing you/I am thinking right now is the picture of the Nazi Bastard that was holding the knife to the face of the old, Jewish man. He was cutting off the man's pais, and he had a malicious, mother-fucking, shit-eating grin on his face, and the three other Nazi mother fuckers looked on with smiles as well. The old man was doing his best to be tough, a man, and not to cry, but I saw the rage and frustration on his face as he held in his intense anger. I thought I saw tears starting to stream. I know know, more than I ever did, that Hashem exists -- more than I did after Discovery, more than I did after every Rabbi on this trip tell me. The way I know this is because there is no way that those two people, the young, smiling, knife wielding Nazi mother fucker, and the poor, helpless, old Jewish man who was forced to be still as his pais were cut off, are in the same place. Please don't ever forget this.

Love
Mitch

(Transcript on next page)

Dear Mitch,
The one thing I am thinking right now is the picture of the nazi bastard that was holding the knife to the face of the old, Jewish man. He was cutting off the man's payos, and he had a malicious, mother-fucking, shit-eating grin on his face, and the three other nazi mother fuckers looked on with smiles as well. The old man was doing his best to be tough, a man, and not to cry, but I saw the rage and frustration on his face as he held in his intense anger. I thought I saw tears starting to stream. I know now, more than I ever did, that Hashem exists – more than I did after Discovery, more than I did after every Rabbi on this trip told me. The way I know this is because there is no way that those two people, the young, smiling, knife-wielding nazi mother fucker, and the poor, helpless, old Jewish man who was forced to be still as his payos were cut off, are in the same place. Please don't ever forget this.
Love, Mitch

These letters would be mailed back to our home addresses, waiting for our returns. I wouldn't see mine for a while.

When the program was nearing its end, *Aish HaTorah* offered some of the more serious students an opportunity to stay in Israel indefinitely, and continue learning and living at the yeshiva for free. I told my parents I was going to stay for two more months to take more classes and spend the Jewish holidays in Jerusalem. My dad agreed this was a great opportunity but reminded me it would then be time to come home and focus on my next career move, so I wouldn't "lose the momentum" I had gained from Wharton and TB&A. During these next two months, I fell in love with the yeshiva environment: The philosophical debates between students and rabbis, the brotherhood and camaraderie in the classrooms and cafeteria, and my sense of pride in being a Jew, studying Torah, in Jerusalem. The learning atmosphere was serious, but I had never felt so carefree. My romantic woes and career concerns were worlds away; I was healthy and grounded, in Israel, immersed in Judaism.

These feelings dissipated on Sunday afternoons, after my weekly call to my parents. They both missed me and were excited that I would soon be coming home. I was happy to hear their voices and know they were OK, but they sustained my connection to the outside world. My dad would remind me of mundane things like mail or phone calls I had received, and my mom would express her fear that I might fall victim to the surging wave of terrorism in Israel. All this was a buzzkill, and made me feel guilty I was in Israel, even though there was nowhere else I could imagine being. When I extended my stay to a fourth month, the tone of our conversations worsened and my guilt increased. My dad sounded weaker and more deflated. My absence was affecting him personally, and I knew the wrath of my nervous mom, who I assumed blamed him for my extended stay, didn't help.

And then my plan became clear: I would spend the next four years living and studying in Jerusalem, at *Aish HaTorah*, and become an Orthodox rabbi. I was convinced that overcoming all parental guilt was best for me and the Jewish people, a necessary step in my commitment process. I mustered the confidence to convey my rabbinical plans to my dad. He instantly respected my decision and said he would support me and help me win my mom's support too. Then he paraphrased Abraham Lincoln, saying, "Whatever you are, be a great one." His only condition was that I first come to Armonk to see him and my mom, if only for a short visit. They needed to see me in person. He was being fair, as usual, and I agreed to the deal. After this conversation, I was relieved. I also felt stupid for doubting that my dad would support me, and I looked forward to seeing him. I expected to spend ten days in Armonk and then head right back to Israel to begin my rabbinical curriculum.

I rushed to tell the rabbis at *Aish HaTorah* my great news, expecting them to be elated. But while happy about my long-term plans to become a rabbi, they vehemently disagreed with my decision to leave Israel, even for ten days. They said that leaving at this early stage in my development was a huge mistake—because I might never return. This sounded preposterous, but they said that even for a short visit, the secular world would present me with too much temptation, too soon, which would disrupt my rabbinical plans. They suggested I invite my parents to visit me in Jerusalem instead.

I became riddled with indecision, since I had already promised my dad I was coming to visit. But the relentless reasoning and pleas of my rabbis and fellow classmates were convincing, and soon changed my mind. I lied to my dad that I needed to stay in Jerusalem for one more month to "tie up some loose ends." He didn't argue but half-joked that if I didn't come back after the month was over, he would be on his way to Israel to shepherd me home. My sister told me there was a rumor circling around Armonk that I had been brainwashed and was wandering around Jerusalem, wearing rags, proselytizing. At first, my mom and dad had dismissed the rumor as nonsense. But after I delayed my visit several times, I think they had begun to consider it. Given my recent decision to cancel my visit to Armonk, I feared that my dad's nightmarish scenario of flying to Israel to get me might actually play out. This would be a guaranteed disaster, regardless of whether I obliged him or not.

Stressed out, I left the yeshiva and the Old City of Jerusalem for a non-religious weekend in Tel Aviv, the commercial—and secular—capital of Israel. While relaxing on the beaches of the Mediterranean Sea, I met Amanda, from Leeds, England, who was vacationing with her friends. She was eighteen, with blonde Victorian locks, hypnotic eyes, and a sexy British accent. We talked on the beach for hours. I shared some personal things about my life, including my dilemma on whether to visit America. She shared too, telling me about her on-and-off boyfriend who was attending college out of town. I hoped the "off" part was the present status, and got my assurance at the end of the weekend, when she held my hand and gave me a long kiss goodbye, her eyes staying open throughout.

When I returned to *Aish HaTorah*, my dilemma was right back on my mind, as well as Amanda's eyes. I phoned her in Leeds and said I was still agonizing over my decision. She said I should go to Armonk to see my parents—how could I not?—and if I did I could visit her on my way, since she knew my flight to New York connected through London. Her offer squashed the uncertainty that had been torturing me for months. I booked my plane ticket, non-refundable and non-changeable, and told the displeased rabbis that I would be back in two weeks. My dad was thrilled when I provided my return flight information. He was also curious about "Amanda in Leeds," whom I said I would be visiting on my way home. (I didn't supply many details—I never did in this area.)

My sojourn in Leeds was romantic and innocent, full of more open-eyed kisses and constant hand-holding. As Amanda drove me around the lush green Leeds countryside, cows and sheep everywhere, I felt far from Israel and the yeshiva world. My *yarmulke* was off for the first time in months. Amanda's mom was youthful, friendly and hospitable, and she casually asked me about my plans, including why and when I had made "the big decision" to become an orthodox rabbi. Innocent questions like these can shake the delicate foundation of a *Baal Teshuva*, a Jew who has gone from the secular to the religious life, if he is not prepared for them. I rambled, wondering if my answers sounded believable, even leaving room for a future change back to secularism—it felt strange to be saying this only a few days after leaving Israel.

I arrived at JFK Airport in New York, *yarmulke* back on my head. My dad was waiting for me at the gate. He told me he hadn't known what to expect: Perhaps my new religious lifestyle would render me unrecognizable, like a new person. But he said that when I came out of the gate, he saw I was "still Mitch" with "the gleam" in my eye, and he was relieved. It felt great to hug him, hard, and know I made good on my promise to visit. I didn't think he knew for sure that Amanda was the one who got me home. But when he asked with a smile if "Beauty had killed the beast," I half-smiled back.

It felt good to be home. I enjoyed seeing my friends and the rest of my family. I got comfortable explaining the logical progression I had taken toward the religious life and my recent "big decision" to become a rabbi. I thought about Amanda a great deal too and phoned her in Leeds multiple times. We discussed the possibility of her visiting New York for an extended period of time, which could never happen if I were living and studying in Jerusalem. I soon found myself open to the possibility of finding a yeshiva in America, close to New York. I viewed this as a potential way to have it all—friends, family, and yeshiva—and Amanda. It contrasted with the *Aish HaTorah* way, in which I would be 100% immersed inside the walls of Jerusalem's Old City. This was the exact development that the *Aish HaTorah* rabbis had predicted and most feared.

I visited Orthodox yeshivas in Brooklyn, The Bronx, and New Jersey. Most of them were in old buildings and remote neighborhoods, not nearly as esthetically pleasing as *Aish HaTorah's* historic campus in Jerusalem's Old City. While my classes at *Aish HaTorah* were serious, my studies of Torah and Talmud, the backbone of every yeshiva's curriculum, were at the beginner level. In America, the rabbis wanted to place me in classes with prepubescent boys, where I could learn the fundamentals of Torah and Talmud. They said it would take me eight years to become a rabbi. Studying with kids, ten years younger than I, with whom I had nothing in common was far from the social status and dynamic learning environment I had enjoyed in Jerusalem. There, I had been surrounded by a lively group of international *Baal Teshuvas* in my age-range, with whom I shared so much in common, and received so much attention.

I checked out a few Reformed and Conservative yeshivas that also had good rabbinical programs. But it felt more authentic in *Aish HaTorah's* Orthodox environment, and the different denominations didn't reduce the time it would take to become a rabbi anyway. I reconsidered Israel, but it was no longer my desire to live outside the United States. Out of options, I was in between everywhere and not fitting anywhere. My dad discussed my predicament with our family temple's rabbi. He recommended I speak to Rabbi Ronald Price, the Director of the Union for Traditional Judaism (UTJ) in Teaneck, New Jersey. UTJ was a small Modern Orthodox Yeshiva with a respected rabbinical program. On the phone, Rabbi Price was warm and welcoming, happy to meet with me. And when we met, my *authenticity meter* told me he was a wise and special man.

Rabbi Price understood my situation and empathized with my confusion. He invited me to learn full-time at the UTJ at a very reasonable price. They had only seven full-time students, but all of them were in my age range, dynamic and smart. The friendly environment seemed ideal. Then I asked Rabbi Price the big question: "How long would it take me to become a rabbi?" He replied that if I dedicated myself full-time and showed I was a hardy learner, I had a chance to finish in five years, even though my studies would continue for the rest of my life as a rabbi. I pressed him on whether it could be done in four, and he said it was highly unlikely. (But I pointed out, with a smile, that he didn't say "impossible.") I enrolled full-time at the UTJ and rented an apartment down the street in Teaneck, New Jersey. My dad was happy with my decision to pursue the rabbinate in America, and offered to pay my tuition and rent for my first year at the UTJ. His gracious offer allowed me to begin my studies at the UTJ with no financial worries.

As Rabbi Price had welcomed me, so did the students of the UTJ. I enjoyed the familiar camaraderie of the yeshiva vibe, highlighted by good-natured, passionate debate among students and rabbis. But when the witty banter quieted and it was time to face my books and actually study Talmud, I had my usual hard time "getting started." Talmud felt boring, and the ancient laws seemed impractical and archaic. Less than a year ago, high on adrenaline, I had sped from Binghamton to Bethlehem to pay little Rex's vet bill because his life was on the line. But I didn't feel passionate about the Talmudic debate over who was responsible for paying a vet bill from 3,000 years ago, when a farmer's mule wandered through a broken fence, onto his neighbor's property, and injured his leg by stepping in a hole. Was it the farmer's fault for allowing his mule to stray? Or was it the neighbor's fault for neglecting to repair the hole in his yard? And who was responsible for fixing the fence on the boundary between the two properties? I didn't see how this Talmudic analysis, which rarely led to answers, yet always more questions, would help me be a great rabbi. But when we discussed issues like anti-Semitism, or intermarriage, or anything involving "saving the Jews," I was riveted and effective at expressing myself. Rabbi Price was concerned about this severe drop-off, but he and the other students welcomed me, supported me, and encouraged me to continue studying at the UTJ.

In the evenings after school, I began to go out with my secular friends in Manhattan. It was less than a fifteen minute ride from Teaneck, NJ. And I thought about Amanda, in Leeds, every day. We exchanged letters, this one from me unsent.

Dear Sweetheart Amanda ♡,

You just put me in the greatest mood, you can't even imagine!! I got your Valentines Day card in the mail. It filled me with such warmth and happiness that it was truly weird!! It made me think about you, and remember how great it felt to spend time with eachother, and how we both slowly became more comfortable as the night progressed, and as each day went on. I felt so close to you that "weekend", and I still feel the same way. Don't ever say that my feelings for you are "dwindling!!" That is such bullshit!! I just got back from N.Y.C., where I was out with two friends. I went to the bar where my pre-Israel guitar teacher plays with his band. We had a great conversation, I agreed to take more lessons with him, so we'll see what happens. I must admit, I am slightly tipsy right now, since this is the first night I have been out doing something like this, so my body has forgotten how to party. Anyway, this is supposed to be a love letter, so I better get down to business. I really want you to know how much I do miss you!! This letter is so sloppy, I think I'll read it to you in person, or at least on the phone!! I will definitely not send this, so I'll be romantic, since there will be no evidence of this on paper. I really miss touching you, and kissing you, and smelling you, and being so close to you. I definitely feel like you are someone I can one day really love, or at least be in love with. Is this too mushy? Hopefully, if we somehow see eachother this summer, we can start saying more things to eachother about our feelings, etc...

(Transcript on next page.)

February 1995 (unsent)

Dearest Sweetheart Amanda,
You just put me in the greatest mood, you can't even imagine!! I got your Valentine's Day Card in the mail. It filled me with such warmth and happiness that it was truly weird!! It made me think about you, and remember how great it felt to spend time with each other, and how we both slowly became more comfortable as the night progressed, and as each day went on. I felt so close to you that "weekend+" and I still feel the same way. Don't ever say that my feelings for you are "dwindling!!!" That is such bullshit!! I just got back from NYC, where I was out with two friends. I went to the bar where my pre-Israel guitar teacher plays with his band. We had a great conversation. I agreed to take more lessons with him, so we'll see what happens. I must admit, I am slightly tipsy right now, since this is the first night I have been out doing something like this, so my body has forgotten how to party. Anyway, this is supposed to be a love letter, so I better get down to business. I really want you to know how much I do miss you!! This letter is so sloppy, I think I'll read it to you in person, or at least on the phone!! I will definitely not send his, so I'll be romantic, since there will be no evidence of this on paper. I really miss touching you, and kissing you, and smelling you, and being so close to you. I definitely feel like you are someone I can one day really love, or at least be in love with. Is this too mushy? Hopefully, if we somehow see each other this summer, we can start saying more things to each other about our feelings, etc…

After a few months at the UTJ, I found myself turning down Shabbat dinner offers at my classmates' homes, choosing instead to socialize with my secular friends across the Hudson. In Israel, Shabbat had been the highlight of my week, and I always looked forward to it. In Teaneck, NJ, it felt like a long commitment of time, bordering on isolation, with no phones, no television, no driving—and no girls. Things changed when I attended a UTJ book fair and met a twenty-year-old Orthodox girl named Bayla, the daughter of a rabbi. We had immediate intellectual chemistry with a flirtatious undertone, and she invited me to her family's house for Shabbat. Bayla was born religious, not *Baal Teshuva.* Like her mom years ago, she was ready to marry young, cover her hair, have many kids, and stack volumes of Talmud on her *own* bookshelves. I told Bayla about my experience in Israel, my logical progression toward becoming more religious, and my decision to become a rabbi in America. Bayla said that my path was especially righteous and brave, since it was my own choice, and not something I was born into. Meeting Bayla energized my studies. I even made a concerted effort to apply myself more to Talmud, realizing that my lack of knowledge in this area was embarrassing—given my oft-stated and lofty rabbinical aspirations.

For a few weeks, Bayla and I spoke on the phone every day (except Shabbat) and got together for coffee dates. In yeshiva jargon, we were in the early stages of "dating for marriage," as opposed to the secular practice of "dating for sex," a term Josh Metternich and I had once coined in jest. Bayla was *shomer negiah,* which in Orthodox law meant that I was forbidden to touch her, even on the hand, until marriage. I found myself saying all the right things to prove I was solid in my religious convictions. Bayla, a young-looking twenty, told me how amazing it was to finally be with a guy who knew what he wanted. But my words soon felt inauthentic, my desire to get closer to her likely connected to man's desire to reproduce—heightened to a frenzy by the *shomer negiah* prohibition on all touch. (I could see why Orthodox teenagers got married so young!) In Leeds, when I had spoken with Amanda and her mom, I had downplayed my commitment to the Orthodox life and left room for change. With Bayla I was doing the opposite, while my real feelings were unknown, even to myself. And I couldn't waste her time any longer: I told her I was having some faith issues, and it would be better if we didn't speak anymore. She was surprised and upset but not devastated or damaged, further evidence of the merits of "dating for marriage" versus "dating for sex."

I wasn't ready to admit to anyone that I was second-guessing my entire rabbinical direction. I kept my creeping doubts to myself. Then I found out about the Wexner Fellowship, an ultra-prestigious, highly competitive scholarship for potential rabbis and Jewish leaders in the United States. When you "get the Wexner," your path to the rabbinate and subsequent career is assured. These *chosen ones* receive full four-year academic scholarships and living stipends, all under the guidance and support of the renowned Wexner Foundation. After becoming rabbis, they are expected to make a long-term commitment to the Jewish community and stay associated with the Wexner Foundation throughout their careers.

There were about 500 qualified applicants each year, and only twenty recipients. These were the long odds that got my competitive juices flowing, providing me with a new and exciting goal. I couldn't stop thinking how great it would be to "get the Wexner." I easily "got started" and prepared my application, (with my dad's usual writing assistance).

An excerpt from my Wexner Fellowship application essay:

My goal is to be an "outreach rabbi," dedicated to strengthening American Jewry. While I expect to specialize in working with college students, my door will always be open to any worthy Jewish cause.

Prior to making the decision to become a rabbi, I had other career interests. My earliest goal was to be a politician. I had a promising start by being elected president of the student bodies of my junior high school, high school, and the University of Pennsylvania. In the summer after my freshman year of college, I worked full-time for our local United States Congresswoman, Nita Lowey. I learned a lot about the workings of government, and I was intrigued by the politician's opportunity to bring about change. But I was also confronted with the reality that a politician must temper each decision between what he thinks is right against how it may affect his re-election chances. This was a turn-off, because while I understood the importance of compromise as a means to an end, I could not see myself in a career where I would be forced to forsake my principles.

My second career choice was business. I decided to transfer from the School of Arts and Sciences at the University of Pennsylvania to the Wharton School of Business. The following summer, to test my entrepreneurial skills, I started up and ran my own business. It was quite successful, and I later sold it for a substantial profit. I returned to Wharton with renewed confidence and vigor, ready for greater challenges.

Following my junior year, I worked for an up-and-coming investment banking firm. My job was to screen business plans and solicit potential clients. The president of the company was very pleased with my performance and asked me to return as his assistant after college graduation. I knew that if I accepted his offer it would have meant financial security, but I turned it down. I concluded that in investment banking, an individual's worth is defined almost entirely by the amount of money he makes for himself and for his company. Character, honesty, and integrity seemed secondary. While I must admit that the thought of becoming wealthy was tempting, I was searching for a career that would have more meaning to me.

After much deliberation, I decided to spend time in Israel, where, undistracted, I could learn more about Judaism, experience firsthand what a career in Jewish affairs might be like, and then make a specific career choice.

When I arrived in Israel, I began to live as an observant Jew. I studied the Torah, initially for a few hours each day, but within a month I had switched to full-time. The more I learned, the more I wanted to learn. The more about Judaism I experienced, the clearer my path seemed. I decided I wanted to become a rabbi, and I stayed in Israel for 5 months.

One day my study group was discussing the meaning of the statement in the Torah (Leviticus 19:16) that says, "...Thou shalt not stand idly by in the blood of your brother." Each student had his own interpretation. The experience of reading a passage in the

Torah that so directly paralleled my feelings toward the Jewish people, especially our need for leaders, made me shiver with emotion. If my brother was bleeding, how could I stand idly by if I honestly believed I could make a difference?

I made it to the final round of the selection process. There were 40 out of 500 applicants left, with 20 scholarships available. All that remained was my final one-on-one interview, now my forte, where I could look my interviewer in the eye and say to him, "There is nothing I have ever wanted more than the Wexner Fellowship; and if I get it, I will not let you down." I liked my chances. My interviewer began by telling me I had a great chance of getting the scholarship. He had read my essay, and asked me to elaborate on my rapid path toward becoming more religious and my "big decision" become a rabbi. By then I was an expert at fielding this question, and I expected it to be asked. My answer was polished, logical, and devoid of ramble and doubt.

At the end of my monologue, the interviewer asked if he could be candid, based on his experience giving hundreds of similar interviews and hearing the "logical progressions" of hundreds of other *Baal Teshuvas.* The tone of our meeting soon resembled a therapy session. He said he saw "doubt in my eyes" regarding my long-term commitment to the Orthodox life. He didn't doubt my desire to be "a great Jew," or to help "save the Jews," but said I appeared to him like the "typical case *Baal Teshuva*," who goes to Israel non-religious, often to "fill some kind of void," gets enraptured by the spirituality there, and becomes Orthodox. He said this "typical case *Baal Teshuva*" doesn't usually sustain the religious lifestyle over the long term—the temptations of secular life tend to win out. He warned me that if I were to accept the Wexner Fellowship and not complete the four-year program, or if I completed it but did not remain in the rabbinate long-term, I was "stealing someone else's opportunity." I hated being called "typical," a term he used over and over—possibly to evoke a passionate response. I was about to tell him he was wrong, dead wrong, and that he was sitting in front of a future rabbi that would change the world—if I could just "get the Wexner!"

But this time my real voice spoke: I admitted I was confused—I missed Israel, but didn't want to go back. I enjoyed Shabbat, but didn't understand the rationale for restrictions on television and driving. I liked the idea of studying Talmud, text that was thousands of years old, but found the subject matter boring. I was being honest, which felt good, but my entire existence suddenly felt inauthentic. I was sweating, and nervous laughter, my old nemesis, threatened another visit. It was time to leave the meeting—there would be no Wexner. I received the rejection letter a few weeks later, but I already knew that my road to the rabbinate was over. When I told Rabbi Price that I was withdrawing from the UTJ, he encouraged me to at least continue attending their once-a-week evening Talmud class—at no charge. I accepted, which felt better than a clean break. It helped preserve our relationship, and allowed me to save face in front of friends and family.

As I packed up my Teaneck, New Jersey apartment, I thought about my canceled path to the rabbinate, and my dad's *King Kong* insinuation at the airport when I returned from Israel. He was right again: It wasn't parental guilt, or lack of interest in Shabbat, or mules with broken legs 3,000 years ago. "*Beauty* killed the beast." Meeting Amanda on the beaches of Tel Aviv shifted my course in ways she never knew. But she was *across the pond* and would stay there—I never saw her again. And beauty didn't just kill the beast, it also created it: If Hillary had not broken up with me, I never would have gone to Israel! Then I thought more about her and the powerful force that beckoned that morning on the Jersey Turnpike—when everything was "great-times-great." But I was twenty-four, single, and suddenly secular. New York City called me right back.

Chapter 5

Right Back

"The truth frees you."

I WANTED TO RENT AN APARTMENT on the Upper West Side of Manhattan, and a broker named Nygil Cox presented me with a rarity: A rent-stabilized one-bedroom in a brownstone on West 80th between Broadway and Amsterdam—large, quiet, and only $720 per month! I had to get that apartment, but I had no job, no credit, and no landlord references. So I pulled fictional names and numbers out of nowhere and wrote them on the apartment application. Hours later I comprehended my fuck-up: Any respectable management company would attempt to verify my answers. I would be rejected from West 80th and possibly blackballed from future apartments. In a late-night panic, I called Nygil Cox and told him what I had done. He said, "The truth frees you. Get me a cosigner and call me in the morning." My dad agreed to cosign, and I got the apartment on West 80th.

For immediate cash, I got a job as a waiter at Chaz & Wilson's, a restaurant one block from my new apartment. Chaz & Wilson's was the city's hottest Sunday night joint for live R&B and celebrities, mostly African-American. Our customers included Mike Tyson, Prince, Madonna, Lawrence Taylor and my sports idol Patrick Ewing. I knew nothing about being a waiter and had lied on this employment application too. On my first shift as a waiter, my first customer ordered coffee. I went into the kitchen and picked up a bag of whole coffee beans. I poured them into a mug of hot water and began to stir, wondering out loud why they wouldn't dissolve. A cute biracial waitress named Michelle politely inquired, "What the fuck are you doing?!" Then she taught me how to make coffee. I soon became a decent waiter.

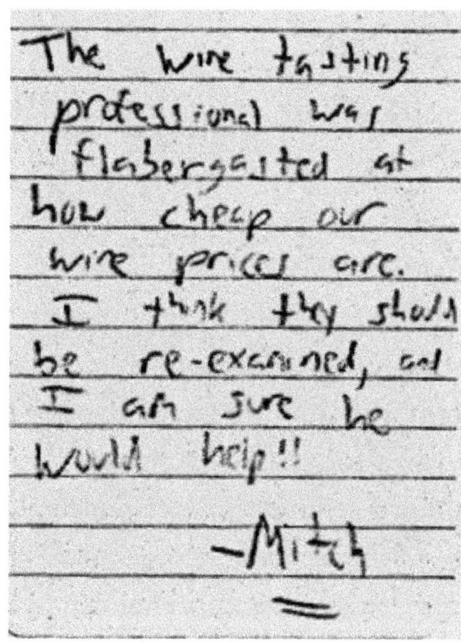

The wine tasting
professional was
flabergasted at
how cheap our
wine prices are.
I think they should
be re-examined, and
I am sure he
would help!!

-Mitch

The only drawback to my West 80th apartment was that it received no natural sunlight. Without the lights on, the apartment was pitch-dark, regardless of the time of day. The weather was a mystery until I got outside. I would get home from the restaurant around 2 a.m., wired, wind down until 4 a.m., and then sleep until noon, leaving only a few hours before my next shift. I never saw the sun, wasn't getting anything else done, and I started feeling depressed. For career waiters and spirited restaurant staffers, this was their normal schedule. It explained why the Chaz & Wilson's staff always appeared so close to one another, forming a proverbial second family—their nocturnal lifestyles rendered them unavailable to everyone else!

To combat my creeping depression, I reduced my work schedule to two shifts a week, Thursdays and Sundays, and answered a Help Wanted ad for a leasing representative at the Brooklyn Army Terminal (BAT). (This was a large complex of industrial buildings in Brooklyn, formerly used by the military, now for rent to manufacturing and industrial companies.) I had no real estate experience, but my dad coached me well for my interview, and the osmosis I had undergone from hearing him talk real estate on the phone for many years also helped. I said to my interviewer, "If you give me this opportunity, I won't let you down." The magic line worked again—I got the job. My hours were perfect, Monday through Friday, noon to 5 p.m. It was a municipal job, with no preparation, follow-up, or thinking required. I would sit in my office all day and wait for potential tenants to show up, and when they did, (about once a day), I would give them a tour of the vacant buildings.

There was downtime galore. I watched a great deal of the O. J. Simpson double-murder trial on a television right outside my office, and I also started my journal.

August 17, 1995

I want to write a portrait of myself, how I am now, how I feel now, and who I am now. I do not want to write an autobiography, a boring story riddled with unimportant facts. Who gives a shit where I was born? If I tell the story well, the important stuff will come out. You will know enough about my childhood, my adulthood, the places I have lived, the things I have done. My goal is to let my mind and my desire dictate how I tell the story, not some chronological story that places equal importance on the hospital I was born in to the restaurant that I waiter in. Clearly, what is going on in the restaurant, what I learn there, and what I think about in my spare time now is the most important part of my life. The proof is that these are the things that are compelling me to write this portrait. I do not know if this is something anybody will want to read, but a record of this time really should exist. I wish I was less lazy in terms of keeping a daily diary, and perhaps this manuscript will become that. To stop doing and start recording what has already been done takes discipline, something I sometimes wish I had more of and sometimes wish I had less of. This will be a manuscript, full of stories, insights, and designed to leave a record of me for others to read. For some reason, I know that I have been gifted enough to know that it is time for me to cut the bullshit and start writing some shit down. I keep thinking it is too late and that if I have not started writing yet, there is no point. But that is so damn ridiculous, because I am at the height of my consciousness, and this job, while in some ways is monkey-izing me back to being a societal pawn, in other ways has provided me with a wonderful writing atmosphere.

It is trepidation for the future that has made me really start to wonder what the fuck I am going to do with my life. I really do not know what will eventually make me happy. I constantly have, and I had to say this cliché, delusions of grandeur. I am not exaggerating when I say that there have been specific and distinct times in my life, when, in a sober state, I have honestly felt that I could be a professional athlete, President of the United States, a professional musician, a famous writer, a famous rabbi, a great boxer, a groundbreaking philosopher, a stand-up comedian, a successful gambler, and the list probably goes on. The part of this that sort of amazes me is that I still feel that most of these are attainable. Yet I know none will probably happen, because I have so many conflicting forces that drive me. For instance, I think I have the charisma and ego to be a very electable and successful politician, and the public appearances and press would do my ego good. But at the same time, I have an appreciation and a love for what is real, a true realization that politics is basically a bunch of shit, and while I could actually enjoy myself, eventually the realization that I have sold out would make me want to leave. And, since I am basically not one to not follow my impulses (in other words, I follow my impulses), I would seek out something else. Sometimes I wonder if this conflict is actually an internal strife between attaining what I believe is important versus what I believe others feel is important. To take this further, perhaps I do not know what I actually believe to be important. Is my public opinion actually important to me, or do I want others to talk about me, or do I want to really do what I feel is important. But what I feel is important may not be unrelated to what I think others will find special, crazy, weird, cool, and original. Take a look at the things that I have wanted to become. If you were to take a cursory look at them and compare them superficially, a professional boxer and a rabbi would seem to be so different, and the mere fact that the same person, sane, could want to be both would probably boggle the mind and confuse the simple minded.

But in my mind, it is not at all weird that the same person could want to be both. They are both people that lay their entire existences on the line every time they pursue their profession. A boxer, who risks everything physically, in obvious ways, and also mentally, who must be ready to deal with a crushing defeat, in front of everybody, after he has trained so hard, talked so much shit, and convinced himself he would win. When he leaves the ring, he is annihilated, destroyed, in every way. He is risking everything he has, or has risked. When he loses, and realizes he is not unbeatable, not the best, what does he have? Take the rabbi. He has studied his entire life in a Yeshiva, building his foundation for belief in G-d, for an obedient existence, for living for one purpose – to serve G-d and be worthy of creation. What happens when his innermost beliefs change? When he wakes up one day and has some doubts? Not doubts that are common, that are easily shrugged off and beaten away by trained ignoring or reviewing some previously known proofs. The doubts I am talking about are real doubts that G-d might not exist, doubts that do not go away. What does the rabbi do when he has devoted his entire life, his entire existence, to something he is now unsure of? What about his followers? What does he tell them? What about his family? What about his students? Most importantly, what about himself? What does he tell himself when he can no longer pray? How does he lead a prayer? How does he tell his students to lead a life that he is unsure that he himself can live by?

And here probably lies my problem, which maybe I am discovering while I write this manuscript. I am afraid to commit to anything because I do not know of anything that I fully believe in. I cannot think of a cause that I may not grow tired or weary of one day. I am fickle, or I think too much. I love guitar, but I know I will never be a great musician. I love sports, but my athletic skills, while better and more well-rounded than most, are not at the professional level by any means. I am fascinated by religion, but I am not pious enough and too tempted by pleasure to be a religious model of obedience and wisdom, of humility and generosity. I am entrepreneurial and love the idea of creating something new, and the possibility of making a lot of money from this. But I realize how much hard work goes into this, and I am not sure if I am not too lazy deep down. I do love money, and I really enjoy having a lot of it. This is not for the true rabbi. Granted, some rabbis must really love money, and secretly wish for more luxuries. But I am not capable of being this kind of rabbi. If I did it, it would be all the way, 100%. This is the case with everything, and that is why I find myself quitting so often and changing my mind so often.

Because when I change my mind, I don't ignore it. I don't continue half-assed. I stop and pursue something that will occupy and enrapture me 100%. But my fear is that this does not exist. If it does not, then how different am I from the beaten boxer, or the rabbi who doubts his own faith? What happens when I discover, which I probably will, that nothing exists that is capable of enrapturing me 100%? Haven't I devoted my life to a cause that is unattainable, and haven't I though it to be attainable the entire time? Just like the boxer in search of invincibility and the rabbi in search of that ultimate peace that comes when one has discovered the truth, the unwavering, undeniable, bliss that comes when something is right in a permanent way.

August 24th, 1995

I feel like writing about my friends, and the struggles that I have been having in my mind regarding them. There really is not one friend I have that I am not disappointed with. This is kind of fucking crazy, when you really think about it. Perhaps the reason why I am disappointed with everybody is because I initially was insecure and glorified my relationships with them. I liked to say things to others like "xx is my best friend," like Josh Metternich. And actually, he really is. But I think we are better off at long distances, where our phone calls are soothing reminders of the loyalty we have to each other and the desire that both of us have just to share our lives with each other and talk to each other for hours on end. His stubbornness makes it difficult to spend a great deal of time with him in person, and a minor argument can make my blood boil. I have even purposely pissed him off a few times to make him feel how I do when I am so frustrated with him! Actually, Josh is not the problem. I love the guy and have already learned to kind of pull back, sort of attempt to not get so emotionally involved in convincing him of anything or attempting to win an argument.

Competition is a bad thing, I think. It only brings out bad qualities in people. This is something I can write volumes on, and I am inclined to. This will be revisited. But my real problem, which I have touched on, is that most of my friends fall short of what I want them to be. Toby I find too immature to take seriously, too selfish, and deep down too simple minded and stupid. He has no concept of reality, he is paranoid, and I have warm thoughts for him because he is a decent person, and we have great memories together. Lovitz is a great guy, but he is immature, and will lie for no reason—not to pick up a girl, not to get money, but just to appear more interesting—like lying is almost his truth in a weird way. Again, though, he is a great guy, and this is just one fault. I realize that the problem really lies in the fact that I place great expectation on these people, when I should not. I should take them as they are and no further, or else I become disappointed.

But I can't take anything in a half-assed way. Not even friends. I want to explore a person, a relationship, at full speed until I become sick of it. I want to squeeze the juice out of a person until I have given and gotten all there is to give and get. The problem is, most people dry up. I figure them out and there really is not much more to get. Then I have a problem, because of course I have not dried up to them, and we have a strong relationship. These usually must be broken. That is why so many people contact me from my past. I have had a major effect on their lives and then I have cut it off. I have devastated girls because in a short time I have made them love me and then I have grown bored. This is not to say I have never been rejected, but it is to say that I know how to make a person care for me a great deal. I am not being devious, or anything else when this begins to happen. I actually put initial faith in them that I will not grow sick of them, that they will challenge me and take me to the heights of companionship, an everlasting relationship full of on-going discovery and challenge and happiness. But then I gain the ability to sum them up. Once you can sum a person up, you have no more need for them. You know how they will react to a situation, so why do you need them to be there? Actually this is probably too cynical, because people, while predictable, can also provide companionship, humor, etc. But that is not the point. You can get this without investing so heavily in their character or their friendship. The real issue is that I wish I did not have so many close friends that have fallen short of my expectations, because it eventually causes me to either upset them, blow them off, or get upset myself when I realize how alone I can be even with so many friends.

August 30th, 1995

A lot of shit is going down in my life right now, and I have the feeling that I am on the verge of doing some pretty exciting things in the near future. Socially, I am going to the US Open with Michelle from Chaz and Wilson's on Thursday, if I can cover my shift (I know I will.) I am looking forward to Silvia's visit, although it might be a disaster. (It really might be.) I should admit, however, there is not much else going on woman-wise.

Guy friends are the same, although Lee and I had a good time last night hanging out. I really like him one-on-one, as opposed to in a bar situation, or a group, where he is uncomfortable and pressured to act cool. We sang and played guitar, and our third take of

"Patience" bordered on decency. I realize that I must get together and form some kind of band that meets once a week. Maybe with Scott? Two guitars and a singer are all we need, if it becomes something more, a drummer, but for now that is totally unnecessary. I just want a cover band for now, or I would not mind playing with other people that are writing stuff, but I do not have the talent/inspiration for anything original that is half-decent. But I really want to get into a band – soon. I must make it happen. So why the fuck did I just screen Scott's call? Stupid motherfucker.

Let's talk women, a subject that I have been doing some thinking about. I think I want a relationship, but I cannot bear to be in one unless I am totally into the girl. But I would not mind having something, just for the adventure and the regular lay. I know that sounds horrible, but I have not had that in a long time, and except for Norma, it would have been even longer. I could use the experience. Silvia has a lot of amazing qualities. If I am sexually attracted to her, things might work out. She is long distance, which might work even better for me. I am really intrigued by Michelle from the restaurant. I am not sure if I like her or I am just trying to amuse myself. But I remember the night I first met her, after the coffee incident, and then when we shared a candy bar. When I was lying in bed that night, I had this premonition that something was going to develop with her. Not happen, but develop, a saga type of thing. I might be into that. When I have these premonitions, I usually end up being right. I say to myself, "I will get that girl," and I usually do. I am not saying every time I set my eyes on a hot woman I do this, it is only once in a while, at the beginning of some sort of extended engagement in which I will be seeing a group of people on a regular basis. I look around, and pick one girl, and say it. Michelle is hot, not jappy, funny, and very down to earth. She has a fire to her, and I really find her so intriguing. I do not know if she feels the same way about me. I am nervous about our date. As I sit here and write, I cannot believe that I am about to let myself fall for a non-Jew. She is also half African-American. I do not care. I really have a strange relationship with religion, which actually is really a strange relationship with all temptations that I have once proclaimed not to succumb to. Pot, dating non-Jews, cigarettes, veggies, I have declared how I will never do them until it was right in front of me, and then I did it. I have a weakness in my temptation to adventure, or temptation to anything. I basically will do almost anything. But is this a weakness? Or is this really wrong? I am unsure. Sometimes I think that religion is so oversimplified, that the concept of G-d and Torah, and doing good, and beating the evil inclination, all of this seems too simple to be how things really are.

Reading Herman Hesse's *Narcissus and Goldmund* and *The Steppenwolf* have changed me. It talks about the life of obedience versus experience, sex, violence, travel, etc. in *Narcissus and Goldmund*, and it talks about the needs of the bourgeois versus the loner *in The Steppenwolf*. Both of these topics have set me into deep thought. I will start with *The Steppenwolf*. Harry is a lot like me to a greater extreme. He is a loner, and spends his time pursuing things on his own. He realizes how pathetic the masses are, and does not want to be swallowed by them. But he also succumbs to them quite frequently, like when the professor invited him to dinner, and he was so bubbly and happy to be noticed, known, invited anywhere. That is so me. I think I am so cool and such a great loner, but maybe the reason is that I just do not have that many people that I really like so much that are always including me. When I am invited to a party, or some sort of gathering, I am almost always happy to go. Pathetic people invite me. But in my defense, maybe I am just using these situations to meet women. And speaking of women, why the fuck don't I have 30 women that all like me that I like back? Why are there always only one or two? Maybe because I don't play the game in the social scene as much, like hang out with Toby or something. But he is so fucking shallow and so are all of his friends and endeavors that it is almost painful. I shouldn't say Toby is so shallow, because he does have an interesting side to him that I am intrigued by. But he really is fucking weak as shit when it comes to his inner self. Who cares?

Back to *The Steppenwolf*, Harry. Harry makes the mistake of oversimplifying his existence, thinking he is fighting between the wolf and the man. The man is the bourgeois, and the wolf is the loner, the madman, who is being attracted and slowly killed by the depths of sadness, loneliness, etc., but who is being pushed to greatness by this extreme form of life, in his sadness, etc. I am not explaining this well, but my point is that I oversimplify things as well. I have this religious side of me which is kind of sort of maybe dwindling. I also have the side that wants to experience everything. Do everything, smoke everything, drink everything, play everything, fuck all women, sing in a band, etc. I think when it all plays out, Judaism will be a culture that I will have no desire to hurt in any way, and I will definitely marry a Jew, but being religious is probably not me. I believe in being a good person, not fucking with others unnecessarily, etc. I do not think that G-d cares who we pray to, and for that matter, G-d does not care about anything, because he is not a finite being who can do these things. I am sick of people trying to oversimplify G-d's word to make us do certain things. The laws of Kosher, the prayer details, all of this is so ritualized and so regimental and so invasive!! Shabbat can be a nightmare if there is something going on that you would rather be doing. What about every once in a while doing a Shabbat? The religious say, if you really knew how to experience Shabbat to the fullest, you would realize how great it is and not want to do anything else. But what if they experienced having a party with friends and watching the Tyson fight after going out to dinner on a Friday night? And seeing a movie on a rainy Saturday, or watching college football. This is culture as well. I am not sure of the way, but I keep on realizing that proselytizing is not the way to go. Tell a person to be good and act as a kind person, but do not tell them what to do, or what to eat, or when to stay home. Present it to them in moderation, so that one can find a happy medium. Extremes are often bad also, as I have learned in my life, and very difficult to maintain. I realize the importance of the Jewish people, and I know there will always be a Jewish people. I feel it is my duty to be a good person, marry Jewish, and raise my kids in a Jewish home. The Jews are largely responsible for bringing ethics and humanity into this world, and our culture and smartness have made this world a much better place in terms of the humanities, sciences, arts, education, etc. I will continue this faith.

But orthodoxy is too separatist for my taste, at least that is how I feel strongly now.

August 31, 1995

I want to bring up the issue of oversimplification one more time, because I think it brings out some light on my extremist attitude about a lot of things. Since I think I am fighting between Narcissus and Goldmund, or the Wolf and Harry, I tend to do things in extremes. But since there are so many degrees between the extremes, and in reality, we all are all of these degrees, or least special people are, then I must give more credence to moderation. Being moderate is good, and if you go to the extreme too much, other people tend to ostracize you and do not take you seriously. In some ways, and in the realest ways, this does not matter. But if one wants, and I think I do want, to still associate socially with some of these people (especially women) that may not be so extreme, then it may be important at times to be moderate. More importantly, to take this a step further, moderation helps to allow the person to gain public stature. Like public office, or some other position that will bring prestige and money. I do not like the way this sounds, nor do I know if I fully agree with this or am just writing about it. But it definitely is an interesting thought. The most important thing I must keep in mind when I write this is that I am not performing, I am writing. I cannot worry about who or what or when this will be read, and how it will sound. I must just write, anything and everything that comes to my mind that I deem worthy to write.

What is up with Silvia? Why is she so pathetically involved in this stupid phone communication? I feel so horrible to say something like this, but I realize I am just filling a void with her, and the word I can use to describe this whole thing is stupid. I feel stupid opening up to someone on the phone who I do not even know. And she is so cliché and corny, a geeky wannabe, that I think she is a dork. (That is really fucking funny, the sentence I just wrote. If she only knew I just wrote that, she would be totally devastated in a big way!!) She just got back from a trip to China, and I was like, I do not want to talk to her. In fact, I do not want to talk to her more than a few times until she comes. And I only want her to come for a standard weekend. None of this Thursday thru Sunday bullshit. I am not giving up no three days to be stuck with her. Believe it or not, there is a possible good side. She is kind, and understanding, and honest, and Jewish, and smart, and nice, and has class. If she is pretty enough, which I do not think she will be, then I may be psyched. I do not want to change her, but I think that she will be willing and ready to change if I so choose. Not to sound dominating, but she may be too straight. But perhaps I could do with a long-distance relationship. A few weekends here and there, and no full commitment. This may work. The real question, I guess, when it comes down to it, is that I hope I am attracted to her. I remember her white legs, almost purple, actually, that freaked me out and still do. But she may be a fair-skinned beauty, another stack of wheat in the name of Annie.

Annie was Andy Metternich's red-headed girlfriend, always bright and beaming, always sweet and cheerful. I was a big fan of hers. Around Andy, I hummed The Cars song, "My Best Friend's Girlfriend," to mess with him. In my West 80th apartment, the three of us shared some great laughs, such as the time we called a hospital and asked to speak to a doctor to verify the rumor that a human intestine, when stretched out like a string, could span five miles. The hospital administrator refused to connect us to a doctor, but opined herself, "it couldn't be that long," and then reprimanded us for wasting the hospital's precious time. On another occasion, the three of us cooked a huge bowl of chili at my parents' house while they were out of town. We were dog-sitting Frosty, my mom's passionate American Eskimo who couldn't resist the smell of fresh meat. As we prepared the chili, Frosty's excitement climbed until she was trembling with desire. We placed the bowl of chili in the center of the table, impossibly out of her reach, and began washing some dishes before our feast. While we looked on, Frosty assumed a contorted, cobra-like stance, and used internal leverage to catapult all fours onto the kitchen table. Then she dove headfirst into the chili. When she came up for air, she stared right at me—her white face had turned to red, dripping with meat, saliva, and pride. Vicious growls warned us not to approach. It was *her* chili now.

August 31, 1995 (cont.)

I do not want a strong-willed bitch, which Michelle deep down may be. Tonight at the US Open, I will act cool and not fawn all over her and kiss her ass, for once. I will attempt to get the real me to come out. Her attitude will be interesting to observe. Anyway, there is little more to say about my skepticism with the Silvia thing, the fact that there is no challenge right now, and the Michelle issue. Why am I writing about them simultaneously? Because I think they are related. My feelings for Michelle are definitely stronger right now, and this is weighing on my lack of attentiveness to Silvia's call last night. We'll see…

Last night I had this dream about Frosty fighting another dog, which I picked up and took away, not being afraid of getting bitten. This must be a continuation of my veggie trip when those two dogs were growling at each other all day, and then started to fight, which freaked me out, and I was a wimp trying to break them up, while Josh and Andy laughed. I just did not want to get rabies from those sick, fucking ugly, non-cute dogs.

I kind of want to start writing about Fredda now, but I may get too mad. She is supporting her drugged-out boyfriend Wendell, literally. Not only does she pay for his everything, but she actually gives him a damn allowance!! He has no pride in the world, and he is actually able to accept this, and then he is jamming with his friends instead of looking for a job. He is going to have free rent in her fucking apartment soon, and it makes me sick. But do I tell her? Do I do anything? I want to write her a letter and tell her, more importantly, I want to scream at her and make her realize!! I do not know when to step in, but I must do something soon. I will use the angle that Rob gave me to figure this out. G-d forbid she finds a guy with a job who can support himself!! I am not saying he has to support her, or even pay for her one time in 20, I am saying he must be able to pay for himself 100% of the time or he should not be doing anything except finding a job!!

I must make a deal with my father, so I can stop taking money from him and be totally financially independent. As soon as I get rid of this Visa debt, actually, after his next payment, I will no longer take money from him. I know I always say that, but I really want to stick to it now. I really want to bet big on Bowe/Holyfield III. Riddick Bowe will knock him silly, no doubt about it. What I am hoping is that the odds will be something like 3 to 1. If they are, I want to bet 10k. If they are 4 to 1, I want to bet 12k.

September 12, 1995

It's been a long time since I've written. Some good stuff. I am not sure if I have written about it, but I have recently realized that all of my friends, literally, all of them, leave something to be desired. They all have flaws, irresponsibility, mostly lack of maturity, flakiness, etc. This bothers me, a little. I do not feel like talking about this subject, except to say that when I get paranoid now, and think I am acting weird, strange, or whatever, I realize it is not me. The fact is, the people that I am hanging around with are causing this, and that I am right on target and normal with my actions. I see things the right way. I must be confident with myself because of this. Self-confidence is so fucking important, knowing when to stand up for yourself, and to hold your ground. Last night, when the chef Andre was giving me shit at the restaurant, I stuck it right back into his face. I then realized I did not feel guilty. I know I am a nice person, and I treat people with respect and kindness. I have to be confident enough in my own personality to realize that this is the case, and when people try to tell me that I am not being this way, or I am being weird, or obnoxious, I must be confident enough to either think or say, "No I am not. I am acting perfectly normal. You must be the one with the problem." I must hold my ground when necessary, and not take shit. I strongly wonder if Andre will ever do it again. And if he does, I will again stand up for myself

I gotta start playing and taking guitar lessons on a regular basis, because it is important that I get better. I have been stagnating over the last few months, but I really think my singing is getting to the point of decency. ("Wendy let me in, I want to be your friend, I want to guard your dreams and visions. Just wrap your legs round these velvet rims, and strap your hands cross my engines…!")

Short Story:

He walked into the bar and looked for the man that had wronged him. His eyes quickly locked on his target, the sole reason for his trip. As he approached the man, he fantasized of the violence to come. He was unsure of whether he would win the fight. He did not know whether he would live through it. But he knew he would leave his mark. His enemy would be hurt, and hurt badly. Joey was in a vicious rage, and he prepared himself for the battle. It was not too long ago that they were best friends

September 13, 1995

I am not really in the writing mood right now, so I think I'll read *Exodus*, which Nana gave me. See-ya soon…

September 14, 1995

I am disappointed today because the deal that would allow us to buy the Yeshiva (UTJ) building and us to own it with no money down fell through. Sometimes I feel that the world is playing a cruel trick on me, and that I just don't understand what my calling is. I see some of the actors in the restaurant, and I know I am better than them. I know I have more charisma, more humor, and I am more motivated and success oriented than them. But why do I even think about acting? Acting is playing somebody that you are not. I don't really want to live a life like that. I do not know what the fuck I want to do with my life. I really wish my father and I could buy some type of property!! I feel so strongly that if we could just beg, borrow, and steal to somehow purchase something, with or without a partner, but hopefully without, we would be on our way to equity. Then we could little by little build up a mini-portfolio, which would turn into a portfolio, which, in five or six years, could be worth a few million on paper, with equity built and building up.

September 21, 1995

This girl, Rachel, who I met at a bar, and made the fatal mistake of not talking to her long enough, told me where she lived and the company she worked for. I tracked her down and called her Monday, no return call. I called her Wednesday, she came to the phone at work, and said she would call me that night. No call. Poem for her:

Call me pathetic, a deluded romantic,
although that's not important to me.
I met you at a bar, and had to leave quickly,
a rather egregious mistake certainly.

You probably think I'm average, a regular Joe,
who gets woman's numbers each night.
And after two calls, which went unanswered,
my friend Josh said to give up this plight.

But I wanted to show you, I'm one of a kind,
in this short poem I've sent through fax-mail:
That you seemed special and nice, you glowed in the night,
and in great attempts it is glorious even to fail.

So here is my last shot, a stalker I'm not,
I promise now I will leave you alone.
If you need a reference or two, Becca (formerly) Meyers will do,
So tempt destiny and pick up the phone!

Believe it or not, and I'm asking myself that question right now, I just sent that fax to her! I have only spoken to her for five minutes, or less. Maybe two minutes. But this makes up for that lack of time. I can see that two calls would not do the trick. But if a fucking poem does not, then that is obviously it. I will not call her again…

Silvia is coming in this weekend from North Carolina, she claims she is thirty pounds overweight. I hope she isn't. This is continuing my girl push, or my attempts to step up my woman social life. I had two dates and a girl coming this weekend. The dates were both not worth pursuing, although Mindy is OK. She looked older, and slightly chubby, perhaps a Hillary in the future… But there are always more prospects, a spanner in the wings, although I don't know what that is.

I am really enjoying playing and singing Bruce Springsteen's "Thunder Road," etc. Ballad-like songs. That book was fucking worth all of the $75 I paid for it!! I gotta get into a band of some kind. I think I will advertise in the *Village Voice.* I bet I will get some replies… I must do that soon. After the weekend, or maybe before…

Chapter 6

The Goddess of Fertility

"Mr. Greenwich Village"

September 27, 1995

So you can imagine my chagrin when a large beast, heavily disguised from what I thought (hoped) Silvia would look like, showed up off the plane. I was waiting at the airport with flowers and hope, and I got Annie Wilkes from the movie *Misery*. Luckily, I saw her before she saw me, and I threw the flowers in a garbage can behind me. Anyway, I was now stuck with a girl I totally was un-attracted to for a whole fucking weekend. But I forced myself, with the help of constant *Sean Bradley* (marijuana), to have fun. The art museum, where I fell in love with the impressionists, to Kate's party, to going to a bar or two, until the final night. After I told her how I felt, she still wanted to fool around. Since I made the resolution that I have to increase the amount of notches in my belt, and since I had been perfectly clear that I had no intentions of dating her (ever), she still wanted a piece. So I told her I am an extremist, and if we fooled around, I would not want or be able to stop it. She said, no problem. When I tried to back out, she called me repressed, etc. So I had sex with her. It was quick work, not much foreplay, not much kissing – just sex. Penile-vaginal intercourse, sucking tits, a few kisses, and a good fuck. After we were done, she alluded to the second condom I had taken out. But I knew that I would never, not in a million years, ever touch her sexually again. She wanted it and she got it. But just once. The next day I drove her to the airport.

When I got home, Rosh Hashanah was nice with my family, although we conducted business (my dad and I) on the second day, when we bought a car to replace the one that died on the way home from dropping my sister off at the airport!! When I got home from Westchester Tuesday night, I called Rachel, the girl I had written the poem to. We had a really nice talk, and she told me her favorite singer is Neil Young. Uh oh, time to fall in love… I hope to see her tonight, and I must admit that I am honestly nervous. (So what a fucking week – two dates, a girl in for the weekend, a poem to a beautiful prize, actual sexual intercourse, a car dying, buying a new car, and the emergence of a great prospect – a girl whose favorite singer is Neil Young. Is this Hashem telling me that I have now met THE ONE!!??) This week I made the effort to really step up my efforts with women. I totally created the situation with this girl, from the dating introduction, to the two unanswered calls, to the poem, to the call at work, to last night's great talk. We'll see…. I am predicting something good out of this one, but I am hoping there will be mutual attraction. (Please, because I am into a little relationship…) Maybe I'll marry her—the pieces seem to be there.

Life is so fucking difficult at times to figure out, but at other times so easy and obvious. I know that I will be very rich someday, hopefully by the time I am 30, but more likely by the time I am 35. It all comes down to logical thinking. If I take the fucking bull by the horns, I always win. I can get any girl in this world if I just play it right. It comes down to sweeping them off of their feet, and I do not know if this girl is even worth it, but I will soon find out. Rachel reminds me a bit of Jeremy's ex-girlfriend. There is a soft sweetness in her. (Why do I always kind of like my friends' girlfriends?) But one thing I am going to try to do is give her a chance if she lets me give her a chance. I must be relaxed – I am also, for the first time in a millennium, worried that I am not going to be handsome enough!!

How many fucking guys write poems to girls that have blown them off twice already?? How many guys will fight anybody? How many guys study Talmud every week? How many guys work to have an amazing relationship with their family? How many guys have a burning entrepreneurial desire? How many 24-year-old guys play a musical instrument religiously? How many of these guys are also great looking? Healthy? Nice? Well-rounded socially (from the Jeremys to the Robs to the Andy's to the Jasons!!) And mentally (from violence to art to music to love to capitalism to dreams to reading Herman Hesse and about Booker Washington and Henry Miller?)

I am the fucking shit, and every girl in the world will eventually feel this way if I want her to!! I want a girl who is optimistic about me, who is admiring of me, who talks about me to others, who knows I am going to be totally great one day and that I am already totally great!! And I want to feel about her the same way, but she can't be too overbearing or domineering!! NO HILLARYS OR HOLLYS ALLOWED! But they can't be too wimpy either, because I can't deal with Silvias or Rachels or Jills or Heathers, or those loser, overly aggressive husband searchers. No way. I will not fall for their home bred, mother-instilled, nervous Darwinistic crap about how they are looking to settle down and reproduce, with a simple fucking conservative lifestyle in a simple motherfucking presentable life. The right girl will make me want to settle, but I will not be the one to do anything until I am good and fucking ready!! Most girls, almost all, in fact, are easily understood. They have so many weaknesses and hang-ups, and they are basically way uncool about everything. Even though I tend to put my eggs into one basket, and think each girl is the one, I must force myself to write, because I really believe this, that if not her, it will be the next one, or the next one after that. I can tell that wherever I go, girls like me, and that will not change, at least not soon, G-d willing!!

I wanted to spend a few minutes discussing my art revelation that I had over the weekend. I had not been to the art museum with full consciousness, ever. I do not mean sober, but I mean actually being excited and understanding of the sheer fact that a mere mortal human being has created something so perfect and immortal and genius and beautiful!! Without this, which is what I will call art common sense, art means nothing. But one must think of the man that created the art, for that is where the art is born. I want to read about these painters, especially the Impressionists for now, find out about their lives, and eat their pictures for dinner. I am going to buy some prints in the next few days, and my apartment will be one step closer to greatness, although much money and steps are between the current state and future greatness of it. Art is fucking awesome, and I must know more about it. Gotta go, but this was a choppy yet important session…

September 28, 1995

Last night I went out with Rachel, and I now am more depressed than ever. I am really into her, or at least I think I am. I think she has class, beauty, style, and cuteness. She might be the beauty and the cutie. I am so pathetic when it comes to girls I really like, I know I am a true romantic. I just want to fall in love with a great girl and have it work out. I am sick of bullshit, and while I love to be alone, I also love to be with a great girl. I fucked up the end of the night, when I started babbling about our next date. I looked desperate, especially when I said that I might have nobody to go with to the Springsteen cover band. She said, in reference to my asking her out again, "You can call me." Then she offered her cheek from a mile away, and I kissed a lot of hair and a little cheek. I walked away feeling stupid and depressed, miserable, like a true romantic.

I called all of my friends, Jeremy, Lovitz, Rob, Lee, but not Josh. Why not Josh? (I'm calling him now actually.) I ended up speaking to Lovitz, who told me that this could be going either way and that I must relax, and chill out, and keep the game up a little. I can't tip my cards too soon. But I want to call her up and say, "Let's cut the bullshit, commit to a relationship, and see where it goes!!" Of course she would think I am totally crazy and pathetic, and I guess I would actually appear that way, but I fucking like her, and things seem to fit nicely. Is she a snob in any way? I slightly sensed she is not into my un-richness, but I can't let that bother me. But now I am upset that she does not like me, either she did not find me good looking enough, or something else. Did I appear too desperate? Did I talk too much? Did she think I was lying about anything? Who knows, but it seems that the best thing for me to do is to leave her a message on her machine on Friday, and casually let her know I am planning on seeing that band Saturday night, and if she wants to come she should call me, or she should call me either way. If she calls back, this is great. If not, then I will be miserable all weekend, and very upset. So we'll see. But I fucking want her!!! Lovitz seriously warned me to chill out, and realize that I love the challenge very much, and that the conquest for me is what is making me want her so badly. But from a birds-eye view, things have been progressing nicely. A brief meeting, a phone call unanswered to her apt, a phone call unanswered to her work (she said she would call me back but she was busy), a poem to her apartment, a call from her, a lukewarm talk at her office, a great talk Tuesday night, and a good date Wednesday night. And now, misery on my part – motherfucking misery. But I do have a chance. I think, honestly, that there might be a second date. If there is, I am smoking first, actually I won't, and I will have a clean slate with her. I need a girl's advice. I am a romantic, true and pure, and I worship women, especially ones I like!! Ahhhhhhhhhhhhhhhhhhhhhhhhh!!!! I am in misery!!!

It is weird though, because as I write this, I realize that if this girl totally disses me, then I can complain to myself, and my friends, and wait by the phone, and just enjoy the sadness for a while, and maybe even try something drastic (another poem), actually she will get no more poems unless things are working out. I gave her one of my favorite CD's, *Rust Never Sleeps*, by Neil Young. Technically she should call me and thank me for the CD, or at least tell me that she liked one of the songs. But she won't, and that is okay also. My honest, up-to-the-minute prediction as to whether she is now, at this minute, interested (pause for a minute): No. I wish I could write about something else, but I can't. I actually should talk more about the Silvia incident, which showed me that I am truly serious about increasing the amount of girls I have sexual intercourse with. I had no intentions of ever seeing or dating her, and I made that perfectly clear. She wanted to fool around, and she wanted it bad. So I told her why I laughed ("But oral sex wouldn't hurt, anyway") and she jumped at the opportunity. I told her if we fooled around we would have to have sex, no less. She said okay. And I fucked her with not much more desire to kiss or touch her than I would have if I were fucking a prostitute. Pretty fucking crazy, as I described earlier. My friends could not believe that I told her that I would not fool around unless she had sex with me. But that is what I did, and now I have another notch in my belt. Go Mitch. But I must be respectful to her and return her calls, at least for a while. Now I must pay for the fuck. RACHEL!!! I want Rachel!!! I want a nice little cute little girlfriend. Rachel. Wife, lover, friend, cute, be with her, take her everywhere, enjoy her, love her. I am pathetic and desperate.

Meanwhile, I am slacking off on this Enfield Marketplace shit.

ONE OF MY DAD'S FRIENDS owned a chain of Christmas stores, which were only open during the holiday season, and my dad liked this concept. (He explained that more than one-third of a retailer's annual business is done between Black Friday and Christmas.) He learned of a vacant department store in the Enfield Square Mall in Enfield, Connecticut, which was an eyesore to the mall owner and its shoppers. He made a deal with the mall owner to subdivide the department store into a Christmas flea market, which he would call the Enfield Marketplace. My dad's plan was to fill it up with local businesses and artists, collect rent from each, and close down after Christmas. He said we could be 50-50 partners on the profits and paid me $1,000 per month to help him. My only responsibility before we opened was to call local businesses and artists to ask if they were interested in renting space. If they were, I would turn them over to my dad to close the deal. I planned to make these calls during my downtime at the Brooklyn Army Terminal, since I had so much free time there. As usual I found it "hard to get started."

Something is really bad about my slacking off, but I hate making these phone calls. I want to write a letter to Neil Young. If the letter if fucking unbelievable, I think he will respond. I want to join him and be his right-hand man.

Dear Mr. Young:

This is the most important letter I have ever written in my entire life. Since I was old enough to appreciate good music, you have been by far my favorite artist. I love your lyrics, your voice, and everything that I understand about your music. You are the reason I took up guitar, and your music has had a profound impact on my life. However, that is not why I am writing.

When I read about your two sons, and also about the fact that you are purchasing Lionel, LLC, my ultimate goal in life came into my head: I want to be your right-hand man. I want to help your business grow, and basically make things run perfectly. It would be an honor to work for you, and I know you would like me. I had no idea you had an interest in business, and when I found out, it all seemed perfect to me.

The only reason why I have the guts to write this letter to you is because I know I too am special. I am a dreamer, a romantic, someone destined for excellence. I love music and the arts, but I also have a burning entrepreneurial fire inside my head. I have a business degree from the Wharton School, which some say is the finest in the country. My work experience has proven valuable to the growth of my business skills and all-around maturity. I know you would agree. I think that if you were to give me the chance to meet you, you would one day look back on it as a risk that truly paid off.

I am begging you to please call me. I would come wherever you wanted me to on the same day you called me if necessary. I am currently employed, so please do not think I am some desperate guy looking for a break. I am writing this letter asking you for the chance to elevate my life to true greatness. If you take a chance, it would only take a few minutes to meet, I promise I will not let you down. I know your time is as valuable as gold, but I am no slouch either. Please take this chance!!

October 10, 1995

A lot of shit has been going down lately, far too much to make it worthwhile to write. I bought a Guild guitar with turquoise inlay, one of only 200 made, for $1200. Instead of putting $250 into my old guitar, I used it for a $300 credit towards the Guild. It is fucking great, and I am a better player already because of it. It is so much more satisfying that I can't even believe the difference…

I am really attracted to Lee's ex-girlfriend, who I keep seeing every time I go to UPenn stuff. I know she allegedly has problems with lying, meanness, eating issues, etc., but I have this weird idea of fixing her and making her perfect. I might only want the sex, but that is a different story and definitely not worth it. She is the devil, and I am the devil's pawn. I recognize that this whole thing is bad news, and I also realize that it can only lead to bad things with Lee. But he has come out and said he has no problem with this, which I know is bullshit, because he still loves her. I should stay away, but I do not know if I will, for the first time in my life. That is again a test of my integrity, like when I proclaim things, like not intermarrying, or not cheating, and then, when the temptation arises, I may succumb. I either should not proclaim things or I should be stronger. Maybe somewhere in between.

Rachel is still a big if, but probably soon a small "no." She is not worth it. The poem may have had more to do with me than it had to do with her. But this is only because she has been ranging from indifferent to negative, while keeping the small flame burning ever so slightly, but light enough to make me want to speak to her and get upset if we don't. Tonight I will ask her out, and try to play some guitar to her over the phone, and tell her about the museum, and the musical instruments that I saw. I will paint a picture for her of a romantic, which is what I am. Besides this, everything is pretty ok, still working at Chaz & Wilson's Thursdays and Sundays, the Enfield Holiday Marketplace is still coming along, my apartment is great, filling up with art, the guitar is awesome, I am not reading enough, not fucking enough, not exercising enough, but really enjoying life.

I want to write more, and when Rob and I saw the beautiful woman in a wheelchair in Central Park, he said, "She is a bird with broken wings." She was so beautiful, and I fell in love with her, so I will try to write my first novel about falling in love with her. It's called *Bird with Broken Wings*.

October 17, 1995

Why am I such a dreamer? Is one of these things going to pan out? Or will I dream the rest of my life and never be rich or successful or happily married or etc. Now I have youth on my side, so it is okay and acceptable to be in between a lot of things. But soon I will not have this on my side, and if great things do not come by then, I will be depressed. To get involved with the WCC or the UFC (Mixed Martial Arts fight promotion companies) could be very exciting. What about a life in which I do stuff with SCS (My dad's company) and also have an office at SET (Showtime Event Television, Showtime Network's Boxing Department) to work on the fighting events? I know that I truly love the UFC (Ultimate Fighting Championship), and I really think it may be the future of professional fighting. Boxing is basically dead, which is now obvious. But the UFC is pure, not corrupt, and it delivers what it promises. The best fight the best, every night, and they have it in tournament style. I would definitely consider getting involved with this organization, and really try to work my way up. Is it possible? I must be persistent…

I am so fucking deluded sometimes. Last week I composed a letter to Neil Young, about working for him and his toy company. He doesn't need a fucking right-hand man, either that is why I am so pessimistic about that letter (which I did not send) or it is because of the fact that every time I have a new idea, it totally replaces the old idea. Now it is to work with SET and help them promote pay-per-view fighting championships. I would love to get involved with this event, at an early stage. On Monday, I plan to do research at home, get a ton of phone numbers of UFC people, SET people, and others and send out five or six letters with plans to follow up on them later in the week. I will probably also send the letter to Neil Young, which is worth a stamp. I then will have some leads that I can pursue. I have to start heading towards something that will make me happy. I am not sure if it is owning buildings, which may lead to riches, or getting in on WCC stuff, which can also be interesting. It is definitely possible to run a store or another business while working full-time for SET. I am fucking totally crazy, off the fucking wall, deluded, I don't know. Maybe, as my father says, I am waiting to step into shit. SET is a huge organization, but the WCC is not yet. If I could really get involved with this thing, perhaps I could find a group to put one on and make a ton of money. In the meantime, if I am hoping?

I realize, as I sit and write this, that I am in serious trouble of entering a bad stage of my life. Financially, I will be okay when I get my Brooklyn Army Terminal check on Thursday. But not great. Business-wise, even though I have been a lazy piece of shit in terms of helping my dad do the leasing, the Enfield project may go well. I have to make more calls; I cannot believe the fact that I am not doing it, even for my own father and me. I am being worse than his partner Arthur. I must shape up. I really hope we do the Ixchel store

Ixchel was a spin-off from the Enfield Marketplace. One of our tenants there was a Deadhead named Chris, who imported beautiful sweaters from Ecuador and Peru. (The name of Chris' brand, Ixchel, was derived from "*Ix Chel*," the name of the Mayan goddess of fertility and procreation.) His sweaters sold fast—that hippie was making big money! We got along well with Chris, and my dad suggested we open up an Ixchel store in Westchester County—that same holiday season. Chris said we could use the Ixchel name if he could be our exclusive supplier. My dad was excited, scribbling financial projections right away.

PRO FORMA - 10/19/95
IXCHEL OUTLET - RYE/PORT CHESTER, NY

1. ASSUMED SALES — $100,000

2. EXPENSES

Rent @ 10%	$10,000
Credit @ 4%	4,000
Payroll @ 15%	15,000
Bad Debt @ 2%	2,000
Insurance	1,200
Utilities	800
Advertising @ 6%	6,000
Capital Costs	7,500
Sub-total	$46,500
Cost of Mdse. @ 25%	25,000

Total Expenses $71,500

3. PROFITS BEFORE TAXES, DISTRIBUTION $28,500

The numbers looked good, and my dad said we would be 50-50 partners again if he could find a suitable location for the store. (I knew he would.) My job would be to manage and staff it for the Christmas season, which we also planned to shut down February 1. My schedule was busy, but I said I could handle a less-than three month commitment. I quickly assembled my staff: Andy Metternich, his girlfriend Annie, and our two friends Jarrett and Shiva.

When my dad searched for locations, he found "locations, locations, locations"—his favorite real estate mantra—which emphasized its supreme importance for any retail business. Uncovering the best ones was his specialty. Nobody was better.

October 20, 1995

If I can put $20,000 into my bank account by the end of the year, I will be starting off 1996 in a very good position. I feel it is time to take a chance. It may sound frivolous, but I must take a chance. I have to build up something, I do not know what. I am sitting here and brainstorming, and I realize that the pay-per-view concept, more specifically, the fighting concept, excites me very much. I really want to put on an event. I want to get involved with something that is totally exciting and controversial. On Monday, I will do some serious legwork, and hopefully send out a number of letters. Boxing is not the way to go. The way to go is these new bare-knuckle tournaments.

I just called Jock McLean of Showtime. I realize how important it is for me to write, because it inspires me to do. I think that if I can get one interview with this company, I can be on my way to big stuff. Pay-per-view is huge, and will be for a while. In reality, all I really want is the black Showtime jacket!! I would be so proud to wear that thing. My love for excitement and combat may be rewarded with a job with Showtime Event Television. Now I am sitting and waiting for this fucker to call me back, and I hope he does, but he probably will not. Would he be that much of an asshole as to not call me? I don't think so. But nothing surprises me. If I could get a meeting with him on Monday, my life could change. It is time to take action!! Avenge!! Sue for damages!! Go for it!! Combat!! The women will come, so will the fun. But I need that Showtime Boxing jacket, and all that it represents!! Come on Jock, call me, you stupid asshole, you dumbass corporate piece of shit. I hate waiting by the phone. My goal is to get a meeting with this guy, any way I possibly can. Well, I guess I must sign off now. The phone has not rung yet, but I will not give up.

I met Rachel at the Union Bar Saturday night, the one that I wrote the poem to. She was completely unimpressive. Granted, she is very pretty, and I was open for something. But maybe I did not give it enough of a chance. I don't know. She was not that fun to be around, and she brought up stupid things, like her friend dying in a car accident, and being responsible, and she was at the whim of her friends, and had to leave whenever they wanted. The point is, she is lame. I tried to make a date with her alone, and she would not commit. Indifference towards me does not cut it. I told her I was leaving, because my friend Rob (who I invited to tag along) felt really uncomfortable. She said, "Where are you going?" I said, "I don't know." Then I said, "I'll see you around." What a weird ending to a girl I wrote a poem to.

Right now I have no prospects at all. I want to love a girl, fall for her, be with her, have a great relationship with her. I do not know why this is not happening. I know I am picky, and if I look back over the past months since I have been back from Israel, I have had a lot of prospects, and I have ended each and every one. I have not found someone special. Rob says I am looking in the wrong places. That could be true. But if I look at a synagogue, I will wind up married. And if I look at a club, she will not be Jewish. I must keep going girl hunting, and when I go out, get numbers, and create prospects myself. I am still trying to get Amanda to come from England, which would be unbelievable, but I do not think she is mature enough to see why she should definitely come. She is still technically with her on-and-off again boyfriend from out of town, but this is a once-in-a-lifetime experience for her, America, NYC, free rent, a job, love, new friends, everything her heart desires!! Or she can stay in Leeds and see her boyfriend every weekend if she is lucky!! The point is, I am frustrated with people. I am a true romantic, I want to show complete love to someone, and not be brought down to reality. But the girls disappoint me. They don't understand, they are half-assed, or, sadly enough, not pretty enough. But the struggle still finds me a happy man.

I love my apartment, I just decorated it with some nice art posters. I love my guitar, and I know I am getting better. I enjoy my social life, for the most part. I love reading, although I have not had enough time to do this. I love the music I am getting into, twenty years too late. Pink Floyd has been captivating my listening waves. I have a newfound interest in art, and I have been going to the Met somewhat regularly. Basically, I am really sucking in the culture of

New York. It is great. If I wish too hard for a girlfriend, I might just get that. This may take away some of my freedom, which may hurt me in some ways. A nice casual relationship would not hurt, full of sex and fun, but I am not capable of this. I fall in love. To date a non-Jew is a trap I am capable of falling into, and I must not. It is not worth the risk. The fact is, I am not a lonely or unhappy man, but I do feel alone sometimes late at night, and it would be nice to have a girl around, someone special. I know I will eventually find this, but sometimes I do not know. That is the weird thing. But I want a girl who looks up to me, who really thinks I am a beautiful person, who accepts me, fights me if necessary, but not unnecessarily.

Right now, if I had to pick any girl in the world that I already know and marry one, I would pick Amanda. I must get her to come. That is my next goal…. And in the meantime, have sex with three more girls from now until Jan. 1, and maybe a small relationship in between. Mary. I just called her, adding her into my life. Who else? Gretchen? Okay, I'll call her now. I just called her and spoke to her. She is interesting. She said, "You live on 80th street and don't recycle??!!" I was like, "Yeah, but *now* I do!" We talked for a few minutes, and then I told her I would call her soon.

Women. All you have to do is be aggressive. Lee said last night, "Fortune favors the brave." I agree. There are 10,000 different expressions that speak the same lesson. One is enough. Actually, one is not enough. That is why English is such a great language, because there are so many synonyms, and so many ways to say similar things!! Just now, when I wrote, "one is enough," I portrayed an example to myself of something I want to change. Sometimes I say or do something not because it is what I really want to do. I'll say or do it because it sounds or looks good. What I mean is that I at times have a flair for the dramatic, and I don't know when to separate that from my life. I am running full speed into another corporate position, this one with Showtime Event Television. This is literally the only corporate position that I would consider taking. It is getting involved in a brand new sport, and riding it to the top of popularity if things work out. I can be a spokesperson for the sport. Defending its pureness, etc.

Does my father think I am abandoning him? I do not know, but I also must do what is best for me!! I do not like taking money from him. Enough of this bullshit. I am not really in the mood to write, so I will sign off for now. More to come in terms of my interview tomorrow with Jockstrap McLean.

I thought about this when I was talking to Lorena the other night, after Sean Bradley (marijuana). My father is 59, and he is more entrepreneurial than ever. He thinks of the future, of owning a building, starting an empire, and he is so optimistic about all of this. I am 24, with anxiety about my future. I love my father, he is my best friend and biggest hero. I do not want to let him down, and I do not want to be a source of disappointment to him. But sometimes I feel stifled by his nurturing, and I let him do too much because he can and will. My father is getting older, I see it in him when we spend a whole day together. He slows down as the day goes. Granted, he wakes up very early, and others think he is fine, which I guess he is, but I am afraid of his getting old and not being financially capable of a decent life. But that won't happen, G-d willing. I want my dad to be happy. But what if the World Combat thing really pans out? What if it takes us out of business together? Am I abandoning ship too fast? Am I screwing my father over by leaving before? Am I a quitter? I am just a dreamer, with no real direction or clue as to where my life will take me right now.

I hate taking the $1000 from my dad as a retainer, even though this Enfield thing will bring us back to date. And the Ixchel store should make us some good money. The fact is, this is real entrepreneurial shit. I said I wanted to be an entrepreneur, but I am lazy in many ways. My father has such a better work ethic than I do, I do not understand it. He says that he is a screw-up too, but I do not see it. I just like to enjoy life. I have not even finished *Exodus*, which is a pathetic truth. I am ashamed of myself. I can read the whole thing in one day, and it is worth it. Tonight I will cancel the racetrack bullshit, because I do not have any money, and I will read

Exodus. My goal is to get to page 500 tonight, and finish it by the weekend. Tonight I will read 133 pages. That is nothing.

Something is telling me to call Rachel, I do not know why. She has disappointed me in every way. NO!!!!! I will not do it. If she has a desire, she will call me. I have done enough. I know she will not call. That is sad, but the way she looked at me when I was leaving, it was as if she wishes she had not fucked up, but was not and is not ready to not fuck up, or to remedy the situation. Perhaps I should have made more of an effort. But I tried. But every time I talk to her I feel like I become a caricature of myself. I tell her stories, and each time I have goals, to portray a certain part of me, or to teach her something, or to appear cool, but I like to impress others, and affect them. But still, something is telling me to not give up on her, although I do not know why. She wants to appear like bad things have happened to her, which means she is relatively high maintenance and annoying, etc. Give up!!!!!!!!!!!!!! Be a man!!

I want to call Renee, Lee's ex. I know it is fucking wrong, I will be taking something away from Lee, something special. It just is not right. But I do not know if I am strong enough to resist her if I ever see her out again. Be a man damn it, be a man!! But Lee is through with her, and that is a fact. He'll never go out with her again, that is also a fact. If our friendship is capable of surviving this, it may even become stronger. She is Jewish, beautiful, and full of passion. She has problems, she has suffered, she is suffering, and she lives life to the extremes. The fact is, she used to be slutty. That is cool. I don't give a shit. But I want to find out about her. Why does she lie? Why is she so insecure? Why so beautiful and seductive? I want to fuck her!!!!!!!

October 25, 1995

First of all, before I even write, I will denounce my previous statements that I have inclination to go for Renee. She is a troubled girl. My friendship with Lee is valuable. Even though I have differences with him, I would be risking our friendship by ever touching her. It would be wrong, and it would totally change how our friendship is. I will not do this. I just hope I do not see her while too fucked up….. NO!!!!

I should keep going to Jake's to meet girls, and see what happens. Basically, my social life is not great, and it may have to do with the fact that my friends are not giving me that type of support group to hang out with and meet that kind of girl. I should spend more time at night with shallow people, like Toby, where I may have a chance to meet more girls. Every time I go to a place, I meet a girl. If I continue to go to these places, I will find someone of quality.

I am also depressed because of this career opportunity with Showtime and Jock McLean. He has not returned my thank-you letter, and I fear I have been "filed away." We'll see. Hopefully I will speak with him soon.

I am also depressed about life in general, in a weird way. I feel kind of in the doldrums. Fredda seems messed up, the Enfield stuff is annoying. But in reality, I am one or two phone calls away from being really happy. If Allison calls, or if Jock McLean calls, then my fortune is turned around. Now I see it. I need adventure in my life. I need to have exciting things going on around me, or I get like this. When I do not have this kind of stuff, I fall into doldrums. I am not excited about guitar, I read less, etc. I must keep creating new adventure. That is why I want to place a huge bet on the Riddick Bowe fight. Because it is crazy and awesome in risk. I want to keep meeting women, and fucking them, or at least experiencing stuff with them. It must pick up soon, and it can only be this way if I make it happen. I will keep calling Jock McLean until he picks up, and I will do the same with Allison. I will not go out with a non-Jewish girl, but actually I would, if she would convert. But who cares if she is sucking my cock every night? If she falls in love with me, she would convert.

Chapter 7

Cali Flights, Castrati Nights

"No longer a letter to Lori."

IN ADDITION TO their Sunday night celebrity scene, Chaz & Wilson's had a popular midweek "early-bird special," which I worked on Thursday evenings. Over the course of a few weeks, I bonded with one of my regulars, an outgoing Jewish grandmother, who said she wanted to set me up with her granddaughter. She was an attractive grandmother, and persistent in her request, so I accepted. She handed me a folded piece of paper, which I didn't read until I got back to my apartment late that night. It said, "Hillary Hoffman, 867-53X9." It was Miss Great-Times-Great!!

October 31, 1995

Halloween. I love this fucking holiday. By the way, I will never date a non-Jew. This is dangerous. I spent time with Hillary the other night, and she came right out and told me that she is dating a Lebanese guy. Who fucking cares about her or her relationships anyway? But it was kind of cool talking to her. She is a good ear. She claims she has not had sex in two years!! I want to talk to her boyfriend and commiserate with him!! I can't believe he is waiting around! I admitted to her that I am only one, beautiful, special girl away from dating, and falling in love with a non-Jew. But I realize this would create so many problems; there are a few unforgivable things, and this is one. I must be strong. I met a cute girl at the Halloween party the other night, Lori. She was dressed as a pumpkin; I thought she was a cat!! Anyway, we clicked, and I called her last night and left a message. She called me back and we had a really nice talk, actually it was okay. At this point, I can take her or leave her, but I will definitely call her after I get back from San Francisco…

I have been slowly getting into Henry Miller's *Sexus*, which Rob lent me, and it is making me want to become a writer. I think I must write something great, and see where it takes me. People have been enjoying "JJ Streets," my one-page fingerless guitar player story, and I know that took no effort:

***

J.J. Streets was the name of our band, and we played blues, and we played them well. On Thursday nights, we used to pack Sam's Hideaway, and the smell of smoke, the dreamy baseline, and the whining anguish of the lead guitar was enough to make a pretty good joint better. When we played, we played hard, and we played sad blues. Some find the blues depressing. For me, they are a soothing relief. It's sort of like letting somebody else do my crying for me. I don't play guitar anymore. Tonight I rolled a joint in my apartment, smoked it on the way to Sam's Hideaway, and found a table in the back. Now the Bombay Gin & Tonics have kicked in, and they're blending sweetly with my high numbness, and I'm letting the music do the rest.

My life doesn't mean much to anybody, not even me. It's a sad harmony of downhill blues, with no end in sight. My dreams have become lies and delusions, some even cruel jokes. That's okay though. I've lived long enough to realize that most dreams die. Mine was to play guitar, and be one of the best there was. My dad used to put me up on stage, before I even knew what I was playing. But I played what I thought sounded good, and not too many people disagreed. I would just think of a story, a sad one, making it up in my head as I would play. I could play with their emotions, bring them up, tease them, and then drop them for being so foolish to think that the blues were going to make them feel better. There was real communication going on in there.

The night after my girl left me, I was too drunk to be driving, and too sad to care. I don't even remember if I saw the red light or not. But that doesn't matter. I lost two fingers that night, which killed my ability to play guitar. I think I miss the blues more than I miss my fingers. But there won't be any crying or anything. I'm here for the blues, to let somebody else do the crying for me.

***

October 31, 1995 (continued)

The best way I can become a writer is to emulate the style of Henry Miller. He was special, and he and others knew it. When he writes, this comes out. He is cocky, yet in a way that is not distasteful because his greatness and specialness is obvious. I know for a fact that I am special. I do not lead a normal life. I am getting very into art lately, but once a week while on Sean Bradley is enough. Edvard Munch blew me away on Saturday, and Florence Stettenheim blew me away the Saturday before. I am really starting to see something in paintings. I drew some stuff yesterday, a few faces and some eyes.

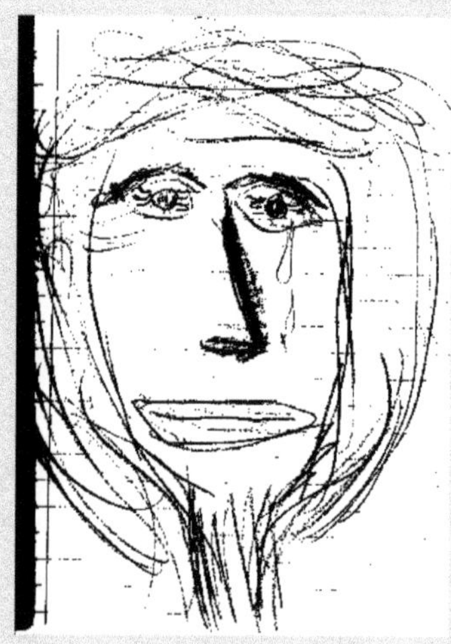

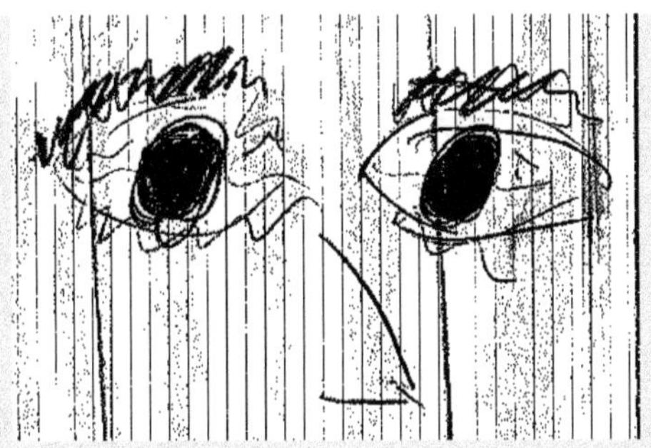

I am not saying they were good, but it was really fun to draw them. I want to get some charcoal chalk to paint some faces, maybe even a self-portrait. I want to be a Renaissance man with money. I want to paint, read, go to museums, play guitar in a band, have a girlfriend, and a sick job. There is so much to do in a day that television is just not good. I still like to be passive at times, though, and watch a sporting event or something. Guitar is not enough to play alone all night. Reading, drawing, these two will start to play a greater role in my life.

I have been thinking about marijuana lately, and I am slowly entering a phase where I will smoke less. I am starting to get to the point where I know how to feel stoned without smoking. However, it is difficult to interact sometimes without it, especially at bar situations. Recently, when I walked into Hi-Life with Lee and his friends, a girl was instantly interested in me, and I liked her too. Instead of being cool about it, I started saying stupid shit, performing, trying to be a caricature of myself. I scared her away. I was a little "too abstract" for her, she said. Last night, when I talked to Lori, I felt like I was trying to be a caricature of myself, and I tried to stop it. I don't know if it was a good talk or not, but I had slight negative feelings about her. But hopefully we will see each other after California. San Francisco with Jer will be great. Pearl Jam, Tyson, Bowe, betting on Bowe, seeing the city, Tahoe, etc. I am also looking forward greatly to the plane rides, where I will be able to read *Sexus*. I hope to finish that book and take a chunk out of *As a Driven Leaf* before returning home. Then perhaps that *Zone* diet book Andy got me, then maybe the short D.H. Lawrence book that I saw on the street, then maybe some of the *Lil' Hegel*. But who knows, some of this reading may turn into some writing, which would be great. But maybe I am not yet ready to write great, that may take some years. But I plan on never stopping.

I was thinking of the time Josh and I became blood brothers before we went to college. When we said goodbye, it was very emotional. I remember it. It is almost like we are bonded together by a despair for life, a sort of cynicism that makes us friends. But when I shed this cynicism, his brother Andy becomes more of my friend. I don't know what I am writing here, but Josh is in many ways a downer to talk to. He has been annoying lately, and he is fucking himself up with bad career decisions. Hopefully he will get this summer job, for once. He is obsessed. That would be fucking great!!

My father is getting older. I see it, as Rob says, every day I see him. He is more forgetful, and not as sharp. I hate it. For the first time ever, I get annoyed at him and I am at times short with him. It is bad. He is very smart, still, and he'll be fine for a while, hopefully longer, but it is very depressing.

If I find an amazing woman, and I mean amazing, I would not be averse to settling down, having a kid, etc. However, I know that this time, being single, and not really worrying about anyone but myself has allowed me to be totally creative, and has allowed me to explore my life in such a way that would never be if I were with someone. I want so much out of the world, and I am just beginning to see all of this. I am not ready yet. Dating is one thing, but marrying and giving up this time is not right yet. What the fuck is the rush? This should give me more confidence with women, because the more I get them, that is great—but the more I don't, the more my art is inspired. Loneliness is good for art. I still have to put the ad in the *Village Voice* to start a band:

"Intermediate rhythm guitarist wants to form acoustic classic rock cover band, with originals to follow. Rolling Stones, Bruce Springsteen, Neil Young, etc. Looking for a strong lead acoustic guitarist, a drummer, and a keyboardist. I can sing a little, hopefully you can, too. No real goals, let's just have fun and play.721-XX17."

I just placed this ad in the *Village Voice*! I realize now that writing compels you to do stuff, I am convinced of it, at least with me. I have just placed an ad, and I am sure that some people will respond to it. This can be very fucking cool if it works out…

November 1, 1995

I have lived a life that has been extremely fortuitous. I always have gotten lucky, in so many situations. Like Henry Miller, I only operate properly under pressure, when things have to get done. I do not do well when there is time, and even a small task does not get done under normal circumstances. But then I get into productive mode, like the day of the Larry King satellite broadcast for *Aish HaTorah*, and have awesome days. The point is I do well from crisis to crisis, and not in between. I just realized that I am a fool for not bringing up the *Aish HaTorah* satellite broadcast when I interviewed for Showtime!! What an egregious mistake. But there is nothing I can do now, and I can't believe that stupid son of a bitch has not called me back. What just happened? I just called, and he told me that Mike Tyson hurt his thumb, and Marina Capporo is going crazy, and that they will both be in touch next week. He just is very busy, and he is also inconsiderate and a bad businessman. But if I fight through this bullshit, and somehow get my ass in there one more time, it is a whole new ballgame. I will call next week.

So the next seven days will prove to be very exciting. I have a call planned to Lori, a trip to San Francisco, a bet on the Riddick Bowe fight hopefully, and a call planned to Jock McLean. A lot will unfold. He said that Mike Tyson hurt his hand… It was kind of cool to be talking to somebody whose life is affected by Mike Tyson hurting his hand!

My life is up in the air, but I am happy, I think. But my Darwinistic impulses are kicking in, and I am starting to plan more for the future. I am not sure what will pan out with a lot of this stuff, I am not sure what to make of the Ixchel opportunity, does it really have a chance? We will see… My woman situation is weak, although it never is really very weak, because every time it is, I go out and find something. I will see what happens with this girl Lori. I think she is really cute, but I was also on Sean Bradley and alcohol, and in a good mood. I don't know, but I want something to have for a while, I guess someone to fuck would not be such a terrible thing. I have to buy some nice clothes, and start building up a nice wardrobe. Why did I write that? To impress a girl? Well, I do not want to look like a kid when I go out. Time to go. California tomorrow!

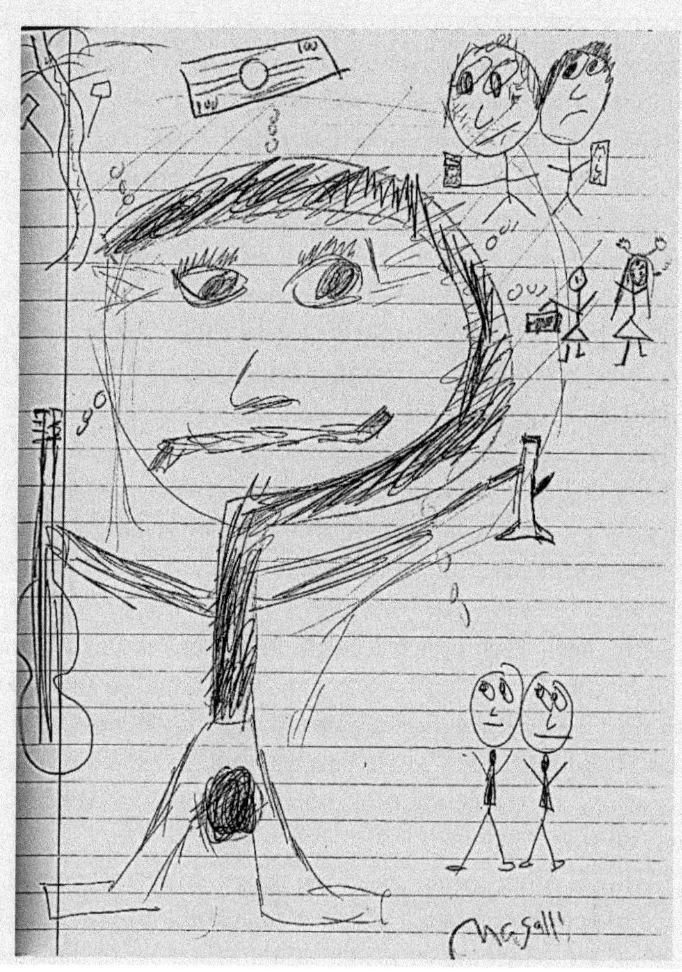

11/2/95 — Flight to SanFran to visit Jer
Dearest Lori-
I met you at a Halloween party.
You dressed as a pumpkin—I thought a cat.
Your cuteness came over me instantly, like I was spattered with cold water after just waking up from a daytime slumber (sleep was fine, but waking is more exciting.)
I can't describe myself to you, not even to myself. I'm changing now, and to try to attract somebody would be futile. I am glowing like a candle, with a life ahead of me full of uncertainty and brightness.
My concept of greatness changes every day—
does it mean to change the world?
I don't know.
I enjoy challenges, I like to be talked about—
my family is supporting

me as much as they are holding me back.
I love having money, but I don't
need
a
lot.
I am friends with bankers, lawyer, future doctors, and they all are, in some way, afraid of me.
I am loving of my newer friends –
Andy – Rob —— but I love myself the most.
It is when I think someone else or something else is so great that a few things happen:
I AM INSPIRED
I ACT
I DO
I RISK
I BECOME BRAINWASHED
But I can't lose myself, but I do not know who I AM, even

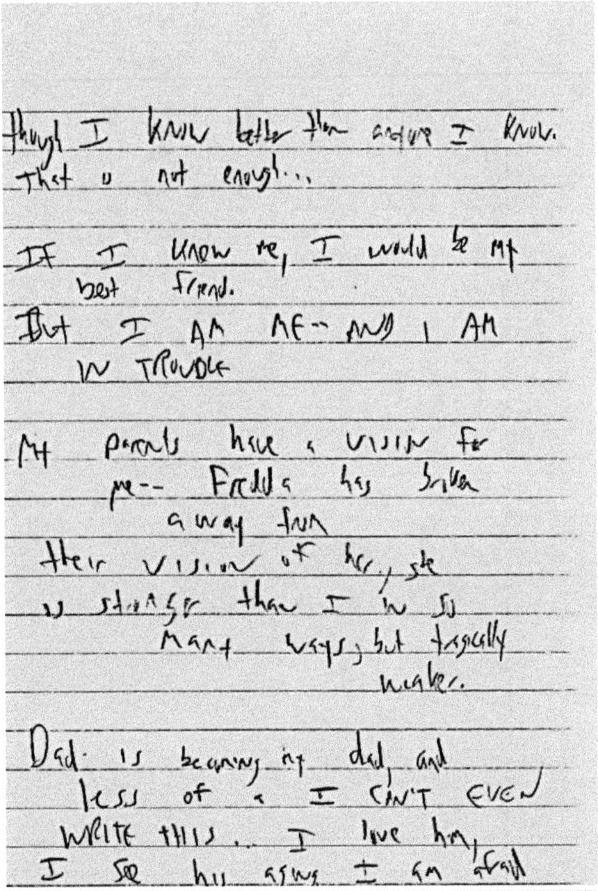

though I know better than anyone I know.
That is not enough…

If I knew me, I would be my best friend.
BUT I AM ME – AND I AM IN TROUBLE.

My parents have a vision for me—Fredda has broken away from their vision of her, she is stronger than I in so many ways,
but tragically weaker.

Dad is becoming my dad, and less of a -I CANT' EVEN WRITE THIS… I love him, I see his aging. I am afraid

if I leave him for Showtime, am I abandoning him? What do I owe him? Not owe in a sense of guilt and debt, but good owe, owe because he is the most giving, generous, greatest man I have ever met!! A man like that should have everything GREAT.
But we will always be close, and if I get rich they will get rich,
but I sometimes feel
stifled
like a little boy
a brat
spoiled
lazy
But…

I AM LAZY, if you define it in terms of the rigid, scheduled, business work ethic world that their generation grew up in

Their Generation (to) Our Generation

From poor, not having material things; to having things due to hard work, time for money; (to) being desirous of <u>more</u>, philosophy, dreams, love

I need to be spiritually satisfied, but I need material wealth too. I take risks, big ones, and I

want to start by making a huge risk—let me get lucky once…
but that is not enough
that is stupid and not responsible, failure can lead to huge problems.
What about SET?
What ABOUT IT?
What will it offer me…
It will offer me:

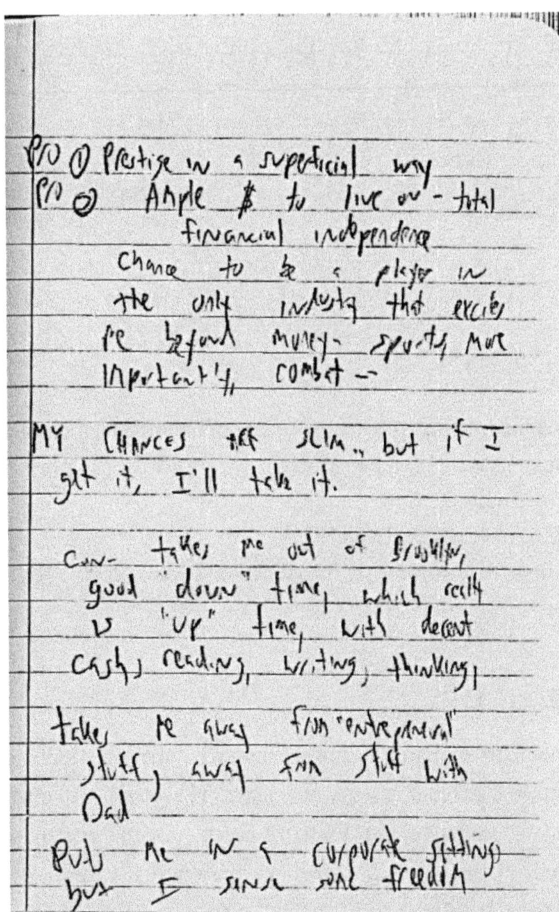

Pro 1: Prestige in a superficial way
Pro 2: Ample $ to live on—total financial independence. Chance to be a player in the only industry that excites me beyond money—sports, more importantly, combat—
MY CHANCES ARE SLIM… but if I get it, I'll take it.

Con: Takes me out of Brooklyn, good "down" time, which really is "up" time, with decent cash, reading, writing, thinking,
(Con:) takes me away from "entrepreneurial" stuff, away from stuff with Dad.
(Con:) puts me in a corporate setting, but I sense some freedom

If I could be travelling to these site, promoting I can stay for a few years, maybe be promoted, I would be a player in the industry--finally.

So what do you think, LORI??
Just kidding, of course this is no longer a letter to LORI.

If I could be travelling to these sites, promotions, I can stay for a few years, maybe be promoted, I would be a <u>player</u> in the industry—finally.
So what do you think, LORI??
Just kidding, of course this is no longer a letter to LORI.

November 7, 1995

Got back from San Francisco yesterday, to visit Jeremy. It was a crazy fucking weekend, to say the least. We went to Tahoe, we saw Pearl Jam, we met two chicks from Spain (Gema and Amparo), we rollerbladed around the city, and we watched the fight. I bet 5,000 on the Bowe-Holyfield fight, and I only really had $2,000. I knew Bowe would win. When he went down, almost for the count, I literally thought in my heart that he had lost, and that I had lost $5,000. I was not really mad, I just could not believe what had happened. I said to Jeremy, "I just lost $5,000 dollars, and I can't believe it. I just lost $5,000!!" I was really in trouble if Bowe did not get up. He somehow staggered to his feet, and I said to myself, he is out on his feet! Holyfield was trying to get a right hand in to finish Bowe, but he could not. HE also had nothing left! Two rounds later, Bowe was up, and now Holyfield was gassed. Then Bowe took him out with a right, saving me from a huge disaster, one that would have taken over a year to climb out of, and one that would have seen me probably getting a part-time job to help pay off this egregious debt. I have learned my lesson. I will never do that again. Betting on sports is stupid and crazy, and it is designed for you to lose. Boxing is so fucking weird and unpredictable, that I cannot believe I took that chance. But it confirms my earlier suspicion that I have major balls or stupidity, or both. I am willing to take risks. This is when I feel best. I have more balls than anyone I know. Anyway, now I have to wait a month and live like I would have if I had lost, while I wait for Harrah's to send me my checks for the bets I won. I am waiting for checks that equal $5,000.

November 21, 1995

This may be my last entry from the Brooklyn Army Terminal. I cannot believe it, but it is true. I have much to talk about – Amparo, Ixchel, quitting here, Bruce Springsteen, the band I am trying to start, etc. And the other day the manager at Chaz & Wilson's said I can't work just two days a week anymore, but didn't offer me other shifts. So no more waitering.

As expected, my dad found and secured the perfect location for Ixchel, a vacant store in a shopping center in Rye Brook, New York. We opened on November 15, a week before Thanksgiving and Black Friday.

November 22, 1995

I know much has been lost forever due to this lack of attention to the importance of this journal. But I wanted to discuss so many things – I am so psyched for the woman that I am hoping to meet, and have been meeting. I know I am becoming a chick-magnet, and I enjoy it very much. Let me first discuss Amparo. I met her at the sea (I do not know which fucking sea) that separates San Fran and Catalina. It overlooked the Golden Gate Bridge. This was a great weekend with Jeremy, where I bet 5,000, 3,000 of which I did not have, on Riddick Bowe. I am fucking crazy (that's true and that is also another story). He almost lost, he was knocked down and almost out, and I would have been dead… I hope I never do that again. Anyway, back to Amparo. I introduced myself to her, and told her she was elegant. She said that she did not know English, that she was from Spain, and we began talking. Jeremy was talking to her friend Gema about things like where she was from, what they have done in San Fran, and we were talking about life. The concept of language barriers, consciousness, what traveling does to one's mind, the ability to know one's self… We discussed music, and art, and she told me she loved the opera. She had never been to the opera, and I told her that if she came to New York I would take her. She is beautiful and elegant, a woman lawyer of 31 years (I told her I was 27). That night we agreed, the four of us, to go to dinner. She looked stunning, because she is, and Jer and I were both interested in her the entire night. They then said they wanted to come to the airport with me that night, so they accompanied us in the car, and Jeremy got two separate moving violations in one shot. In the airport, I told her that I really wanted her to visit me. I kissed her on the cheek goodbye, and she had tears in her eyes.

She called me in New York two days later, and that is when I started to realize what a beautiful romantic she was. "I am a woman with all of the letter. I need love because I like to give love. I am very sensual. I am very sexual." She loves the opera, and when she comes home at night she turns off the lights and lights candles. Then she pours herself a tall glass of wine and then she takes a warm bubble bath and turns on her opera music. She puts lotions on her body, and she is an emotional woman. She demands to be loved, and she says how she feels. It is amazing that I ever went for a girl like Rachel, who is a true sensual prude. It is ridiculous to chase after those that are not worthy, although I do often. Anyway, we had wonderful conversations, and we talked for hours on end. I spoke in Spanish and she spoke in English. She said she could come to New York to visit me for the week on her way back to Spain. I knew she was Catholic, and she mentioned that she wants us to sleep in separate rooms. I told her that would be fine. Neither of us had any idea what would happen.

She showed up on Friday night at the airport. I was exhausted from 3 hours of sleep after going out the night before, I had no time to shower, or do anything. She looked great, and things were not very awkward at all. We got to my apartment without much time to spare, with the opera starting at 8:00 PM sharp. She showered and got dressed in the other room, and I got dressed in the bedroom. I took a whiff and smelled her perfumes, and lotions, and creams, and I followed the scent into her room after she called to me and told me she was ready. She was a beautiful vision to behold, beautiful and sweet and sensual and elegant to the millionth degree, and I wanted to take her in my arms and make love to her right there. I felt like a kid, with nothing great to really wear. So we went to the cab, and still there was no physical contact.

At the opera ticket window there was a problem with my tickets, and the ticket woman kept us until after 8:00, and then she told me the tickets I bought on the phone were for the night before. I could not believe it, and she felt bad, so she gave us two tickets in the orchestra. We had to watch the first act in the viewing room because it was after 8:00, and we held hands for the first time. She held my hand hard, there was passion in her, and I held hers hard too. She leaned her head on my shoulder, and I touched her arms, and her wrists, and her fingers, and I was enraptured with her body, and her elegance. We were in the main area for the second act, and it was great. I will not forget seeing her eyes look at the stage, and holding her hand, and smelling her, and wondering how beautiful a woman could possibly be? After the opera, we went for a late dinner and drank wine, and talked about how much we cared for each other.

We arrived at my apartment after 1:30 and she took her shoes off. We began listening to the "Castrati," "the man with a woman's voice." I told her about how many times I like to close my eyes and sit in front of the speakers of my stereo and listen to music. She said we should try to do that, and we lied down on the carpet in my living room. With only the lava lamp on and the wine in my blood, and her beauty, and the music so strong and passionate, it was the most romantic moment of my life. I told her, all in Spanish of course, that I wanted to kiss the point on her face where her nose ends and her cheek begins. She said okay. I kissed her cheek, her forehead, her hands, and then our mouths met. Our kissing was magical, as was she. We lay on the carpet floor, and kissed and embraced for hours. I felt her wonderful breasts, and kissed her neck, and smelled her skin and her hair. Then we made love, and drifted off to sleep at around 3:30, and awoke together at around 5:00. We went into my room, kissed more, and went to sleep. I lent her my Boston Chicken t-shirt. She was adorable. In the morning, I had shit to take care of. I was worried about the store, and I wanted to get Bruce Springsteen tickets, and for some reason I was not in the mood to make out, and she is sexually overbearing.

Amparo stayed with me in New York City for an intense week. I had never met such a sensual and passionate woman before, and sleeping in the same bed brought us close, fast. I liked being with someone who liked me so much. There were no debates about my authenticity, or our compatibility or chemistry. There were no on-and-off boyfriends to circumvent, or worries about my excessive abstractness. Amparo was available—and ready—willing to give and receive everything. She came to the Ixchel store with me a few times, playfully modeled some sweaters, and hung out with the staff. (Annie knew I had been in a dry spell and joked that *Ixchel*, the Goddess of Fertility, hadn't wasted time!) Amparo didn't speak English, so I was the only one who could communicate meaningfully with her. My Spanish had come a long way.

Amparo thought I was a few years older, the lie I had uttered when we met, which was now too late to fix. She also thought we were together, building something—but soon my feelings didn't match hers. I needed to be alone, as soon as possible, in the quiet of my West 80th apartment. I was relieved when the week ended and she left for Spain. She called me a few days later from Madrid to invite me there—not to visit, but to move in with her! My job in Spain would have been to relax in Amparo's apartment, do whatever I wanted, and wait for her to come home from work. Then we would enjoy each other. She was a sophisticated, beautiful woman and a successful lawyer, offering to support me in Spain. It was an offer out of a romantic movie or a Henry Miller book, which Andy suggested I accept. But my feelings for Amparo and my life situation prevented me from seriously considering it.

Amparo was shocked when I rejected her offer. She said that for her, a relationship was "all or nothing." So it was nothing—and it was over. She expressed her pain as intensely as she did her love, crying hard and loud in a raw bellow. After we hung up, I cried too—from guilt that I had lied about my age and led her on.

Chapter 8

The Center of the World to the Squared Circle

"Standing together—in different hemispheres."

At Ixchel, we sold a lot of sweaters, met some strange customers, and laughed a lot. And the Goddess of Fertility blessed me again. While waiting on line at the bank one afternoon, I spotted a girly girl about my age named Danielle, ultra-sweet and bubbly, with a high-pitched voice. These qualities reminded me of Annie, and Danielle became my girlfriend. She wore high funky shoes from Steve Madden and sent me lipstick kisses and love notes on funny postcards almost every day. Her dad was Italian and her mom was Jewish, which looked good on the sexy Danielle—I liked the mix. And according to Jewish law, she was Jewish!

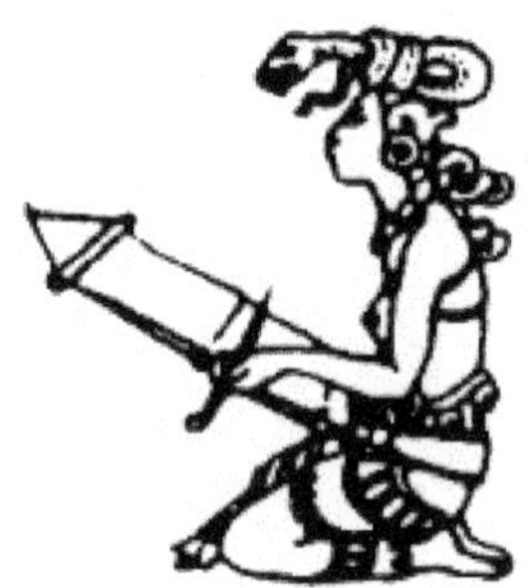

We closed Ixchel on February 1 as planned. In both the Enfield Marketplace and Ixchel, we didn't make the profits we predicted, but we didn't lose; and we learned a lot. "*Dayenu.*" My dad and I remained intrigued by certain items, such as the Alpaca sweaters, which cost us $10 and sold for $55. Customers had come in every day looking for them. The more we stocked, the more we sold. (I realized too late that I could have priced them at $75 and sold as many.) My dad thought we could open a year-round store—not just for the Christmas season—importing and selling these Alpacas, along with some of our other popular items. But Chris was too unpredictable and unreliable to be our exclusive supplier: He would drive to our store once a week, often a few days late, his "dancing bear" stickered van full of goods. He often brought too much of what we didn't want and not enough of what we did, but we had to take everything—or risk a week without enough merchandise to make the store presentable. For a year-round store, this system would not work.

My dad and I wanted to try importing from Central America directly, sans the middleman, and decided the best way to do this was to travel to Ecuador together to find "the perfect supplier." We did some legwork in advance, by dealing with Ecuador's Office of Foreign Trade, and lined up some prospective exporters. But when we got to Ecuador, none of these leads panned out. My dad didn't know Spanish, so I did all the speaking for him. (This reminded me of how Aaron communicated on behalf of Moses, and it felt good to be my dad's Aaron.)

We stayed in Quito, the nation's capital and commercial center, and did some sightseeing while looking for the (perfect) supplier. We visited *La Mitad del Mundo* (The Center of the World) and took a cool picture of my dad and me, standing together—but in different hemispheres. We journeyed to the poor Indian villages, like *Otavalo*, where huge packs of stray dogs roamed, full pigs slow-cooked over street-side bonfires, and old lady artisans knitted in local marketplaces, their skin so wrinkled they looked a hundred years old. It was cool to see who actually hand-made those hand-made Alpacas, which gave me some emotional attachment to the venture. (My dad had this attachment already.) We wanted to do business with those old ladies, but we needed a partner who could handle the red tape of exporting and provide us exactly what we wanted, when we wanted it. So we kept looking.

We focused our search back on Quito and came upon a beautiful store called Ecuadecor, filled with the clothing we knew would sell big in America. We also loved the name. Then we met the owner, Marcel, who was experienced and professional and looked like the "perfect supplier" we were seeking. We took him out to dinner, where he told us he had previously been interested in expanding to North America. (So our timing was "perfect" too.) We made a deal in principle to import our goods from him and use the Ecuadecor name for our year-round store: He would receive reimbursement for his cost of goods and shipping, plus 33% of our store's profits. The next step was for my dad and me to return to New York and find a location. After that, we would fly in Marcel to see it, get better acquainted with us, and sign a formal contract.

The Dream Team headed to the airport with a sense of accomplishment. My dad was excited about Ecuadecor, our first year-round store, which he dreamed would soon be a chain of 50, or 500, scribbling flowcharts and expansion plans on the plane ride home. As he nodded off, I glanced at the napkin on which he penciled out the empire—exporting from Ecuador, the center of the world, with me, his son, the center of *his* world. We were standing together, in different hemispheres.

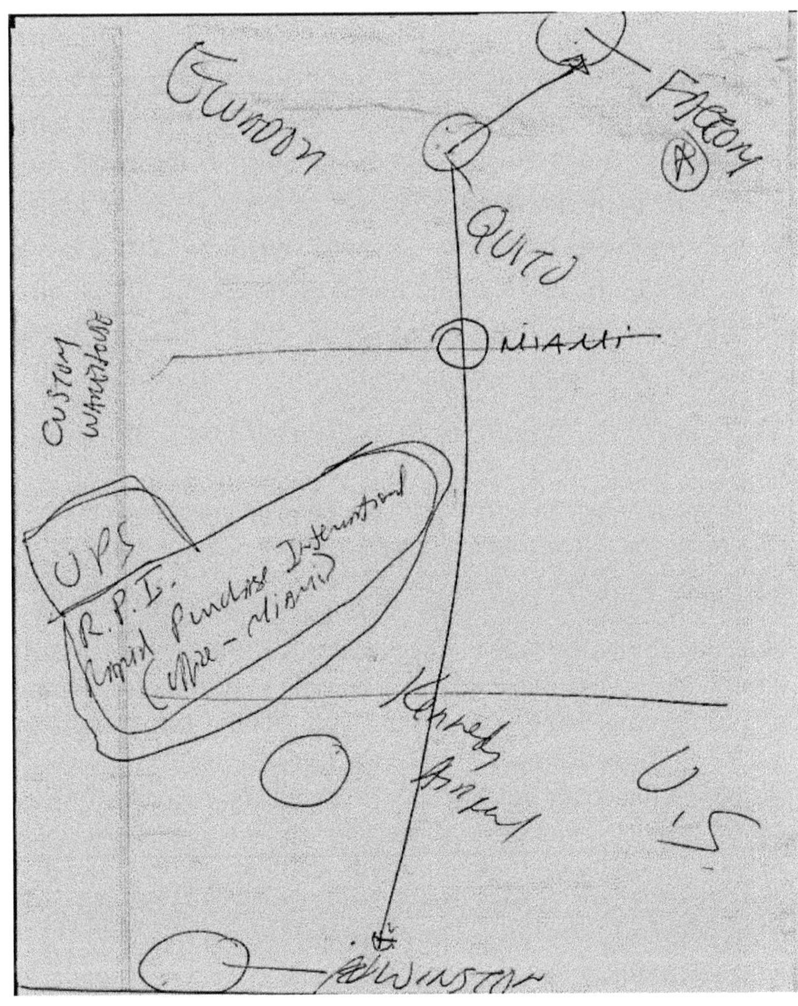

As usual, my dad was trying to set me up for big success, and it made me feel guilty because I wasn't sure about this path. If Ecuadecor panned out, the retail life would be my life and my career, and I had major doubts whether this could satisfy me. Things had snowballed, from Enfield to Ixchel to Ecuadecor—from a few lazy cold calls, to a three-month stint working with my friends, to a potential lifelong commitment.

This was the most recent byproduct of my propensity to tell people what they *wanted* to hear, through loose words or silence—analogous to the Amparo situation. These subconscious tactics, motivated by fear and guilt, provided positive feedback and a happy *present* but ignored the likely cost of *future* rejection: My dad, still dozing next to me, would soon be out there, all-systems-go, looking for the flagship location for Ecuadecor—the first of many. And when he looked for locations, he found *locations, locations, locations*! We were standing together, in different hemispheres.

March, 1996

In attempting to sum up the essence of me, I obviously have much difficulty. How is one able to capsulize something that is so vast and complex? But if I had to describe what is the most prominent characteristic that I embody, it would be that I almost always go to the extreme of any thought process that I endeavor. At the same time, I usually can be simultaneously found at the opposite end of that same extreme. For example, I was interested in learning a little more about religion. Two months later, I decided to become a rabbi and left for Israel. But while all of this was happening, I still maintained an intense love for a martial arts competition that is known to be the bloodiest, goryest, and most barbaric event of our time. Let me pose another example. I have intense ambition to make something great of myself, or succeed in some grandiose way. In some aspects, I have accomplished this with the best of the young people that I know. But I can also be found very often vegetating on my couch, unshowered, lazy, and indifferent, with less ambition than anyone I know. Another example: I love the company of women. In fact, I have pursued them at lengths that I have not witnessed in other's actions. Yet I love to be alone more than anyone I know as well, and miss this greatly when my female pursuits are successfully rewarded. These examples lead me to believe that I am a man of passion, and whatever I do, I do it to the extreme. Whether it is pursuing such opposites as piety versus barbaric violence, ambition versus laziness, or company versus solitude. The type of goal is unimportant -- I go all out.

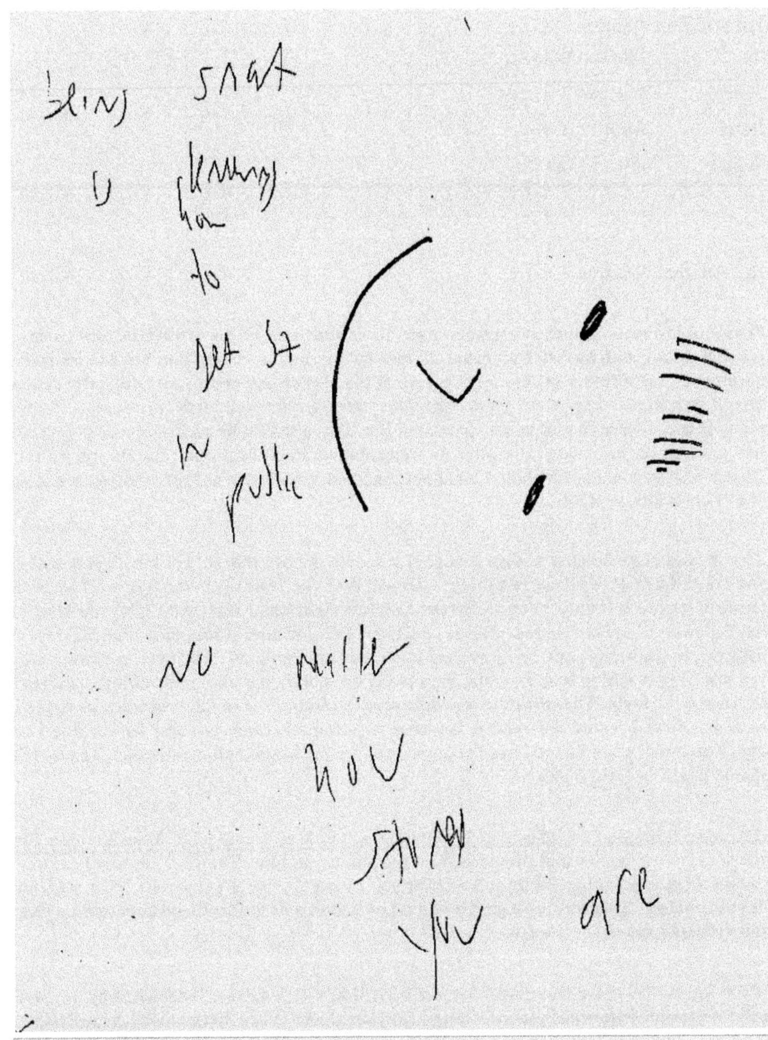

Being smart is knowing how to get by in public
no matter how stoned you are

InterOffice Memo

To: Mitchell Winston
From: Mitchell Winston
Date: April 12, 1996
Subject: What I Must Do

CC: Mitchell Winston

First and foremost, you must organize your file cabinet and all paperwork in your room. There is nothing wrong with having a separate cabinet for personal stuff and another one for essential documents, but either way, you must get rid of the clutter and create a working file system. There should be a file for important documents, like your passport and birth certificate. There should be a receipts file. There should be an apartment file. There should be an Ecuadecor file. Your basket will serve as the in-basket for unfiled or unacted upon items or documents. Do you get the picture? Do not wait any longer for this. You almost had your phones turned off, and you are almost 25 years old. This is unacceptable.

Second, you must develop a more stringent schedule for two things: Guitar playing and exercise. If you are diligent about these two things, you will reap the rewards in the future. This is crucial. In terms of guitar, it is easy. You do not need lessons right now. But each night, you must block out one full hour of uninterrupted, serious practice. This includes scales, base note playing, and really listening to the sounds and being critical about improving them. When you get into a life routine, you must begin taking lessons again, because at this point, you have some ability, and your learning curve may be high. The excercise schedule may fall into place in the next week or so for two reasons. First, because the weather is warmer. Second, because you may be working 12-5 every day, which will allow you to have the mornings free for basketball, tennis, etc. The YMCA on 63rd should again be looked into.

One more thing that would be nice is to pursue a couple of dream jobs. Take Extreme Fighting, or one of the other bodies that promotes the events that you like. The 12-5 job may be a way that you can do these other things while still making some cash (16*.8*25 per week), $320, with no rent for the time being. This is enough, and it will allow you to have basically no debt and survive while the store either pans out or does not.

If you follow the above-mentioned Mussar activities, which are not far fetched by any stretch, you will be happier with what you are doing with your time. When more money comes, hopefully down the line, you will then take some steps to re-decorate your home, with such items as a new comfortable pull-out couch set with love seat, which would be a nice start.

1. **Get Organized**
2. **Play serious guitar**
3. **Excercise**
4. **Dream Jobs**
5. **Money**
6. **Redecorate with new couch**

My dad found some attractive potential locations for *Ecuadecor*, (of course), and we drafted a partnership contract and sent it to Marcel—he quickly replied that it was perfect and didn't request *any* changes. The ease of this step made me happy but concerned my dad. Then we scheduled his trip to New York and purchased his plane ticket. A day before his departure, Marcel told me he was having marital issues and asked to postpone by two weeks. This change cost $75 and worried my dad more. In the meantime, I did some office temping at a few document processing centers in Manhattan's financial district, and resumed my journal.

May 1996

This is the revival of the journal. Much has happened since I last wrote. Without getting into too much plot summary, I have quit the Brooklyn Army Terminal job, opened a store, closed a store, journeyed to Ecuador, gained and lost and gained a few women, acquired a serious girlfriend, the flower Danielle, been in a fight defending Jeremy, temped for a month, learned Freelance Graphics, begun this job at the JP Morgan Presentation Services Group, applied for a job working at the Ultimate Fighting Championship (UFC), gotten better at guitar, gotten better at Talmud but no more religious, and watched the Knicks lose to Chicago…. Again. What a crazy life it is. I turned 25 this week, and 24, just like 23, and just like 22, was crazy as all hell. Since school, I have basically been all over the place. I am still completely unsure about what I am going to do with this life. But I am proud of the fact that I will not settle for anything that is not going somewhere great, at least in my mind…

I just did this critique for UFC IX and handed it to the producer, Michael Pillot. I tore the show apart. He said to call him on Monday. There is nothing more that I want in my career at this time than to get involved with an event such as UFC.

I have to decide if I really want Ecuadecor to work out. Do I really want to own a store, or do I just want to have something to do with my life? In some ways, I can make a good argument for both. But when I walk on the streets I see the stores, and the merchants, and I wonder, is this really me? I am not so into decorating things, or keeping them immaculate, or anything like that. I do not like to deal so much with kissing people's asses, etc. Plus, it is nice to have weekends free. The question is, what the hell am I going to do with my life? There are 3,000 ideas, but none seem perfect. I want to be involved with something I love. I think I could be very creative, if given the chance to work on a production. But is there a future? I think there is, because maybe one day I could be producing my own shows, or promoting events all on my own!! This would be exciting, and definitely has potential. At least I would be involved in something I was really excited about. I think it is untapped, and it has a future.

When I talk to Michael Pillot, I must be firm with him. If he says, we are pretty well covered for the Providence promotion, I am going to speak my mind. I have played by his rules all along, and now I feel I am owed a chance. If he did not like the critique, then I hope he will tell me why and let me prove my worth!! Just give me a chance!!

Anyway, what if it does not work. What are some ideas?

I will have to get a list of dream companies and apply to them

I will have to search my soul

I have no clue what I will do

I should get involved in computers, because it is not too late. What about our starting a computer school? With Lovitz? He would laugh, but hey!! WE could be the most user-friendly school around! I think I will get involved with the computer industry. It is not too late. The internet is still getting larger and larger. It is not yet saturated, not even close…

Actually, instead of starting a computer school, maybe I should learn more about the industry, get involved, find out what is going on, and Lovitz can direct me in where to do this.

What else? Music is not an option, but I had to write it. IF I were only good enough…

Jewish studies is not a desire for a career right now…

It looks like computers may be the way to go. It sounds like there is a definite need for a really good computer school in Westchester. We could start with one class, and rent out a computer room somewhere, two people to a computer. This could work. The philosophy would be no manuals, no flyers, no nothing. It is all about learning, not memorizing!!!

Twice more, Marcel postponed his trip to New York. He first blamed more marital problems, and then his busy schedule. My dad was more disappointed than I, as Ecuadecor was placed on business life-support. Then Marcel's phone demeanor changed; he no longer sounded enthusiastic, not even friendly. The energy was gone from his voice. If I had been more passionate about the venture—as was my dad who didn't speak Spanish—I would have tried harder to convince Marcel to "get on that damn plane" and take advantage of this "awesome no-risk opportunity." But I wasn't, and I didn't. My Moses-Aaron analogy was thereby tarnished, and Ecuadecor was soon pronounced dead.

May 28, 1996

I called the UFC prick on Friday, after delivering the event critique to him on Monday. What did we discuss?

-He appreciates my enthusiasm.

-He does not have a large budget.

-He would rather hire me as a freelance guy, because there is no staff position available.

-He is busy with *Pancrase*, that horrible show where they slap each other a couple of times, all to a background with no noise and no excitement. He asked me what I thought about it, and I said it was a little more technical, and geared towards real fight fans. He said he wanted to get me in on UFC X, and I may be a big help to him, with "your laptop computer" which he does not know was stolen from me (a landlord dispute with the asshole at Pine MGMT is soon to be in court regarding this matter). Anyway, he is going to LA, and then Providence, and then I do not know or care where, but he would not commit. I said

-Am I spinning my wheels here?

-Don't you need somebody to make your life easier?

-Can't I start now?

-I'll quit everything!!

He said to call him on Thursday, because of course he would not commit. So of course I will call him on Thursday to see what the story is, and hopefully he will say, okay, I will see you here on June 10, to start on UFC X. I will then be able to get my shit together, and see what happens… I must save some money this month, because I see financial hard times on the rise, especially with the UFC thing and how little it will pay me.

What the fuck is going on with my life right now? I have no job, except this stupid temping thing, I have no ideas except this stupid redneck ass-kicking dumb idiot competition, and I am waiting around for something good to happen. But tonight I will get my computer, and with it fax capabilities, and with it letter writing capabilities, and I will begin my hunt for something worth catching, latching on to, making grow, fighting for, you know…. a career that I could actually care about.

You are the thing that I remember after I forget how lucky I am.

You are what I think about to remind me how much I have.

You are the first thing on the list of things that I force myself to remember after I forget how lucky I really am.

I am depressed right now. I do not want to join some dumb corporate life. I do not want to be poor, however. But I do not want to be someone's slave. But I do not know what I could do on my own. Unfortunately, I am in a loop.

Now that I have the computer, I must start being very proactive about my life. I must search out opportunities and act on them.

What about trying again with Marcel? I do not even want to be involved in a retail operation right now anyway. I would like to start some sports-related business from my own home, but not a gambling/betting service.

Sports ideas:
Local minor league team in marketing, etc.
Boxing 900#
Hit '1' for latest fight schedule
Hit fighter's last name for info on him.

May 30, 1996

It sounds like that stupid boxing 900 number idea is probably stupid, like many of my other ideas, but I will put it on the back burner for now. Spoke to the Ultimate Fighting flake and he told me to come in on Monday at 5:00. So I will. I am not optimistic…. but of course just a little...

I got my computer. I want to get into the internet now and become an expert at designing my own homepage on the internet. Perhaps then I could start a company that sends somebody to your business for a week and designs your homepage, or just knowing could be a good thing. A boxing homepage may be a future possibility. 900 # fighter info (see previous list)

I want to put on an event. I really can promote a full-contact sporting event at the county center. I know people will attend. I can make a lot of money…. I must look into this. If the UFC thing works out, I will do it for as long as possible and then perhaps do it myself. You can make a shitload of money just by promoting one or two of these things, and it does not seem like many people are doing it.

That is something that I am honestly excited about. A creative ad could generate some very interesting fighters, and could also promote the event, if they bring all their friends…. What about the NY State Full Contact Fighting Champion - FCFC!!? Think of how popular this could be. The county center holds 4,000 people.

4,000 tickets @ $25 = $100K plus merchandise, food, (profit is 40,000). The first event will be small, but one every two months could generate a couple hundred thousand. This is exciting, and if the first one is a sellout, this can become big. Granted, approvals and other things may be difficult, but I have lived in Armonk my whole life, etc…. Maybe another venue is the way to go.

If you rent out a center, I am sure that they provide you with the info necessary, how and where to sell tickets, food vending, merchandise vendors, etc.

I WANT TO DO THIS!!!!!!

What are the things you need?

I know people will go to an event like this. If I could just make it more profitable on paper…

You are the thing that I think about when I need to remember why I'm happy

June 10, 1996

I lost a very important entry when this fucking computer crashed last time I entered stuff in. First, a hit song:

Come my sweet, lay soft on my shoulder, and I will take care of you.

Come, my sweet, and heed my command, and everything will be all right.

Hopefully some good words will come to me one day, like the ones I wrote. But I feel that I am not at the level where I am capable of writing songs that are good.

Anyway, the career of the week is production, and I must not just do it blindly. I want to work on a show or something, so I can learn some of the nuances that go with the concept of planning an event.

I have already landed a week's work at UFC X in Providence, RI. I will hopefully work there that week and see what happens, but I will not depend in any way on this after that week, but it will definitely help my resume. I have contacted USA Tuesday Night Fights, and I have sent my resume to Brad Jacobs. Other shows… HBO *Boxing After Dark* (wait for Scott).

MSG Boxing – tomorrow morning!! No fucking around!!

Anyway, two calls tomorrow, next Monday HBO, Steve Griffith? (not in Berwyn, PA!!, but who knows!!)

By the way, Pine MGMT will get theirs.

June 11, 1996

I should call all of the companies that have events on pay-per-view, starting with WCW (World Championship Wrestling). For some crazy reason, young kids love this stuff and it makes tons of money!! Well, WCW is not in NYC, but WWF (World Wrestling Federation) is in Stamford, CT, and I want to call them!! I just called WWF, and I got the name of the man to send a resume to. I must think of all of the pay-per-view events that are held, and apply to them.

I am not afraid to let you know that I am going to be requesting great change in the future, and I am unsure of what it will specifically entail. But just beware of the future, and expect the unexpected, unless you already do not expect it, in which case, expect it!

I will call USA Tuesday Night Fights on Friday, and see what I can do. I do not want to compromise on the type of job I will take, and that does not mean I won't start at the bottom, I just want it to be an opportunity in which I will be able to grow and learn and do what I gotta do to become the "big shot, the little shot that kept on shooting!"

Why not just plan an event, though? Why not pick an exciting event and plan it? Instead, I will be stuck doing some bullshit thing at some bullshit place, then what is the point? How about planning a concert of the best local unsigned bands, and try to invite record companies and labels to attend? 4,000 * 50 = $200,000.

The doldrums seem to come up on me so easily. I wake up one morning and things are great, and then later in the day I feel so depressed. Who am I that I go through this? Where will all of this stuff that I am going in and out of end up? I really have no idea. Basically, I love to think and dream, and pursue things, but when it comes down to it, I do not know if I like to follow up on them. It is easy to blame this on money, which does not mean that money is not really why, but who knows. I want to be someone who enjoys his work.

June 14, 1996

When a Taurus is determined, he will go all the way. I forgot what it was like to be determined. For the first time in so long, I feel free to do whatever I want in my career. There is no pressure to get a certain type of job, or enter into a certain field. I want to get into special event planning and promotion, with the goal of one day doing it myself. I want to eventually manage fighters, have a facility, etc. Right now I know nothing. But if I work for someone for a while, this will change. I will meet people, etc. On Monday, I will be sending stuff to Cedric Kushner Promotions, HBO, WWF, Battlecade?? (not in NYC), and hopefully Main Events. I will call Darcy from MSG today to see if anything at all is available, and if she says it is above me, I will say, nothing is above me right now if I can at least make a living. If not, she must know people… Carl Moretti, etc. There has to be something!! None of these are very solid leads, but each one has small hope. What about Bob Arum in Vegas? I have to call him on Monday. It is not good to call people from here, because I cannot really be myself.

July 11, 1996

Anyway, one of those "small leads" turned out to be a job – I am now Cedric Kushner's personal assistant, and I am in the fight game!! I will be a player!!! In 40 minutes, I leave here for good. This is the final journal entry. I really enjoyed this job – the people, the independence, the ability to get away with being lazy, the phone calls, the learning about computers, etc. It paid well, in addition. Anyway, sign off…. Until the next entry!!!!!!!!

Chapter 9

Uptown, Saturday Night

"Don't write checks you can't fucking cash."

CEDRIC KUSHNER, a Jewish boxing promoter from South Africa, was short with a walrus moustache. He was highly obese, weighing about 350 pounds. His company, Cedric Kushner Promotions (CKP), promoted more fights per year than any boxing promoter in the world. In our interview, I promised him I wouldn't let him down, and it worked again—I was excited to start at his headquarters in the Hamptons. Gregory Laurence, from Philadelphia, a polite guy around my age with reddish-blond hair, was hired to be Cedric's publicist and began the same day. Cedric lent us his spare two-bedroom house for two weeks, or until we could each find our own places on the East End. Greg and I slowly became friends. An unexpected perk of my job was that Cedric paid the rent for my West 80th apartment, which allowed me to keep it. He worked two or three days a week from his Manhattan apartment office and needed me (his assistant) with him. Our working relationship gelled quickly, and we also became friends.

The CKP office in Sag Harbor, NY had once been a store, and Cedric's office was in the storefront, drenched all day with sun. It was hot and stuffy. I didn't have my own desk, and sat directly across from Cedric at his. I watched in disgust as he allowed the two office dogs to lick all over his neck, face, and deep inside his ears. They would occasionally pause to chew whatever it was they had extracted, and then get back to work—all *three* creatures moaning with delight. Cedric *tried* to be clean; he showered every day, but he was a very stocky man and certain parts were hard to reach. And he didn't wear underwear, resulting in the most severe cases of "plumber's butt" imaginable. Part of my job included mundane things, like bringing Cedric his bran muffin with walnut cream cheese every morning, or Tab sodas from the fridge every hour. Every Monday, I would drop his laundry off at the cleaners, and the girls who worked there would always giggle when I came in. When I finally inquired, they said they had a nickname for Cedric: "Poopy Pants!" (I neither required, nor desired, further elaboration.)

Cedric was a man of letters, and when he wasn't on the phone, he dictated them to me. I would fix them up and make them shine. We were a good writing team (but never as polished as the Dream Team). Cedric was always nice to me, but peculiar and particular in how he wanted things done. I think he liked being thought of as an eccentric. His legal signature was a scribbled smattering of lines fused into a jagged rectangle, with no letters anywhere. This forced me to explain to everyone he wrote checks to that "this *really* is his signature." I knew how to keep Cedric productive, seemingly by instinct. I was in step with the man and his needs, and he was pleased with my performance. I was usually in the office with him until 8 p.m., and I sensed he was happier in the office than at home, where he was alone. His past three assistants could not take his quirky, demanding style, and had each lasted only a few months. I knew my experience would be different.

Every major boxing promoter had a "number two guy," a non-administrative right-hand man, a proverbial *consigliore* who was often a minority partner. Occupying this role for Cedric was Joe West, a smart guy who had already been with him for six years. Since Cedric was on the phone for extended periods of time, he told me to ask Joe West for a project that would use my downtime efficiently. I was hoping Joe would assign me a meaningful task so I could showcase my real skills. But he gave me the boring administrative exercise of updating an old database.

When I was around Joe, I felt somewhat competitive, which emanated more from me than from him; he was always friendly and respectful. My dad thought Joe West's tenure and stature at CKP placed a ceiling on my future advancement there, and said my eyes should always be open for other opportunities. I was thrilled to be where I was—I couldn't consider that now.

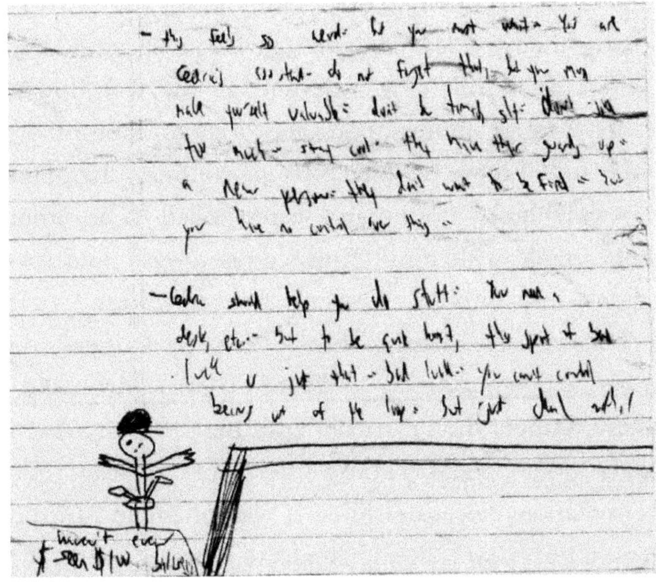

--This feels so weird—but you must wait—You are Cedric's assistant—Do not forget that, but you must make yourself valuable—Don't be timid, shy—don't joke too much—stay cool—they have their guards up—a new person— they don't want to be fired—but you have no control over this.
--Cedric should help you do stuff—You need a desk, etc.—but to be quite honest, this spot of bad luck is just that—bad luck—you can't control being out of the loop—but just deal with it.
--I haven't even seen (the new) $100 bills!!!

I would screen and qualify all of Cedric's incoming calls, which gave me instant status in the boxing industry. I spoke daily to boxing industry legends like Don King, Bob Arum, and most important to Cedric, Lou Shafer, the head of HBO Boxing and his good friend. HBO was the leading network for boxing, by far, because it had the largest budget to buy boxing programming. Lou Shafer decided which fights HBO would buy, so every boxing promoter with HBO aspirations had to first sell Lou, who was therefore wined and dined often by Cedric and other promoters. Whether in Manhattan or the Hamptons, part of my job included going out to dinner with Cedric—after a full day's work—along with boxing industry leaders and television executives like Lou Shafer, the lawyer Milt Chwasky, and all the way down boxing hierarchy to local promoters, managers, matchmakers, and trainers. I labelled many of these people "boxing groupies," lifelong industry nuts who worshipped Cedric and were thrilled to be sitting at the same dinner table with him. (And Cedric always paid for dinner, which didn't hurt either.) At these dinners, Cedric would "hold court," boisterously sharing funny boxing stories and crazy experiences with an adoring audience. It was all boxing, all the time. These dinners didn't usually end until 10 p.m., and I would rather have gone straight home after work instead. I accepted Cedric's invitations because I knew it was smart, and I experienced some great dinners, stories, and laughs in the process.

When Cedric wasn't holding court, he had the tendency to fall asleep instantly, often while he was on the phone. It happened when he was forced to listen rather than speak. But he also had the uncanny ability to wake up, just in time, and say something that fit the conversation. When he missed his cue, or was questioned whether he was paying attention, he resorted to yelling, "OF COURSE I'M LISTENING!! WHAT THE FUCK DO YOU THINK I'M DOING?! CARRY ON!" And then he would doze off again. His doctor told me that his narcolepsy was due to obesity and severe pre-diabetic symptoms.

Before he got into the boxing business, Cedric had been a concert promoter, and he often got tickets for his clients. When there were more tickets than clients, he sometimes invited me: We attended an R.E.M. concert at Madison Square Garden together in the tenth row. He slept through it, while I suffered from lack of taste for the slithering Michael Stipe and lack of marijuana—the first (and last) concert I ever attended without it. I never told Cedric I smoked weed. On another occasion, Cedric got great tickets to Fleetwood Mac at The Meadowlands arena in New Jersey, a more appealing musical proposition, and invited Lou Shafer, Gregory Laurence, and me. We were driven there, as usual, in Cedric's red limousine by Larry, Cedric's full-time driver, a pothead whom Cedric always treated well. We sat together in the sixth row, directly in front of lead guitarist Lindsay Buckingham. I never saw someone play guitar like that. He mesmerized me with his finger-picking solo for "Gypsy," his notes weaving in and out, filling the stadium. I looked over at the dozing Cedric, in and out too. Lou Shafer was also in and out—to the parking lot to meet Larry and right back with a joint—which Greg and I inhaled, in and out.

Cedric's stable of boxers included many world champions and rising stars, and working for him required a great deal of travel to their fights, about two or three times a month. For one of our world championship fights at Mohegan Sun Casino in Connecticut, I invited my dad up from Armonk, a two-and-a-half hour drive, and Cedric made sure he had a great seat. My plan was to meet my dad for dinner after my post-fight responsibilities, which included paying each fighter, partially in cash, after reviewing and explaining each purse deduction line by line and getting their final signatures. There were often discrepancies between what a fighter expected to receive and what I expected to pay, which I tried to resolve without calling Cedric or Joe for help. I was proud that Cedric trusted me with this responsibility, and I often carried over $100,000 cash in my briefcase. That night, there were more post-fight discrepancies than usual, and my dad was already sitting in the restaurant alone, waiting for me. I feared I wouldn't be free for another hour, so I told him to grab a bite and get on the road before it got too late. I felt guilty that my dad had driven so far, more excited to see me than the fight, and we had barely gotten to spend any time together. Then Cedric arrived at the restaurant, ready to hold court, accompanied by his usual circle of executives, managers, and boxing groupies, all eager to hear his stories and enjoy a great meal. Cedric saw my dad sitting alone and invited him to *his* table—and seated my dad right next to him. He proudly introduced him to everyone as "Marshall Winston, Mitch Winston's father." My dad was a boxing groupie that night, and he never forgot that dinner, the stories he heard, and Cedric's touching gesture.

In the year since I started working for Cedric, my life had changed. Whether I was traveling to a fight or working late in the Hamptons or Manhattan, I never had enough free time. Danielle and I fizzled out and broke up. Soon afterward, she and her sister started going to huge all-night clubs featuring house and electronic music from DJs like Danny Tenaglia and Paul Oakenfold. These were the same all-night clubs my sister used to attend, a scene I never checked out—because I judged it as weird. A few times, after leaving the club around 5 a.m., Danielle floated tipsily into my Manhattan apartment, wearing tight pants and sexy shoes. She would change into one of my tee-shirts and boxers and join me in bed. These were the moments I found her the sexiest, the most desirable, and I was thankful for her visits. I also wondered more about those clubs.

Soon afterward, I was set up with a trendy Upper East Side girl named Jessica Marlene Ridgeway, and we met at a trendy Upper East Side restaurant. Jessica reminded me of a trendy Upper East Side girl named Jennifer whom I had been obsessed with in college, even though we had nothing to say to each other and nothing in common—our only date had been a travesty. But *this* date went well. Afterward, I crossed Central Park and headed back to the Upper West Side. I found myself singing her name in my head, over and over. It was a call and an answer to a melody that flowed.

Jessica Marlene Ridgeway, Jessica Marlene Ridgeway.
Jessica Marlene Ridgeway, Jessica Marlene Ridgeway.

Dear Jessica,

I am not sure what I am going to write as I start this letter to you, but I guess we'll both find out, I as I write it, you as you read it.

Obviously, for a guy who is interested in a girl, more specifically, myself in you, last night was the worst of all possible scenarios: ...Guy meets girl, likes her, calls her the next day, she says she is tired, he forces the issue, she doesn't object when he asks if he should never call her again...

When I hung up the phone, I felt stunned. I felt like the ultimate personification of Delusions of Grandeur, as we discussed. I am not saying that every woman I meet should be in love with me, and, as you know first-hand, this is not the case at all!! However, I feel like I really know who I am, and, at the risk of again having delusions of grandeur (which obviously is going to be the theme of this letter), I will now state that I know that I am:

a romantic;
nice
smart
athletic
cool
gentle
caring
strong
tough
musical
easy going
sensitive
happy to be me
in a great career opportunity
cognizant and proud of my religion
friendly
honest
funny
unique
handsome
healthy
in good shape
intuitive
insightful
spiritual
grounded
good listener
good advice giver
well-traveled
competitive
happy to be alone
happy to be together

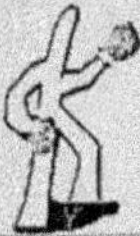

aware of myself
aware of who I was
aware of who I'll be
articulate
courageous
adventurous
responsible
street smart
close with my family
intent on self-improvement!!

(Wow, that was so much fucking fun to write that list!!!!! Whether or not you now think I am a complete nut, I strongly recommend you do one of those lists for yourself!!)

Anyway, my point is this: I do not know you well. I have, however, met many different women in my life. Some I have clicked with, and some I have not. Most of the "have nots" have drifted out of my life, and I have only really missed somebody significantly on one occasion. I know when to move on. I have things to do.

BUT AS I JUST WROTE THAT LIST, I ALSO THOUGHT ABOUT YOU. AND I REALLY HAVE A VERY STRONG INTUITION THAT YOU ALSO POSSESS EVERY ONE OF THE QUALITIES ON THAT LIST!!!

The first quality on my list is that I am a romantic. I believe in special people, special circumstances. I have extremely high expectations of my friends (which most do not live up to), family, girls that I associate with, and my own life's goals. I believe in greatness, and the strive towards it. Jessica, I know I am not being delusional. I know I am rare, one of a kind. And I think you might be too!! How do I know? I don't. But one quality that a romantic has is that he trusts himself and his own opinion, and he is not afraid to convey that.

So without going on forever, let me close this letter in this manner. Maybe we did not click at Mesa City. Maybe I blabbered. Maybe we were too tired. Maybe I turned you off. Maybe I was nervous. The point is, I think that we are letting something go by without giving it a full chance, something that can really turn out to be important. To be geeky and use a political science analogy, **"I THINK WE POSSIBLY ARE BOTH SUPER POWERS, AND DEFINITELY MEANT FOR ONE MORE SUMMIT!!**

So, Jessica I have told you how I feel. If this letter inspires you in any way, or makes you think, or does anything to you that makes you want to call me, then I urge you to do it:

Home: (212) 721-5917 (leave message)
Work: (516) 287-0700 (leave message)
Hotel in Albany: (518) 462-6611 room 318

If not, like I said on the phone, I totally respect that and will leave you alone forever. And definitely don't feel guilty, because I will never regret writing this letter.

DELUSIONS OF GRANDEUR? ILLUSIONS OF GRANDEUR? OBSERVATIONS OF GRANDEUR?......(Only time will tell!!)

Sincerely, Mitchell Lloyd Winston (Mitch) MH

A week had passed since I faxed that letter to Jessica Marlene Ridgeway, and subsequent calls to her were unanswered and unreturned. The uncertainty of the situation was difficult for me, and so I called *again*. Finally—or mercifully—a guy answered and told me that Jessica wasn't interested and not to call again. (Implied rejection, by omission or attrition, was sufficient for some; *I* needed to hear it.) Josh and Andy both cracked up when they read my letter to Jessica. I liked to make them laugh together, even at my expense. That didn't happen enough. I joked that I was the "Metternich Court Jester"—and sharing that embarrassing, unrequited letter was proof.

By then, Josh was committed to the Orthodox Jewish lifestyle. After "dating for marriage," he wedded an Orthodox girl. Unlike the "typical case" *baal teshuva* I was labeled at my Wexner interview, Josh was a *baal teshuva* who stuck with it. He never desired to be a rabbi, but once G-d's existence was logically proven to him, he never wavered from the Orthodox life it prescribed. This supreme logic brought Josh stability and community, the permanent kind. It suited him.

I was committed to fun, which bordered on gluttony, and by then was hanging out more with Andy. We would order those typical New York City plastic containers of intense hydroponic weed, delivered right to my West 80th door for $40. After partaking, Andy and I would play our guitars, and I would sing. I also dabbled in harmonica, which came more naturally than guitar. We only played covers, songs by Bob Dylan, Bruce Springsteen, and Neil Young. We would grade our performances of each song from one to ten, on yellow Post-it notes that we stuck to the sheet music. I joked that we were opposites: I usually gave us eights and nines, while Andy gave us threes and fours. Jamming in the private confines of my apartment was fun and enough for Andy, who had no desire to play a show in public. He often stated that we would make fools of ourselves if we tried. He wasn't shy to say he didn't love my singing voice—and I wasn't shy to say I did.

During these jam sessions, I sometimes wondered out loud if I was meant to be a great singer-songwriter, maybe "the next Bob Dylan." Andy laughed at this and reminded me that I had never played a live show or written a real song. ("Jessica Marlene Ridgeway does not count!") Later that night, to prove him wrong, I wrote, "The Jack Maggan Lukin Blues." It didn't come close to Dylan's "If You See Her, Say Hello," our favorite song to play at the time, and the chords were just a standard blues progression in E. But it was *something*—and it existed.

THE JACK MAGGAN LUKIN BLUES by Mitchell Winston

```
        E                                    E7
Jack Maggan Lukin, his friends called him son of a gun,
        A                                    A7                          E (walk up)
He was a terrible sonofabitch from a town I aint never heard of..
        B7                                   A (walk up)  E (walk up)
and when the going got tough, Jack Maggan Lukin stuck around...
        B7                                   A (walk up)     E (walk up )  B7
he aint the kind of boy that gonna turn around and walk out of town...
```

Jack Maggan Lukin, his hair was black and slicked straight back
He was a tough mother fucker who could scare away a 20 man pack
He had a tattoo of his momma on his left arm and his girl on the right..
but when he was home alone, no one knew that he'd take his pen out and write.

Jack Maggan Lukin, wrote about the girls he ~~let go~~ had seen.....
Jack Maggan Lukin, wrote about the places he'd been
and Jack Maggan Lukin, wrote about the man he ~~wanted to~~ could be..
and when he looked in the mirror, he knew it wasn't the same guy he'd see...

Jack Maggan Lukin, his girl was hotter than a fire in the night..
she was tall and thin and raving and her hair flowed like an angel in flight
and she had a power over Jack that made him scream with all of his might
and she was mean and he was vulnerable,(and she thought in the end she would win the fight..)

Jack Maggan Lukin, heard about his girl and another man..
he had to count to 100, and then 50 more to hold that rage in..
but when he came to the hotel, that his friend had sad he'd seen em walk in..
he didn't want to be counting, he knew he had to commit the sin

Jack Maggan Lukin, wrote about the girls he ~~let go~~ had seen...
Jack Maggan Lukin, wrote about the places he'd been
and Jack Maggan Lukin wrote about the man he longed to be..
and when he looked in the mirror, he knew it wasn't the right guy he'd see..

Jack Maggan Lukin, he was sentenced to a year in the can..
he didn't hate it too much, cause nobody was gonna come around fuck with him..
and Jack Maggan Lukin, had a lot more time to sit and find...
the secrets that were hidden behind his toughness in the shadow of his mind

In late August 1997, Cedric sent Gregory and me to Mar del Plata, Argentina to oversee a boxing event that was part of his successful pay-per-view series, *Heavyweight Explosion.* The Argentinean promoter handled everything that Gregory and I were usually responsible for, so our only duties were to ensure the attendance of our twelve heavyweights to their fight-related obligations and promotional appearances. Greg and I were given a fifteen-passenger van and a full-time driver to make this happen. The people of Mar del Plata weren't used to large groups of giants, and we were flocked to everywhere we went, especially by the women. (I even signed an autograph, "Best Wishes, Mitch.") Sexy Argentinean girls were everywhere, eager to be with us. Someone told me that during this season in Mar del Plata, the girls outnumbered the guys four-to-one—and his claim did not appear inaccurate. With Cedric thousands of miles away, the week soon resembled a party.

On our second night, Gregory and I went to a bar and met two hot girls, who approached us in the aggressive manner that prostitutes would, but refused to accept money! From the moment we met them, they never left our side, whether in our hotel or in public. At first this was good—very good—because both Greg and I were suffering from dry spells back home. But after a few days, their constant presence became overbearing, even a hindrance, since we had to conduct ourselves as professionals. We were forced to lie to them, to escape for a few hours. But when we got back to the hotel, the girls would be waiting in the lobby! They got more aggressive, and weird, as the week went on: I was in my hotel room one afternoon with my girl, a long straight haired brunette with a flat stomach and that sexy Argentinean thigh-gap. We were kissing, and about to have sex, as we had the previous few days. I took out a condom, but she resisted, insisting we have sex this time without it. I refused, and she tried harder—first begging, then pleading, then crying. Dead set on unprotected sex, vampire-like, she resorted to powers of tantric seduction and dominance, which turned me on, wore me down, and brought her closer to her goal. I thanked G-d later for the strength to not give in, never forgetting that a mistake there could have changed my life everywhere.

We walked across the hall to Greg's hotel room, where his girl was acting stranger: Unlike the vampire in my room, Greg's girl had become a snake, trying to convince him that *I* had been cursing him and saying terrible things about him all week. None of us were sober, Gregory liked his girl, and he didn't know Spanish—a dangerous mix. I feared this snake's influence because Greg seemed confused and looked at me differently. To cut the tension, I turned on the television, in time to hear the breaking news that Princess Diana, while in Paris, had been in a serious car accident; and she had succumbed to her injuries. I was ready to get home.

Back in the United States, I was soon back on the road for another *Heavyweight Explosion*, this one in the Midwest. Two heavyweights from separate bouts failed to show up at the weigh-in. We made a few calls and found out that the two pugilists would not be showing up at all to fight—neither of their representatives had been responsible enough to call in advance. But their two opponents *had* shown up, after full training camps, and were facing the reality of not fighting and not getting paid. We were in the presence of two disgruntled heavyweights, standing next to each other, with nobody to fight. The tension in the room made me nervous, and I blurted out to them—in front of casino representatives, state officials, and media—"Why don't *you* two fight each other?!" More fights meant more casino revenues, more state fees, and more stories to write, and everyone joined in with a chorus of approvals, now looking over at the two fighters for theirs. One of them, a journeyman with little to lose, who in Cedric's words would have "fought King Kong for a payday," said, "Okay, let's do it! I'm in!" The other, Jesse Ferguson, a proud veteran who had gone six rounds with Mike Tyson and had recently fought Riddick Bowe for the heavyweight title, stared at me deadpan and remained silent. Both he and I knew I had made a mistake: I wasn't the one who determined the matchups, a crucial process assigned to Cedric's full-time matchmakers, which also required Cedric's approval. None of them were at the weigh-in. I had put Jesse Ferguson on the spot, and challenged his ego, without even holding the authority to make the fight. I tried to mitigate my error—and displace Ferguson's stare—by explaining to the crowd that I was kidding, and had nothing to do with making the fights. I held back nervous laughter, awkward silence ensued, and we concluded the weigh-in. Before I could leave the room, an unsmiling Ferguson approached me. He got really close and whispered into my ear, "Don't write checks you can't fucking cash." Lesson learned.

Cedric promoted me to Director of Events, which made me the number three guy at the company, behind Joe West. Before this would take effect, Cedric assigned me to find and train my replacement, his would-be new assistant. I did so in a young, spirited up-and-comer named Ron Rizzo, who wanted badly to get into the boxing business, and said in his interview, "I won't let you down." (That line got him hired!) My promotion gave me some breathing room; I was no longer glued to Cedric's side. But it didn't change my salary or the fact that when I was around Cedric, I still felt like his assistant. My dad feared he would always perceive me that way. He pointed out that even though Cedric was great, I was destined for greatness too, and huge success. He said that wherever I worked, I should strive to become a partner, an owner, or at least to earn a huge salary. He reminded me that I was "working for peanuts"—like the boxing groupies who were content to just sit at the same dinner table with their charismatic king, Cedric Kushner. Maybe my dad was right, that I was enjoying the perks too much: With countless adventures from the road, apartments in the

Hamptons and New York City, and a red limousine to take me to and fro, it was hard *not* to be Cedric's boxing groupie.

Due to a late development, one of Cedric's most popular fighters, New York heavyweight Lou Savarese, was promised an upcoming fight on HBO's *Boxing After Dark* series, but only if we could find a suitable venue in Manhattan. (This HBO series was Lou Shafer's brainchild, and he wanted only *sexy* fight venues, ones with panache.) Finding a boxing venue with panache was hard enough, especially one that was suitable for HBO and available at the last minute on a Saturday night in New York City. The event would be canceled if we didn't find something fast. With my recent promotion to Director of Events, I wanted to be the one to save the event. This motivated me. I came up with the idea to place it at the world-famous Apollo Theater in Harlem. It would be the first boxing promotion ever held at this iconic landmark. I found out that the Apollo was available, and I liaised with the production staff of HBO, the New York State Athletic Commission, and theater staff, cross-checking everyone's technical requirements against building specs. Lighting, camera positions, and seating were complicated due to limited space and low ceilings. (A ceiling jack was not considered.) And due to the Apollo's cinema-style seating, the boxing ring would have to be placed on its very small stage, which I circumvented by locating a tiny yet (barely) legal boxing ring that would be trucked in from Buffalo. I found a way to make everything work with inches to spare. HBO and Cedric were thrilled to be the first ones to bring boxing to the Apollo Theater in Harlem. Cedric named the event, "Uptown Saturday Night."

A week before the fight, I attended the press conference, which had a great turnout of local and national sports writers. The idea had built a buzz. As Cedric graced the podium, holding court with the media in his usual charming way, I was hoping hard that he would credit me with the idea—but he didn't even mention my name. Then Lou Shafer of HBO got his turn and announced that bringing boxing to the Apollo Theater was "Mitch Winston's idea." That was cool of Lou—but it should have come from Cedric.

That night, Gregory Laurence came to my apartment, and we baked a tray of pot brownies, mixing in almost three ounces of ground grown Jamaican weed, which wasn't as strong as the NYC-hydro I was used to. We were inexperienced in this culinary art, not realizing that using this much marijuana was insane, regardless of potency. We sat and ate the whole tray—and soon we couldn't stand. It was the most drugged I had ever felt, overcome by total fog, and the feeling didn't subside all week. Greg didn't move from the couch that night, but somehow made it to his meeting the next morning. I managed to get off the sofa and into my bed, but I overslept for work the next day, the first time I ever did. At 11 a.m., I was still sleeping, until Cedric's call woke me. My head was whirling, the room was spinning, and Cedric was annoyed, asking where I was. Fueled by adrenaline, I mustered a lie and delivered it aggressively: "I'VE BEEN AT THE APOLLO SINCE 9 A.M., DEALING WITH TICKETS AND LIGHTING! I TOLD YOU THIS LAST NIGHT AFTER *YOUR* PRESS CONFERENCE!" He apologized and didn't question me further.

Greg and I remained in this semi-catatonic, fully-drugged state the whole week of "Uptown Saturday Night." Each morning, I woke up hoping that my haze would be lifted, at least partially—but my spinning head and blurred vision told me otherwise. At one point that week, I dragged myself to the bank and withdrew a $6,000 cash advance from my credit card, wired it to Las Vegas, and placed a bet on a different fight. I won, receiving back my initial $6,000 plus winnings of $5,000. The next day, I floated into the luxury watch store on 58th Street and purchased a silver Breitling, the same watch brand that both Metternichs wore. I felt cool—like a real gambler. To this day, I can't remember what fight I bet on, nor much else from the week of "Uptown Saturday Night." But I do remember how good it felt to win that money.

Chapter 10

Kid Lightning Is Born

"The Jamaican Tea Incident"

AFTER FIVE YEARS with Wendell, which seemed to take an increasing toll on Fredda's "gleam," she decided to break up with him. But he told her he couldn't move out of her apartment until he found a new place. Months passed, and he was still there; enabled, in my opinion, by Fredda's guilt and pity—that thing she had for lost causes. I still suspected Wendell was using zombie drugs while wasting my sister's time and taking advantage of her kindness. This frustrated me, because he had the option of moving in with his parents, and I didn't understand why providing shelter had become my sister's responsibility. But Fredda had asked Mr. Greenwich Village and me to remain passive and not intervene, and we obeyed. Then, according to Rob, my spy into Fredda's social life, some troubling things started happening: Strange people were showing up at Fredda's apartment, her vinyl records went missing, and Wendell was getting caught in multiple lies about his whereabouts. I told this story to Andy's street-smart friend Stevie Stone, who agreed that Wendell might be using zombie drugs.

Stevie said that zombie drug addicts die young. He also said they will do anything—lie to or steal from even their own mother—for one more hit. And when zombies go down, they "take the ship down" with them. Fredda was the ship! He said, from experience, that the Gandhi-like tactics Mr. Greenwich Village and I were using would never work—I had to change my approach now or regret it forever. Stevie had woken me, and my rage was building when I dialed Wendell that night. He answered the phone sounding small and weak. Then I *pulled a Vickers*, warning him that if I found out he was doing the zombie shit near my sister, I would be on my way over to deal with him physically, and would then throw him out.

Wendell was a scrawny, peaceful guy, a comic-book lover and a bass player. I believed him when he swore on his life and his mother's that he wasn't using zombie drugs—even though Stevie had prepared me for those exact lies and tactics. *Pulling a Vickers* on Wendell didn't make me feel powerful. Instead it gave me a taste of the pity and guilt that my sister must have been experiencing in her efforts to let him go. (Maybe we both had that thing for lost causes.) I hung up the phone without resolution, still worried about the *Fredda-ship* going down.

Fortunately, we got an unexpected opportunity, more like a blessing, which solved the problem in a better way. Fredda loved designing funky clothes—wacky purses, skirts, dog outfits, and clown costumes—the latter being her latest specialty. She showed me a yellow newspaper called *The Loot,* full of classified ads, where she found her costume-less clowns. While leafing through it, I came upon a FOR SALE listing of a Manhattan studio apartment on East 26th Street, between 3rd and Lexington, at a price of $50,000—about $75,000 less than the current market value! I assumed it was a typo, I didn't have any extra money, and I wasn't in the apartment market—but I pursued this "freakish" rarity to satisfy my conscience. Without even visiting the apartment, I submitted an offer of $45,000, expecting never to hear back, or to learn that the ad was a cheap way to solicit phone calls for another purpose. But the owner quickly countered at $47,500, which I accepted, and I was soon holding a signed contract for the apartment. I went to see it: It was very small, and on street level. But it was in good condition, the building was nice, and the neighborhood was great. I called Lee Deerman, who agreed with me—in about thirty seconds—that this opportunity was clearly a "freakish rarity." We made our first real estate deal: He put up $20,000 cash, and I qualified for a 10% mortgage for the rest. We closed on the apartment, and the perfect tenant—*The Fredda-ship*—sailed in alone, away from the dark clouds and danger that hovered over Wendell.

My dad was proud that I had purchased my first piece of real estate by invoking his favorite strategy: Locating and controlling a deal, at excellent terms, *before* approaching the investor. He taught me that if I were successful at these first two steps, I could earn substantial equity in a property without putting in cash. He also pointed out that I had a keen sense for real estate, and I would be much better off as a real estate developer, where I would get rich, as opposed to my current status as Cedric's "boxing groupie." That was a term I had taught him, which he used with a smile, but also his truth.

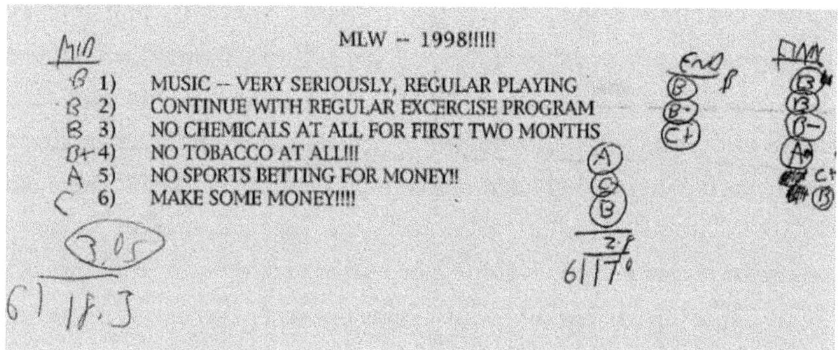

MLW -- 1998!!!!!

1) MUSIC -- VERY SERIOUSLY, REGULAR PLAYING
2) CONTINUE WITH REGULAR EXCERCISE PROGRAM
3) NO CHEMICALS AT ALL FOR FIRST TWO MONTHS
4) NO TOBACCO AT ALL!!!
5) NO SPORTS BETTING FOR MONEY!!
6) MAKE SOME MONEY!!!!

In October 1998, I decided to accompany Andy and his friend Zuckerman to a golf resort in Jamaica. It would be my first vacation in over two years of working for Cedric, but he had the *chutz-*

pah to express annoyance that I would be gone all week. Cedric hadn't been his usual self lately, due to a recent onset of diabetic symptoms, manifested visibly through red patches and swelling below his knees. I was getting more disgusted by him than usual, due to his obesity and unwillingness to do something about it. He *said* he wanted to lose weight, and a few months earlier he had asked me to find him an (attractive) female nutritionist who was willing to live with him, travel with him, exercise with him and cook his meals. (And he may have had a few other things in mind.)

Locating a live-in nutritionist who could handle Cedric's eccentric lifestyle proved more formidable than finding the Apollo Theater. But I found Susie, the daughter of my mom's friend, who was successful and connected in the health and fitness industry. She agreed to divide the duties among two of her colleagues. One was a well-known trainer who had a proven track record for working with celebrities and reshaping their bodies; he would supervise Cedric's workout regimen and see him every week. The other was a trained chef (and former model) who would live and travel with Cedric, and work out with him daily. Susie would plan each week's menu and coordinate everyone's schedules. I had assembled a mini-Dream Team, and they submitted their proposal to Cedric, to which he agreed in writing. A few days before everything was to start, Susie came to Cedric's New York City office to plan his menu for the first week. She opened the meeting with a simple question, asking Cedric what his favorite foods were. For no apparent reason, Cedric went ballistic, tantrum-like, and physically chased Susie out of the office—and out of his life—for good. It was weird and embarrassing behavior, and I apologized to Susie that night (on her answering machine). She never called me back, which didn't surprise me after that incident. My theory was that Cedric finally internalized that he was about to *give up control* over his food. In the crazy world of boxing, where Cedric and his groupies dwelled, nothing was ever certain, nothing predictable—except, sometimes, a plate of food. It would stay that way.

Cedric and his eccentricities became an afterthought when I got to Jamaica, an especially gluttonous experience, where Andy, Zuckerman and I enjoyed gigantic buds of freshly grown marijuana, too much fast food, and golf. During this week of abundance we laughed a lot, but Andy was also acting strangely, a bit more negative than his usual cynical-yet-hopeful state. One afternoon, the three of us traveled far and paid a lot for three "magic mushroom" teas. When we got back to the hotel, Andy chugged his down, while mine waited on the counter as I prepared for my journey. But before I could take my first sip, Andy grabbed mine and chugged it down too, while staring at me defiantly—reminiscent of Frosty and the chili. After he finished, his face showed deep regret, and he apologized profusely. He wanted me to laugh it off so we could move on. But I was upset by the Jamaican tea incident, egregiously out of Andy's character: It wasn't (just) the tea, which I wanted badly—it was the feeling that I had been betrayed by my best friend. It was only about 7 p.m., but I got into bed and slept until the next day.

Cedric tracked me down at the hotel the next morning and requested I come home three days early. He was stuck in bed due to doctor's orders, and needed me to handle some things in the office. I was pissed at this disrespectful interruption of my only vacation in two years, but I was also secretly ready to leave Jamaica. When I left for the airport that evening, I was mad at both Andy and Cedric. I got over each quickly though. I knew something was on Andy's mind that caused him to go dark in Jamaica. He could be weird, as could I, but not like that. I believed that living in New York City was getting to him. It seemed that he never belonged there.

With my Apollo Theater gambling victory fresh in mind, I considered myself a good prognosticator of boxing talent. Gregory

Laurence wrote a monthly column in a boxing magazine and let me insert a subsection of my own. Thanks to Greg, it soon became my own paid column, "Kid Lightning Picks of the Month." I was Kid Lightning, and my real name was never revealed. I wrote the column in the third person, trying to build the mystery of Kid Lightning through humor and absurdity.

> Kid Lightning grew up on the mean streets of Armonk, NY, rife with famine. He fought for each of his meals. When things got bad, he was forced to drink the blood of rats to survive. Rumor has it that he once killed a man over a stolen sandwich. All of this toughened up Kid Lightning, and taught him who else was tough too. When hunting for prey in the mountains, Kid Lightning camped alone. And at night, under the stars, there was time to kill. He developed the skill "to watch upcoming boxing matches," in their entireties, *before* they happened. And he was *never* wrong. Kid Lightning now receives huge amounts of money to share his insight with gamblers around the world. This made him very rich, but he never forgot his roots. (He still kills everything he eats with his bare hands.)
>
> When Kid Lightning picks the winners of upcoming fights, he isn't predicting—he is reporting. This makes him the best fight prognosticator in the world. Kid Lightning recently watched the upcoming fight between Roy Jones Jr. and Otis Grant. This is what he saw…

Greg and I had fun with this, and we built a buzz within the small circle of boxing media. (And when I was wrong about my "guaranteed" fight picks, I never acknowledged it in my next column.) I showed the columns to my dad. He was happy I got paid $150 for each and said the writing was funny. But he pointed out that Kid Lightning was often wrong about his "guaranteed" fight picks! He warned me that I was a very impulsive person and would make a terrible gambler. He urged me, with all he had, to "never, ever bet on sports!"

Although I had been disappointed by Cedric a few times recently, I knew he respected and trusted me, and I believed his promise about my bright future at CKP. I was surprised when he and Joe West hired Brad Jacobs, the well-known boxing executive and the former head of USA Network's *Tuesday Night Fights* boxing series. Brad was a nice guy, a good television producer, and a close advisor to Roy Jones, Jr., who was arguably the best fighter in the world. I was okay with the hiring if it would bring Cedric closer to signing Roy Jones, Jr. That would "change everything" and possibly make Cedric the number one boxing promoter in the world. Cedric often joked that he would have "sold out his mother" to sign a fighter like Roy Jones Jr.—and nobody doubted him.

Then I found out that Brad Jacobs's hiring had nothing to do with Roy Jones; the possibility of Jones signing with Cedric was never considered. Cedric and Joe West had awarded Brad Jacobs a $135,000 annual salary, double what I was earning, to help produce Joe West's opus, *Thunderfight.* This was an ill-fated boxing series in which real boxers were pitted against one another in real boxing matches. The fighters, however, took on fictional character names and personalities, and rivalries were "created" through staged interviews—a trademark of professional wrestling. Even if the *Thunderfight* concept had been decent, I would have been upset by the salary Brad Jacobs got. But the idea was so bad that I became angry. Everybody in the business (besides Joe and Cedric) knew that an unmarketable journeyman boxer who put on makeup and a cape and pretended to hate his opponent would look the same and fight the same when the bell rang. And professional wrestling fans, the audience Joe and Cedric were targeting, didn't care about real fights. They wanted compelling hero-villain storylines with happy endings, made possible by professional wrestling's predetermined fight scripts. Joe West was trying to blend two things that would never work together.

Ever since I started working for Cedric, I had spoken with him and Joe West many times about my love for the Ultimate Fighting Championship (UFC) and Mixed Martial Arts (MMA) in general, and how big they were becoming. I suggested that if he and Joe wanted to expand to the wrestling audience, they should go in that direction, because MMA was attractive to both boxing and wrestling fans. My suggestions had *fallen on deaf ears*, and I was surprised how little each of them knew and cared about the UFC. The industry rumor was that Joe West had pushed Cedric hard and convinced him to commit a huge amount of funds to *Thunderfight*, so much that they risked the entire future of CKP. More hurtful was that the Brad Jacobs hiring implied that Cedric viewed me as a boxing groupie, not a future partner. My dad had been right again; my eyes were now open for other opportunities.

Right at that time, a boxing trainer whom I was friends with told me about a promising young heavyweight prospect named Robin Johnson. He had just come out of the Army and needed a manager for his imminent boxing career. Instead of running to Cedric like a good boxing groupie, I kept the news to myself. That weekend, I drove to the Poconos (alone) to meet "The Robin" and his dad and watch him work out. I wasn't disappointed. The Robin, a twenty-one-year-old African-American, was a physical specimen: 6' 7", 250 pounds, and the body of a Greek god. He started his workout by hitting the speed bag and dancing in place. His feet were agile and his hands were fast. Then he switched to the heavy bag, pounding it with lefts and rights, each making a loud, crisp thud as it collided with the leather, knocking his trainer backward as he attempted to support the bag.

After The Robin finished his workout, my trainer friend introduced me to him and his dad, and the four of us had a good talk. I inquired why The Robin had flown under the radar until then, rare for such a good-looking prospect. The trainer told me that The Robin hadn't become interested in boxing until recently. He hadn't fought as an amateur, not entirely uncommon for certain gifted fighters who are ready from the get-go to jump into the pro ranks. In addition to his obvious athleticism and imposing physique, The Robin was well spoken and intelligent. I could tell he was sensitive and respectful, always letting his dad and trainer speak first. I believed I was looking at the true package, the real deal, maybe even the next Muhammad Ali! Even though I didn't have a company formed, my plan became clear: I would become The Robin's manager. I explained to The Robin that if he took a chance and signed a management deal with me, an up-and-comer like him, I would focus on his career 100%, whereby other more established managers, with many fighters in their stables, would not provide that same attention or enthusiasm. I offered him a $2,000 cash bonus, looked him in the eye and said to him, "If you sign with me, I won't let you down." He said yes.

I located a talent management contract and The Deerman help me tailor it to Robin Johnson, "the Boxer," and Kid Lightning Enterprises, "the Manager." (The name of my corporation, yet unformed, was an obvious choice.) The Robin signed, and I was now the manager of a serious heavyweight prospect.

MANAGEMENT AGREEMENT

This agreement is made as of the 19th day of November, 1998, among Robin Johnson, (the "Boxer"), and Mitchell Winston, (the "Manager")...

Signed: Robin Johnson, "The Robin," (the Boxer)

Signed: Mitchell Winston, (the Manager)
President of Kid Lightning Enterprises, a corporation to be formed within 30 days.

By signing my own fighter, especially without Cedric's knowledge, I was risking my job with CKP. But managing the future Heavyweight Champion of the World would place me at the top of boxing hierarchy—where boxing groupies dare not go. I knew that if The Robin were successful, given the scarcity of athletic heavyweights and their marketability, Cedric, the consummate businessman, would forgive my transgression and attempt to become The Robin's promoter. (There are roles for both manager *and* promoter in the business.) At that point I would have leverage, but until my client's (successful) pro debut, about six months away, I would have to keep everything a secret. (I still needed my job and my salary.) Right after that fight, I would march into Cedric's office, quit as his employee/boxing groupie, and reintroduce myself as "Kid Lightning, the manager"—and then offer him The Robin's coveted promotional rights at a fair price.

The Brad Jacobs hiring proved to me that to be perceived by Cedric as an equal, rather than a boxing groupie, I needed to bring something valuable to the table—I needed to have leverage: Money, a unique relationship, or contractual control of a special talent. The Robin, perhaps "the next Muhammad Ali," was that talent. And now I had control.

December, 1998

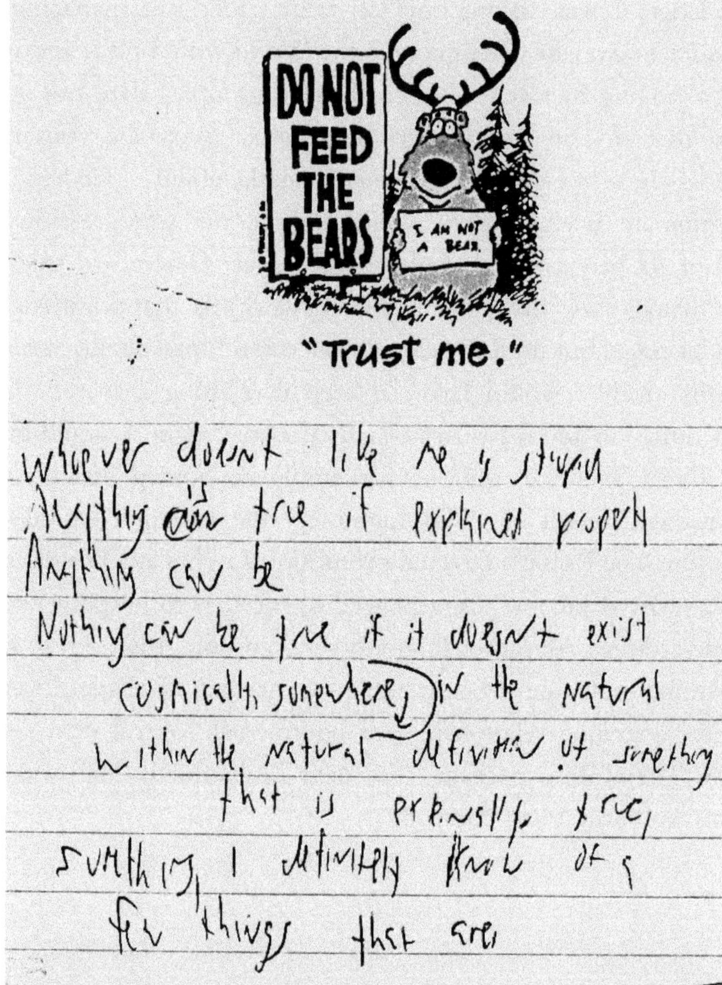

Whoever doesn't like me is stupid
Anything can be true if explained properly
Nothing can be true if it doesn't exist cosmically,
somewhere within the natural.
I definitely know of a few things that are:

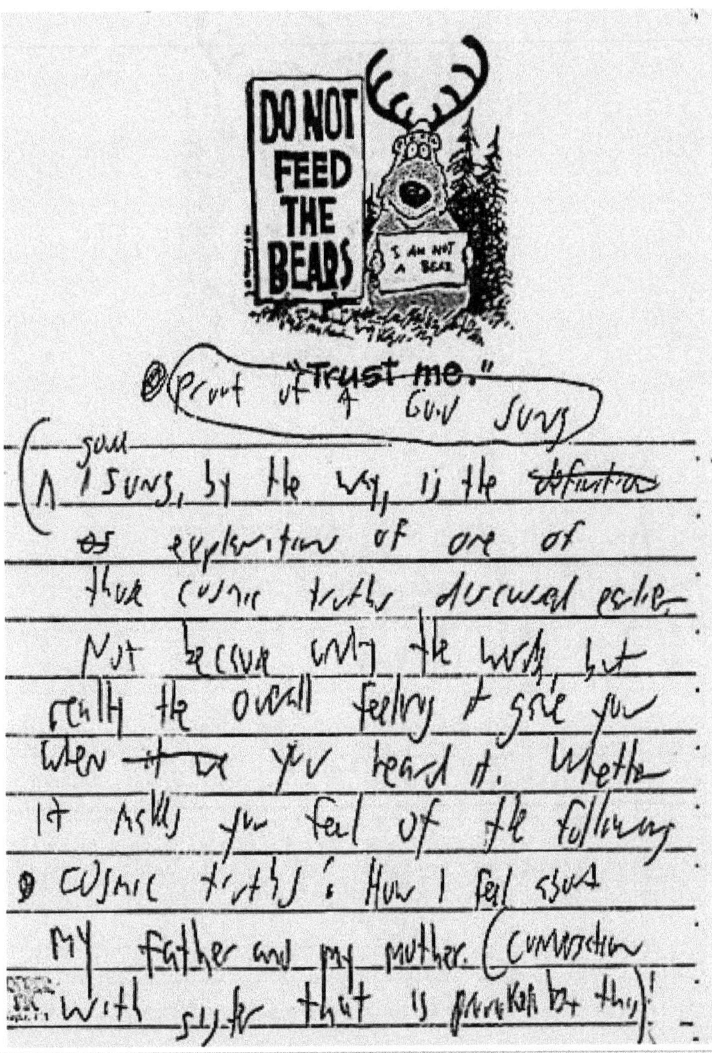

Proof of a Good Song:

A good song, by the way, is the explanation of one of those cosmic truths discussed earlier.

Not because only the words, but really the overall feeling it gave you when you heard it.

Whether it makes you feel the following cosmic truths:

How I feel about my father and my mother (conversation with sister that is provoked by this!)

A good song.
An occasional bong hit.
A moment of euphoria.
A realization.
Parking money?
<u>Stop now!!!!</u>
Resume…

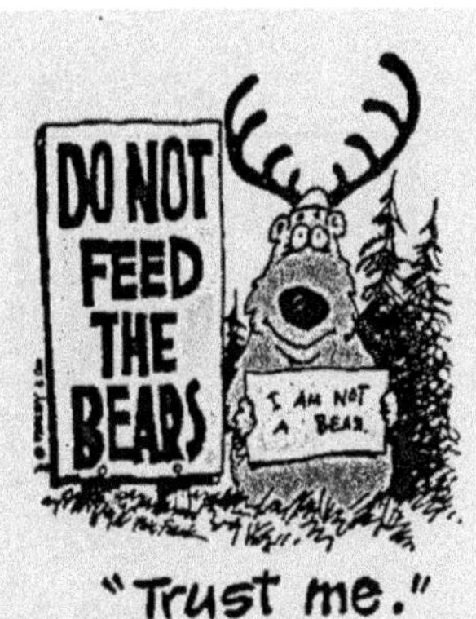

"Trust me."

What is eternally true:
You can't use same word, "true," in the definition of the word true!!
<u>Cosmically</u>, that is the key.
Cosmically, you can easily be a great boxing promoter, or one that can do a big show.

HOW TO SOLVE ANY DILEMMA:
ASK YOURSELF THE COSMIC TRUTH TO ANY QUESTION.
<u>LIVE BY THE ANSWER.</u>
NO SHOULDS OR NEEDS.

About a year earlier, my friend Shiva discovered and briefly managed a talented singer-songwriter called The Cardinal, whose sad songs and lush acoustic harmonies reminded me of Neil Young. I became a fan of his music while listening to him play once at Shiva's house, and I appreciated his waist-long dreadlocks and grungy style, unique for a (white) folk singer. I had also attended a few of The Cardinal's acoustic shows that Shiva had presented. Each time, I was immersed in the music from start to finish—rare for me unless the artist was Bob Dylan, Neil Young, or Bruce Springsteen. After one of his shows, I witnessed the Head of Special Projects at Mercury Records in a state of sheer excitement, guaranteeing The Cardinal a record deal. I was proud of Shiva, on the precipice of taking an unknown artist all the way to Mercury Records, a company with major label distribution! But a few months later, I heard the deal never panned out, and Shiva was no longer working with The Cardinal.

A few of Shiva's friends told me that The Cardinal drank a large quantity of Pabst Blue Ribbon beers daily, even during his recording sessions and performances. That would get him drunk, affect his attitude, and fuck up his sound. All this had allegedly thwarted the Mercury Records deal and soured Shiva on working with The Cardinal further. Shiva was a true music lover, a great judge of talent, and an expert at putting bands together. *My* forte was handling difficult personalities and keeping eccentric people happy. I had excelled at this before working for Cedric—now I was a master at it! And with my recent signing of a heavyweight boxer, adding The Cardinal to Kid Lightning's talent stable would provide instant diversification to my fledgling (and secretive) management company.

I received Shiva's blessing to approach The Cardinal and propose a management deal, promising Shiva a back-end bonus if things worked out. The Cardinal accepted my offer, even before I had to tell him "I wouldn't let him down." Kid Lightning now had two huge prospects: The "next Neil Young" and the "next Muhammad Ali."

Monday, 11/23/98 - Email to my sister

Fredda,

I had to write this to someone. Anyway I feel very great about all aspects of my life. I feel so confident business-wise, personality-wise, musically, socially. I really feel like this is my time to do something big. I have to plunge into deep waters and take major risks in order to achieve something big and great…

I know I can be very delusional at times, when I am doing certain things, feeling certain things. But why should they be delusions? I have succeeded wherever I have gone. I have never thought anyone was better than me.

I could not be an actor. I want to have an audience that I can express myself to and have my ideas be out there, for everyone to know whose they are, and everyone to be able to critique them, whether to my face or to their friends' faces.

I need this to be manifested in all aspects of my life. In business, I must be in a role where my ideas and creativity and balls are tested daily. I have to be "the one". I am the one. I really think so. Therefore, I must have my own company – immediately. I must not open up a bar. That is so fucking common. Buy drinks, sell them. Bullshit people that come in thinking that you like them so they spend their money, and think they should come back. Not to say I would be totally bullshitting, but you know.

But if you are allowed to find some talent, and make people identify with it, and let it grow, in all different aspects of life. Not just boxing, because then it comes down to a few people really affecting whether you succeed. If you believe in the real product, which is you, then your goal should be to get out your message in any way possible. Manage a band, manage a fighter, play your own music, write books, exercise and stay in great shape, get tons of women, just be out there.

This is our youth. This is when we are at our strongest. Why the fuck should we wait until we are in our physical deterioration when we take our biggest risks? Do athletes wait until they are 35 or 40 before they go against the big boys in the major leagues? Oh, but they are inexperienced. Big deal. They are also younger, stronger, freer, more optimistic, and better looking than their counterparts.

I am not going to be homeless. I am not going to starve. I have to make it big. I do not care what I have to do. I will work. But I have to make it fast. Very fast. This is the time, in the next three years to do it, so then when I slowly start to deteriorate physically, as every man does, I will be able to rest on my laurels just a tad, and let my accomplishments in the past when I was most strong help me to enjoy my life in the present and future…

Bruce Springsteen is so fucking great. He has the most energy in the world. When he is up there, he has a special relationship with the audience. He can relate to those people. Seeing Saving Private Ryan and then listening to Bruce Springsteen's music makes me really feel how horrible war is. This is a fucking stupid concept, based purely on economic reasons, but I won't get into that now. The point is, we totally sent young people in to die, and we did not ever realize that this is their only life!! This is it!! Those people never got to live their only life!! They do not even know what the fuck is going on now!! Anywhere!! And this is not their faults.

So if their only life is wasted by concerns outside of their control, then I must believe that I am a human, and my life, too, could be wasted or ended earlier by concerns outside of my control. Then why not live out the real person who believes so earnestly in his own philosophy of life? Why live to someone else's? Just like soldiers dying before living, I am letting myself die and deteriorate without using that youth that I still have to carve out my own life!!! I have to be in the public!! I have to be out there!!!

I also have to perform in some way, whether I write, or sing, or play guitar, or have a fucking talk show, or do something. But if there is one motherfucker out there that can read this and realize that I am someone who must, and I really say must, go far in this world. I must not let myself be wasted. I must do what it takes in my life to get where I have to go. The beauty is, if I am in business for myself, then I will be throwing tons of shit against the wall, and if one or two things stick, I will make myself a lot of fucking money!! With money comes opportunity!!!

I should wind this down again – Whoever realizes that what I am writing now is an ultimate truth, then I urge you to step forward. I urge you to come along for the ride, and join my company, Kid Lightning Enterprises, which will do one thing. It will pursue ventures, all with potential economic upside and great challenge and pleasure both along the way and at the end, with the main theme of the company being the fact that Mitch Winston is a unique and special person, with powers far beyond most, and balls as big as any, who must be "out there". He is the man. Or at the very least, he is the man that needs to try.

Your brother, Mitch

Chapter 11

The Queen Pigeon

"Just because you're paranoid..."

MY DAD WAS PROUD of my recent bold moves, but would have cried if he heard about my next one. I perceived an excellent gambling opportunity coming up on March 20, 1999, because I had inside information. It was a major HBO heavyweight fight at the Emerald Casino in Seattle, Washington, promoted by Cedric Kushner Promotions, between Ike "The President" Ibeabuchi (19-0) and Chris "Rapid Fire" Byrd (26-0). Ike was coming off a big win against another undefeated, highly touted prospect, David Tua, whom boxing insiders had considered "the next Mike Tyson." The Ibeabuchi-Tua fight was a thrilling clash, setting records for most punches thrown in a heavyweight fight—neither man backed up once. Ike Ibeabuchi emerged victorious, a huge win for Cedric Kushner Promotions, who held Ike's promotional rights.

In the eyes of many, Ike was now the "*new* next Mike Tyson." He was a hot fighter and heavily favored by the Las Vegas bookies to beat Chris Byrd on March 20. However, I considered Ike's power and speed to be far inferior to Mike Tyson's, and found him slower and less athletic than Iron Mike. And the general public didn't know that Ike was a troubled soul, suffering from mental illness.

I knew from Cedric's inside sources that Ike's personal life was in shambles. He had barely trained for the Byrd fight. He had been to the gym only once, at which time he sustained a bad cut on his eyelid, which required stitches, while sparring with an inferior boxer whose ring was not removed from his finger before the trainer wrapped his hands. Ike was convinced that this was part of a conspiracy against him: He first attacked the boxer, and then the trainer—sending both men to the hospital and Ike to the police station for questioning. Outside the gym, Ike was showing more signs of paranoia and violence, as rumors surfaced of additional outbursts and run-ins with law enforcement. Cedric told me that Ike had recently picked up a steak knife and waved it around menacingly during a dinner with Lou Shafer. Cedric had joked that this was not the best way to gain HBO's confidence and a big contract offer, but I knew Cedric was beginning to see Ike as less of a long-term prospect. Another time, Ike had to be dragged off a plane because he sensed demonic forces in his presence. There were also reports of Ike demonstrating suicidal tendencies.

With so many strange incidents and the bad cut above Ike's eye, Cedric Kushner had to decide whether to cancel the Ike versus Byrd fight. This would have been a huge financial loss for him and a major disappointment to Lou Shafer and HBO. Cedric did not cancel—and I don't know of any other boxing promoter who would have either. Instead, he flew in Bill Benton to take control of the situation. Bill Benton was Cedric's tough, no-nonsense matchmaker who didn't take shit from anyone. He was instructed to stay glued to Ike's side 24/7, even camp outside Ike's door if necessary, to keep Ike out of further trouble and save the March 20 promotion. Ike trusted and respected Bill Benton, which were rare emotions for him in those days, which made Bill the best choice for this two-week stint. During March, I spoke to Bill every morning to get the daily Ike updates for Cedric. Bill said that Ike was not training in the gym and was not jogging. He was staying inside all day, doing who-knows-what, and going out at night—with Bill close by. Bill couldn't force Ike to train, and he wasn't told to try. His job was to keep Ike out of trouble and get him on the plane to Seattle. He delivered.

Ike's opponent, Chris "Rapid Fire" Byrd, was an Olympic silver medalist and also undefeated. He was in the best shape of his life and also coming off a big win. Unlike Ike, Byrd's life was in harmony, inside and outside the ring. He was living like a professional athlete, training with the best fighter alive, Roy Jones, Jr., and working with a team of professionals that he trusted. After winning the Olympic silver medal, Byrd had moved up a weight class to the heavyweight division, adding size and muscle through a regimented, supervised diet, while maintaining his signature speed and quickness. He fought like his nickname, "Rapid Fire," throwing endless quantities of sharp jabs with both hands, never slowing down. He was a pesky and elusive fighter, hard to hit and hard to beat. His style and speed were unusual for the heavyweight division, and the reason Chris "Rapid Fire" Byrd was 26-0.

Kid Lightning, the best fight prognosticator in the world, recently isolated himself in the mountains of Armonk to pick off a mountain lion, *his* kind of sushi. All that alone time makes a man think, and before the sun came up one day, Lightning *watched* the upcoming fight between Ike "The President" Ibeabuchi and Chris "Rapid Fire" Byrd. Kid Lightning *saw* Chris "Rapid Fire" Byrd out-dance, out-speed, and out-box "The President," painting Ike's face with hundreds of annoying, non-stop, pitter-pat punches. Ike got frustrated, did something illegal, and either got disqualified or lost a decision. (The final seconds were blurry, because Kid Lightning had to strangle the mountain lion with his bare hands.) But the result was as real as the warm flesh on the carcass that Kid Lightning feasted on: Chris "Rapid Fire" Byrd had *already* beaten Ike "The President" Ibeabuchi at the Emerald Casino in their *upcoming* fight on March 20th…

I decided to bet $14,000 on Byrd, which I took from credit card cash advances. (My credit lines had been increased since my recent gambling victory during the week of "Uptown Saturday Night.") This was the most cash I could gather, and I wired it to my guy in Las Vegas, who laid it down. After Byrd, the underdog, prevailed on March 20, I would receive back $36,000—my initial $14,000 plus winnings of $22,000. Andy Metternich, who didn't gamble like I did, bought into my reasoning and gave me $8,000 of his own money to put on Byrd too. Now we had $22,000 on Byrd, with a payout of $55,000 to us after Byrd won. (In the unlikely event that Ike won, we would be broke and crippled with debt.) This scared me but also excited me. I wanted to win the money for both of us.

In the weeks leading up to the fight, I noticed a pigeon that perched herself on the ledge outside the bathroom window of my West 80th apartment, every morning around 5 a.m. Each time, she cooed triumphantly in a flute-like song, both soothing and angelic. She was a tough pigeon too, never letting the other birds join her on the ledge or in her song—she sang alone, for herself and for me. After I told Andy about her, he became a fan too. We named her "The Queen Pigeon," to whose arrival each morning I had become accustomed. On the morning I was scheduled to leave for Seattle, I was rushing around my West 80th apartment to pack my bag and make my plane. I hadn't thought about the Queen Pigeon that morning, but seconds before I left, I heard her glorious song, cooing more passionately than ever. I paused outside my bathroom for a minute to listen and take in the moment: She was sending me off to victory, for Andy and for me. The Queen Pigeon had become a symbol for our *other* feathered warrior, Chris "Rapid Fire" Byrd—the two birds were one.

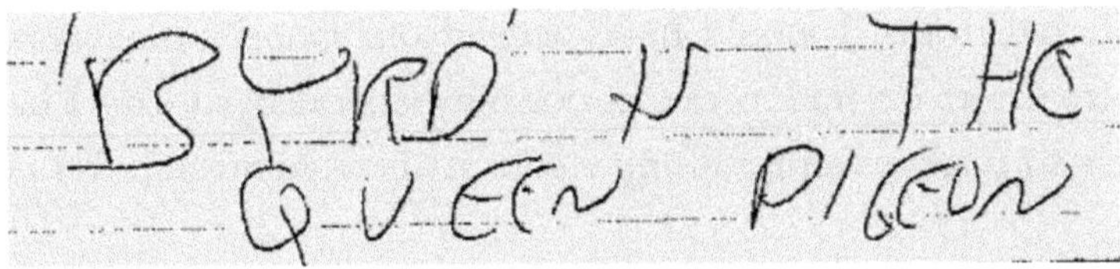

I arrived in Seattle and checked in at the Emerald Hotel & Casino. Bill Benton and Ike "The President" Ibeabuchi were expected later that day. I waited for them in the lobby, where I got my first glimpse of Ike: He was shirtless, with a toothpick in his mouth, wearing jeans and a jean jacket, a black cowboy hat, dark sunglasses, and cowboy boots. He was pissed at the world, intense and unsmiling, and looked to be in perfect condition. (Where was the out-of-shape, unfocused guy who hadn't trained?) His dark aura (and ripped physique) reminded me of Clubber Lang from Rocky 3. It dawned on me that he must have been training alone, a la Clubber Lang, in the private confines of his apartment, away from all conspiracies and demonic forces.

The next morning I saw Ike marching back and forth in the casino parking lot, like a soldier, a ritual he repeated every day. Chris Byrd—the Queen Pigeon—witnessed it too. Byrd's trainers said Ike was "pulling an act," trying to intimidate. In my view, Ike really thought he was a soldier in the military, going into a kill-or-be-killed battle! Byrd, seemingly unfazed, stuck to his regimented diet and fight-week rituals. He prepared not for a military battle, but a professional contest of skill and stamina, with rules, regulations, and a referee.

The two avoided each other all week, never once being in the same room, until the weigh-in the day before the fight. Ike weighed-in 36 pounds more than Byrd, which I expected, but he looked twice Byrd's size. At that moment, if I could have, I would have pulled out my money and Andy's money and canceled our bets—but that was no longer possible. Or, if I had access to additional funds, I would have hedged our bets by placing a secondary wager on Ike, to cancel out our bets on Byrd. But I had no access to further funds, all my credit cards were maxed. *The die was cast.*

On the night of the fight, I sat close to the ring, next to Bill Benton, whom I now wished more than ever had failed in his directive to deliver Ike to Seattle. Ike entered the ring military-style and Tyson-like, with the same countenance he carried all week, angry and fixated. When the fighters faced each other in the center of the ring, I saw fear in Chris Byrd's eyes—the Queen Pigeon was scared, and it didn't look good on her. When the bell rang, Byrd inaugurated his "Rapid Fire" style, throwing a high volume of pitter-pat punches, frustrating lefts and rights, which looked effective. He was keeping the stalking Ike at bay and annoying him. That gave me some hope, because Ike's frustration, possibly leading to a foolish disqualification, had been part of my vision. But Ike didn't follow my script much longer, staying calm and patient while sizing up his avian prey. He was gradually shrinking the distance between the two men, a distance the Queen Pigeon needed to maintain.

In the fifth round, Ike connected with a few big punches and backed up Byrd. Then he caught Byrd's jaw with a powerful left hook and a vicious follow-up right. As more punches hit his face, Byrd's arms became tangled in the ropes—a crucifixion of sorts—and he dropped to the canvas, face-first. The fans were in a frenzy, screaming for more. And Byrd, drooling from his mouth, showed tremendous heart; he staggered to his feet and passionately convinced the referee to let him fight on. When the action resumed, Ike pounced again—showing no mercy—grounding our Queen Pigeon again, and then again for the final time. The fight was over. There would be no $55,000 payout. Our $22,000 was gone. I was in major debt.

Emotionless for the rest of the night, I handled my post-fight responsibilities, including an attempt to pay the victorious Ike in his dressing room. I showed Ike the calculations and deductions from his fight purse, who started shaking his head and pointing his finger at me. He objected to the numbers and asked to speak to Cedric. That was fine with me—I wasn't going to try to convince that man of anything.

On my way back to my hotel room that night, I said, "Fuck you" to myself in all four mirrored walls of the Emerald Casino's elevator. (My dad once told me he had done that after losing $75 in a poker game, but that is where the similarities ended.) In the mirrors, I noticed that my white shirt had been sprayed red with The Queen Pigeon's sacrificial blood. From my room, I called Andy to apologize and commiserate. He had been watching on HBO and sounded drunk, depressed and wired—a worrisome combination and a recipe for my severe guilt. I was usually the one who gave Andy the good advice; *I* was the one who bailed *him* out of bad situations; *I* was the father figure to *him*. This world of shit was *my* doing. Though riddled in debt for the first time in my life, I felt worse for Andy than myself.

I got back to West 80th the next day and went to bed early. 5 a.m. came and went, and came and went a few more times. There was no cooing, no Queen Pigeon—she never did her thing again. Neither did Ike: In the prime of his career, twenty-six years old and the number one contender for the heavyweight championship, Ike "The President" never fought again. Four months later, he went to jail on various charges related to *attempted assault*—and fifteen years later, at the time of this writing, he remains incarcerated. I never educated myself on the specifics of Ike's incarceration, why he is still there for charges that don't seem to match the severity of his crimes, or whether his mental illness was properly considered by the judge. But at a cursory glance it evokes Joseph Heller's *Catch 22*: "Just because you're paranoid doesn't mean they aren't after you."

Chapter 12

No Birds, One Cat, We'll Talk

"If one woman I tried to create, if she would exist..."

THE GAMBLING DISASTER at the Emerald Casino had drenched me in debt and guilt. I never told my dad, but felt his would-be horror and shame anyway. I couldn't mourn for long though: The Cardinal, my "next Neil Young," was scheduled to arrive at my apartment in two days for a period of one week, to record a demo and play a live showcase performance. I contemplated delaying his trip so I could (try to) recover from my loss and (try to) muster up some funds, but his plane ticket was booked in advance, unchangeable and nonrefundable. *Before the deluge*, I had planned to put The Cardinal in a hotel; he crashed at my apartment instead, on the pink leather sofa that Cedric had given me—when he bought himself a new pink leather sofa! (Cedric's pink sofas, like his red limousine and diamond Rolex, were not *my* taste. But I appreciated his generous gift, and the fact that he paid someone $100 to deliver it to my apartment.)

I had become The Cardinal's manager because of his songwriting and organic guitar sound, so recording a stripped-down demo, with just him and his twelve-string guitar, seemed appropriate. It was also the quickest and cheapest way to get something current to shop to the record labels. On the first day of his two-day recording session, I was excited to be in a real music studio—my first time.

We started at 2 p.m., and The Cardinal was already buzzed on Pabst Blue Ribbons. His inebriation and performances both worsened by the hour. Day One was a total failure, resulting in no usable takes. Given my dire financial situation, it hurt to lose that $300.

For Day Two, I needed to push The Cardinal early and hard to get the music—before the alcohol got him. That evening, I conferred with the studio owner and engineer, and we changed our time slot to early the next morning. It felt cool to be *the manager*, strategizing with the studio about how to get the most out of my tormented talent before tragic self-sabotage took over. The problem was that The Cardinal thought he played better when he wasn't sober, (a feeling I understood all too well). But the revised schedule worked, and we ended up with an acoustic demo that showcased the good songwriting and lush, melancholy vibe that I remembered from The Cardinal's performances with his twelve-string guitar.

I had scheduled his live showcase at the famous CBGB music club in downtown New York City, and invited my friends and personal business contacts to check out "the next Neil Young." I had a hard time getting my uptown friends to come all the way downtown, and a harder time getting music industry people from anywhere to answer their phones. I had promised The Cardinal there would be some industry people in the audience, so I resorted to cold-calling local record companies, trying to get anyone who worked there to attend, even their interns. I left many messages and got some maybes, but no firm commitments. I realized that I didn't know anybody in the entertainment business outside of Cedric's contacts, but these were not available to me. (Just as I was keeping my heavyweight a secret from Cedric, I was doing the same with my troubadour. While my managing a folk singer would not have bothered Cedric as much as my managing a boxer, it would have caused him to question my supreme loyalty and level of focus as his most devoted boxing groupie. In order to gain coveted leverage in my future dealings with Cedric, I needed to first prove there was value in both The Robin and The Cardinal.)

About an hour before the showcase, I looked around CBGB and feared the worst: A pissed off Cardinal playing to an empty house, and me looking terrible. I went outside the club and spotted some well-dressed people on their way home from work. I offered four of them $20 each to come to the show and pose as record executives. One person I approached actually was a record executive! He said he liked my hustle, and that I wasn't the first manager who had done this. He accepted my $20 anyway and attended, which gave me one real and three fake record executives. A few of my friends showed up before the show, and one wearing a nice suit became my fifth record executive. We ended up with a decent turnout, and the Cardinal's solo acoustic set was solid. But I viewed my $20 bribes and desperate marketing efforts as a harbinger of the difficult road I would face as The Cardinal's manager: I had no music industry contacts, no money, maxed-out credit cards, and a weakened spirit ever since the Queen Pigeon went down in Seattle. I also realized that while I was pushing The Cardinal toward the solo acoustic "next Neil Young" folk-vibe, his real preference was to play harder rock with a full band. He almost sounded apologetic on stage for the solo acoustic format of his performance, and mentioned that he "missed playing with the rest of his band"—a few of whom happened to be in New York City and in the audience that night.

Later on, back in my apartment, I got drunk and high with The Cardinal and those band members. The Cardinal was drunker than I had ever seen him, and I felt no friendship or connection to him or anyone else in my apartment that night. One guy was cooking something zombie-like on my stove, which smelled bad and turned one of my spoons black. The vibe at West 80th was dark, as was my mood, and I went into my bedroom to crash. A few hours later, the zombie cooker was knocking on my bedroom door, but it was locked. I pretended I was asleep and he went away. Around 5 a.m., I woke to use the bathroom; (I still heard no cooing), and glanced down the hall into my living room. Two unknowns and the zombie-cooker were sleeping on the floor. The Cardinal was crashed on my pink leather sofa—halfway holding his last beer—before unconsciousness had tipped it over on my (pink) seat cushions. And the dirty black soles of his beat-up Converse One-Stars rested on my (pink) head cushions. I needed him out of my apartment and out of my life as soon as possible. I did not dislike The Cardinal, nor did I doubt his talent—but we were never going to connect spiritually or business-wise. Shortly thereafter, I bowed out of the project.

But I still had The Robin, "the next Muhammad Ali," Kid Lightning's number one priority from the start. The Robin was living well and training hard with respected boxing professionals, who reported to me that he was looking great in the gym. I confirmed this when I drove to Pennsylvania and attended his last training session, a few days before his pro debut. He looked like an unstoppable force, mercilessly blasting the punching bag, even harder than I remembered; and when I wished him good luck in his fight, his demeanor was gentle and appreciative. I felt giddy the whole ride back to Manhattan. How did I get blessed with this guy?

On April 10, many of my good friends and family came from Westchester and New York City to The Robin's pro debut at the Fernwood Resort in Bushkill, Pennsylvania. I used half of my CKP paycheck and rented a (non-red) limo for some of my friends, including Gregory Laurence, Andy Metternich, Stevie Stone, and a few others. My sister Fredda, my dad, and a few of my dad's friends drove up separately. There were about twenty people at the fight on my behalf, and each had traveled almost two hours! I felt like a player in the boxing industry, and I knew that my secret from

Cedric wouldn't last long—our big meeting would happen tomorrow, after this victory.

When The Robin's fight approached, I sat in the dressing room with him, his dad, and his trainer. He looked nervous, but I wasn't, because we had picked the perfect opponent: Donald Colbert, whose professional record was 0-4 (zero wins, four losses). Not only had Colbert never won a fight, but he was also undersized, out of shape, and had taken the fight on short notice. The trainer's report was that he was looking to make five hundred dollars and not get hurt too badly. When The Robin's name was announced, we exited his dressing room and walked together, from his locker room to the ring. This was my first ever ring-walk—the entrance music blaring, the atmosphere electric—we strutted with confidence. When the referee called the fighters to the center of the ring, the moment (and their size difference) reminded me of March 20 in Seattle, Ike versus Byrd. Once again, it was man versus boy—but this time, *I* had the man!

The opening bell rang, and The Robin came out as quick and slick as expected, dancing around his opponent and sizing him up. Also as expected, Colbert was slow and plodding, the perfect sitting duck. I saw my father, glued to the action. I wanted this victory for him. The Robin threw the first punch of the fight—the first punch he had ever thrown as a professional—and connected squarely to Colbert's head, who crumpled to the ground! My dad, sister and everyone I knew jumped to their feet, cheering and yelling, counting to ten with the referee as he stood over the fallen Colbert, while I flashed forward to how great this "first punch ever" knockout would be for tomorrow's meeting with Cedric and future marketing efforts for The Robin. When the referee's count reached seven, Colbert showed some heart and stood up, his legs buckling and wobbling. The referee saw him swaying, and was about to call the fight over, but at the count of nine Colbert showed enough stability to continue. I knew the next punch would be the *coup de grace*. But The Robin inexplicably backed off, circled around, and threw no more punches. He was showing mercy on Colbert! We were all screaming at him, commanding him to go in for the kill—but he danced and hesitated, and circled more.

Twenty seconds later, the first round was coming to an end. The partially-recovered Colbert threw a punch of his own, an innocent glancing blow, which grazed The Robin's cheek. And The Robin went down! He wasn't hurt, so I assumed he had slipped. He climbed to one knee, halfway up, using as much of the referee's ten count as possible to recover—a crafty move, I thought, for such an inexperienced fighter. But instead of popping up when the referee reached eight, The Robin stayed on his knee until ten—and *then* sprung up. It was too late. The fight was over. The Robin had been knocked out! He expressed anger, (for the first time that night), arguing that the referee had counted too fast. But it was obvious to me that he didn't wanted to fight on. Evidently, The Robin didn't like hitting real people, only punching bags, and he didn't *like* getting hit either—an impossible mix for *any* professional fighter, let alone "the next Muhammad Ali." Another disaster for Kid Lightning.

I walked my dad and sister to their car. They felt badly for me and wanted to console me, but I wasn't in the mood to talk. I wanted them to get on the road so they wouldn't have to drive back to Armonk too late. Then I walked to The Robin's dressing room to wish him well and politely exercise my right to terminate our management contract. He was sitting with his dad, who was now (also) wondering, out loud and in my direction, why the referee had counted so fast. His dad looked at me for approval and agreement, but I couldn't offer any. Then he asked me what I had in mind for his son's next fight, and I didn't offer any euphemisms: I replied that in my opinion, The Robin was not meant to be in this violent sport. He should use his education, intelligence, and sensitivity somewhere else, anywhere besides the boxing industry. (I remember thinking I should heed my own advice too.) The Robin stayed silent, as did his trainer, but his dad disagreed with me and said they wanted to keep going. I told him I no longer desired to be the manager, so we all shook hands and parted cordially. I was glad to learn, years later, that The Robin had never fought again.

It was a meteoric rise and fall for Kid Lightning, who clearly couldn't prognosticate fights, and had no more "next anyone's" to hype. The practical result was that I was still Cedric's disgruntled boxing groupie, but now disheartened, broke and debt-ridden. Cedric never found out about The Cardinal or The Robin, and the salary he paid me was the only thing that kept me from real financial disaster and lifestyle change after The Queen Pigeon had gone down.

I now lacked financial resources *and* a specific plan, but knew it was time to move on from Cedric Kushner Promotions anyway. Right around that time, I attended the wedding of my AEPi Brother Fink, an esteemed member of "The Elderly Five." That's where I spotted Maggie Felines, a spunky, smart, nationally-ranked college fencer, in her senior year at UPenn. Maggie was twenty-one, six years younger than I, and almost looked too young to approach. But when I did, I was enchanted by her wit and glow, and her cute smile. When I told her about the gambling and management disasters that had happened to me recently, she affectionately called me "weird," a description I had lately been contemplating about myself too, but not from my usual positive perspective. But I embraced "Maggie's weird," because I knew she liked the edge my adventures carried. Our phone conversations in the weeks to come flowed, as did our email banter. Maggie Felines was free-spirited and different by UPenn standards, but far more conservative than I. I imagined becoming far more conservative too, to hit the reset button and start on a new path—with her.

My favorite salutation in those days was, "We'll talk!" When I said or wrote that, it signified how I liked to feel: Stimulated, confident, fast-paced, and on the go. Beauty had returned, to revive the beast.

May 26, 1999

Subj: a babbling crazy man at 7:30am

Maggie Felines,

Believe it or not, I write this 'E' at 7:30am! Right before I went to the movie, Andy called, and said he did not plan to go to Westchester, and wanted to hang out tonight. I still saw the movie, which was good but not awesome, and then called Andy. He then came over here and he and I just basically hung out, and talked about tons of shit. It was good, because he has been pissing me off lately, and I felt we needed to talk – which we did, about everything. I made him realize some major stuff that he already knows, but is not following!! (I'll explain another time.)

For some reason, even though I went to sleep late, I am now wide awake, and decided to write you an 'E'. Did you hear the guitar and harmonica on your answering machine? I know most people will always say this, but please believe me when I tell you that I played so horribly on that message!!! I was actually nervous, I was balancing the phone on my leg, and the harmonica was out of time, and it really was not a fine representation of my playing!! I have actually been slightly epiphanous lately in terms of writing some original stuff—that's the way to do it.

Anyway, I am in such a writing mood that you may think of me as a psycho to write all of this at 7:00am!! But, I am pretending I am reading this out loud to you as if you were here, which is a very good thought. I am definitely experiencing an awesome time period of my life right now, and I feel very good about my venture into the wild (pursuing you or quitting my job?, ha, ha, just kidding, you are the easy part…). I am so full of business and life ideas, and I really believe I have the ability to do many of these things successfully, as long as I have confidence and follow my plans. I am looking forward to a few months to research a lot of different ideas, and basically pursue strongly and seriously all things that I think are important and worthwhile. I am entrepreneurial to a large degree, and three years with one company has been not only very rewarding, but also a great struggle, in terms of the lack of freedom I have been able to enjoy.

So I could not feel any better about this step, even though that $14,000 would have helped right about now!! But the money will come…

Well I am now getting tired, and should try to go back to sleep for an hour or two. I am not going to go in to work until 12:00 tomorrow, which will help! In closing (to sound official), I wanted to also take this time of writing to tell you that I am very happy that we met each other, I think you are extremely unique, and I really look forward to our talks every day. (No, I do not say this to everybody, and even if I did, I am telling you that this time I really mean it!)

Hopefully you will feel good about all of your "boy" dilemmas and decisions (of which I am amazed that you still really have!!). And, of course, don't wait too long, or my relationship power percentage will plummet to like 21%, compared to my current status of 40-60 between you and I!! (Or maybe, your lack of wisdom to see that I am the greatest thing in the world will annoy me, and your power will drop from 60 to 40, and mine will rise up to 60??!!??!!??). Actually, 51-49 is ideal (of course in your favor!).

I hope you had a good night. Call me. If you don't, I'll think the guitar playing was so bad that you never want to talk to me again (which it really was, awful and not the real me!)

We'll talk, Mitch

PS Wise Mitchell Lloyd Winston says: However difficult or perplexing a new decision may appear, one must always be open to the solution that can provide true greatness. And however long a lifespan that each option may appear to have, one must also remain cognizant of the true temporary status of all opportunities… (that actually came out pretty smoothly) (yaavcn)??

Notes while on the phone with Maggie Felines

Maggie wants this kind of guy:
1) Nice, caring, kind
2) Fun, funny, entertaining, good sense of humor
3) Guy who can dance, who won't embarrass her
4) Can sing
5) Plays guitar
6) Intelligent, smart
7) Worldly
8) Wild side
9) Sensitive, but not too sensitive
10) Hard-working
11) Athletic
12) Dark, no blondes
13) "Movie Star" looks
14) Best personality
15) Confident, but not too much
16) Jewish

I was a winner
Now I'm a loser
I took a wrong turn…and I left my baby behind.
Now I'm going back to find her… if she has the time.

Maggie Felines – A girl that I met in April
I had a dream that we'd ride together to the sky.
Our conversations late at night made my sleep so peaceful.
And I was hoping that what we had would never die.

Something happened something changed… I felt the trouble.
I had a feeling she was leaving, but she wouldn't say goodbye.
I made her admit that her feelings changed in an instant.
She said it just happened – she doesn't know why.

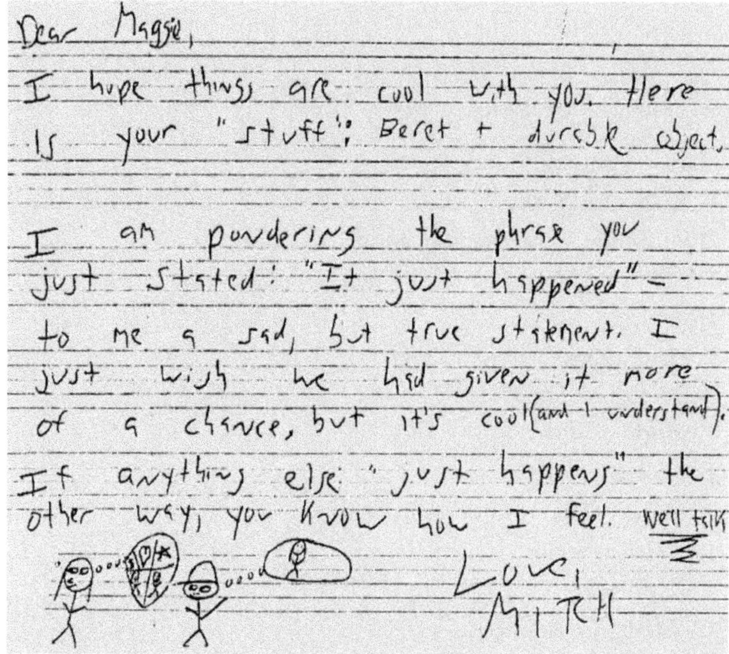

Dear Maggie,
I hope things are cool with you. Here is your "stuff": Beret + durable object.
I am pondering the phrase you just stated: "It just happened" — to me a sad, but true statement. I just wish we had given it more of a chance, but it's cool (and I understand).
If anything else "just happens" the other way, you know how I feel. We'll talk
Love,
MITCH

Dear Maggie,
I hope things are cool with you. Here is your "stuff": Beret & durable object. I am pondering the phrase you just stated: 'It just happened" – to me a sad, but true statement. I just wish we had given it more of a chance, but it's cool (and I understand).
If anything else "just happens" the other way, you know how I feel.
We'll talk.
Love, Mitch

The Felines rejection hurt more than usual and inspired me to write my first *real* song, "Right Back." Getting high alone in my apartment, and playing it over and over, felt right. I also played it for Andy and Zuckerman. Andy admitted it was a real song, and Zuckerman said my harmonica solo told him a story that gave him some clarity. That was cool to hear.

Right Back

I thought you knew I had to be alone.
And the reason why we get along
is 'cause we understand each other.
I'm a dead man now,
If I stop believing,
"The end is near, I'm living in fear, its not easy..."
It's not easy.

Went away for a while, contemplated my confessions.
Trying to get closer to a truth that I knew.
But when I got back home,
I got a little too tempted.
And I had to, right back, do the things that I do...
The things that I do.

Chorus:
It's not easy...
The things that I do...
From the other girls...

It's not easy...
The things that I do...
From the other girls...

A girl I knew hurt me so badly tonight.
That's why I'm sitting here,
Trying to take it all in.
But somehow, this time around,
It's hurting more deeply.
I think it's retribution from the other girls
From the other girls.

(Chorus)

Playing my guitar on a Friday night.
Asking the cosmic question,
"What's the Truth?"
And, "Would this life experience
be less lonely...
If one woman I tried to create,
if she would exist...?"
If she would exist.

Chapter 13

Ray Tico

"Play because you love to...that is the only reason."

AROUND THIS TIME, I began a weekly ritual in my West 80th apartment. Every Friday night, I would get high on marijuana and videotape myself singing, playing guitar and harmonica, and philosophizing. I filled tape after tape—none of which I ever viewed—and had yet to play a show in public. I still enjoyed playing with Andy, who repeated (often, to my chagrin) that if we played in public, we would make fools of ourselves. One day I walked to Central Park and sat on a hillside, where a shirtless acoustic guitar man sang and played to a riveted crowd. I scribbled some notes.

> If you love something, worship its creator.
> Her hands were too good for me to hold.
> Not having a cigarette will never turn anyone off—having one will turn almost everyone off.
> This guy playing is not that good, and he has 300 people in Central Park watching.
> He should wear a shirt.
> He's not that cool…
> He's playing fucking Elton John

Why can't you just focus on playing all day and get a regular gig going?

He is good. He memorizes some good songs.

It works for the park, I guess.

How can you be so fucking nuts…in the sense that you can be so miserable and jumpy, and annoyed, and old, and then you take one hit of pot and then you feel so relaxed, so confident, so right… you feel so fucking good.

Life's a dance you learn as you go…

He is too "Elton Johnny," but not <u>too</u> because people are here.

But it should only give you confidence – when you sing, and you have it going on, you totally have feeling and meaning.

Continuation of pot statement: What is it about pot that makes me so fucking confident?

He is cheesy, but truly happy. In real life? That's the true test!!

You are either looking like a total psycho to these 2 girls, or one of them wants to fuck you. Probably both. Maybe all three (both want to fuck, both think I am psycho.)

I am so "psycho" in my real happy self – when I'm either high or not, but still not hiding anything – it's good to be it when not high. Learn from the substance. Learn from how you feel when you are high. And learn how to get there when you are not high!! That is the key!

These fucking "people" are all looking at me —I am writing like a fucking maniac, and I am going so fast. What is the purpose of my life, what is the meaning of everything I talk about or dream about or think when I don't do about, but what do you want to do?

Right now, what would your perfect lifestyle be?

Play in a band

Have an audience

See if the magnetism is there!!

That is so fucking funny!! I would be embarrassed if I use this.

there is just not enough time to do this at CKP. there is more than there used to be, but still not enough.
JUST DO The thing

There is just not enough time to do this at CKP.
There is more than there used to be, but still not enough.
JUST DO THE THING

What's up now:
- GAVE OFFICIAL NOTICE TO CEDRIC!
-consultant only to CKP, as of 9/1/99!
- lowered economic costs – Andy, dad
Lifestyle I need
- exercise daily
- guitar daily – play out – you need this – get it done
- some public forum = column, radio show, head-shot
- new hairstyle, better clothes = style
- pot is minimal – you're doing well!!
- but you can smoke now!!....done.

Now that I had given official notice to Cedric Kushner that I was leaving, I needed to replace that income. Gambling was on my mind. Without any cash or space on my credit cards to make sports bets, I started to *take* bets from a few acquaintances and place them either online through offshore sportsbooks or in person with a local bookie. I guaranteed myself about $100 profit on every transaction, with no risk, and built up some extra cash. Sometimes, when a person's bet seemed super-foolish, I assumed the risk myself by collecting their money and not placing the bets—in these cases I was "the casino." In all cases, my local bookie's patience regarding when he had to be paid provided me a credit line, and I always incorporated my $100 profit. I only had a few clients, but I enjoyed the cool street feeling of being a bookie and the cash I was earning. I calculated that if I stepped up my volume, I could survive on this income. I would no longer be trading money for time, which would let me pursue music more.

Years earlier, while visiting Las Vegas with my dad to help him at his real estate convention, he pointed out the countless bright lights shining in every casino and asked me rhetorically how the casinos could afford to pay such enormous electric bills. I knew what he was implying—the house always wins—and he was warning me never to bet. (He wasn't suggesting that I become a bookie or open up my own casino, but being on the casino's side of the transaction felt less like a sin against my dad and more like a business.) Many offshore Internet casinos and sportsbooks were based in Costa Rica because it had a stable economy, low infrastructure costs, and favorable legislation to protect the online gaming industry. The problems occurred when these offshore casinos tried to *repatriate* their profits—move them back to banks in the United States, where online gaming was illegal. But the more research I did, the more I learned that revenues from owning my own Internet sportsbook could be enormous. My dad even agreed but urged me to get better educated on the legal side of things, especially on the repatriation of profits back to the U.S.

Close to my last day at CKP, Cedric asked me how I was planning to make money in the future. I told him I had been researching opening an online sportsbook, based offshore. He had also been looking for ways to earn extra money outside the boxing industry, and said he would be willing to partner with me if I could get an online sportsbook up and running. He told me about Uncle Buddy, a friend of his, who had moved to Costa Rica to open up his own online sportsbook, and was always looking for partners. Cedric told me to call Uncle Buddy, introduce myself, and explain my intentions, which I did.

We had a good opening conversation. Buddy confirmed what I had suspected, that revenues through equity ownership in an Internet casino and sportsbook could be huge. He also educated me on the substantial barriers to entry in starting one from scratch. Those included a capital requirement of at least $1 million and various "tricky" legal and accounting issues. The legal roadblocks of repatriation worried me the most, but Uncle Buddy said he had a way to navigate those. He closed our conversation by saying there was a way for me to operate my own offshore sportsbook, under his infrastructure and protection, for an investment of $75,000.

I briefed Cedric on this conversation, and I could tell he was interested. Without my asking, he offered to put up the $75,000 from his personal funds if I could establish this partnership with Uncle Buddy. We agreed we would go 50-50 after Cedric recouped his original $75,000. Cedric's only condition was that I had to keep his involvement a secret, due to his public stature in the boxing industry, which was already highly scrutinized by the media. I didn't have experience raising money, and I hadn't officially decided to plunge into the legally murky waters of offshore gambling—but when Cedric offered the $75,000, I took it—and saved my existential thoughts for later. I called Buddy and told him I had raised the $75,000 and was headed to Costa Rica to make a deal. He said to call him when I got there and come meet with him right away.

Before I left the United States, my dad and I spoke with a lawyer friend of his, who educated us on the legal ramifications of what I was getting into: A few offshore casino owners had already gone to jail when they tried to repatriate their profits to the United States; some were arrested as soon as their planes had landed in America. I explained that under Buddy's infrastructure, I would be protected from this, but my dad was not convinced. To allay his concerns, I lied that I was going to Costa Rica strictly to conduct research, and wouldn't make any moves until we both agreed they were wise. On the plane, I regretted my lie—I was going there to make a deal.

The afternoon I arrived in Costa Rica, it was pouring rain. I checked into a hotel in downtown San Jose, the nation's capital and commercial center. At the hotel bar that night, there were prostitutes everywhere, and I was lonely. I didn't object when a cute one approached me. The next morning, I called Uncle Buddy, who didn't come to the phone, but his assistant told me to head over to their headquarters. With Cedric's $75,000 ready to be wired upon my request, I was eager to make a fast deal before Uncle Buddy (or Cedric) changed his mind. An attractive, English-speaking secretary greeted me and told me that Uncle Buddy had to leave town for a few days and would see me later that week. She said she would spend the morning with me, show me around, and "get me started." (I didn't know what she meant by that.) She led me into the main bullpen on the first floor, which resembled a telemarketing call center. At least 60 people were set up in front of ringing phones and beeping computers, creating a frantic wall of sonic chaos that never waned. (It was football season, a sportsbook's busiest time of year.) The vibe was unsettling, and I was glad when she brought me to a private, much quieter office down the hall.

She said that Uncle Buddy wanted me to get a sense of the business "from the ground up, before I met him upstairs." She added that the best way for me to do that was to open as many new accounts for Uncle Buddy as possible. I should start by calling my inner circle of friends and family, and then expand to their inner circles. Once I had opened up fifteen new accounts, Buddy would be ready to meet with me. Her presentation was planned; obviously it wasn't her first time giving it. And I knew that Buddy *was* in the building. This was probably his standard procedure to gain a sense "from the ground up" of all the new people who walked through his doors.

Buddy would certainly welcome having fifteen new accounts for his sportsbook, and his cold-calling strategy seemed a sensible way for *someone else* to learn the business. But with Cedric's $75,000 commitment already secured, I wasn't interested in cold-calling. I imagined how these phone conversations would go: "Hello, this is Mitch Winston, your former student council President! Maybe you remember my path from Byram Hills to Wharton to rabbinical school? No? Then let me fill you in. I dropped out of rabbinical school, became a boxing promoter, then a failed manager, then a failed gambler, and now I'd like to become your very own, illegal, offshore bookie!! Can I get you started on my same road to success with a new account?" My own sarcasm about the life of a bookie touched a nerve, because I had already been doing this in New York, sans the broader solicitation tactics. I told Buddy's secretary that I couldn't start that day, but would be back in a few days, after I observed the Jewish holiday of Yom Kippur.

Ten days after the Jewish New Year, *Yom Kippur* is the *Day of Atonement*, the holiest day of the year for Jews. On that day, Jews fast—refrain from all food and drink—until sundown, ask forgiveness for their sins, and begin the year with a clean slate. Even during my childhood, I thought I understood why a day without food and drink could help my cleansing process, and I had always made a concerted effort to recall my biggest sins and ask forgiveness for each. My dad and I had a longstanding annual tradition of taking a break from *Temple Bet Torah's* services and embarking on a long walk, where we shared some of our most honest conversations. It was strange for me to be in Costa Rica, so far from my family on Yom Kippur, but I still wanted to observe the holiday by fasting and going to temple.

I started the day with good intentions: I woke up, refrained from breakfast, and took my own long walk, heading for a synagogue in downtown San Jose. It was starting to drizzle when I arrived, and the gates were locked. The security guard told me that the service was in recess and the doors would reopen in two hours. I told him I would be back then. I walked around the corner and sat on a park bench to jot down some notes and kill time. I happened to spot a Pizza Hut nearby—and the drizzle turned to rain.

Yom Kippur, Costa Rica, 1999

Like cars slowing down to see disasters in the night.
Not thinking for a moment of their disasters tonight.

Separately, they are old.
Together, they are new.

Separately, they are new.
Together, they are old.

Unevolved hecklers, creating noise pollution,
make me frustrated.

Silence gone, taken from me, a revelation never born.
Frustrations created, but why should they be born?

I don't want to be walking down the street like a read book.
And I ain't talking about the color.
(When everybody knows what you're all about.)

It rains a lot here every fucking day!!
I should start job searching on the internet,
because it will occupy time.
Travel on weekends, and hang out more at home.

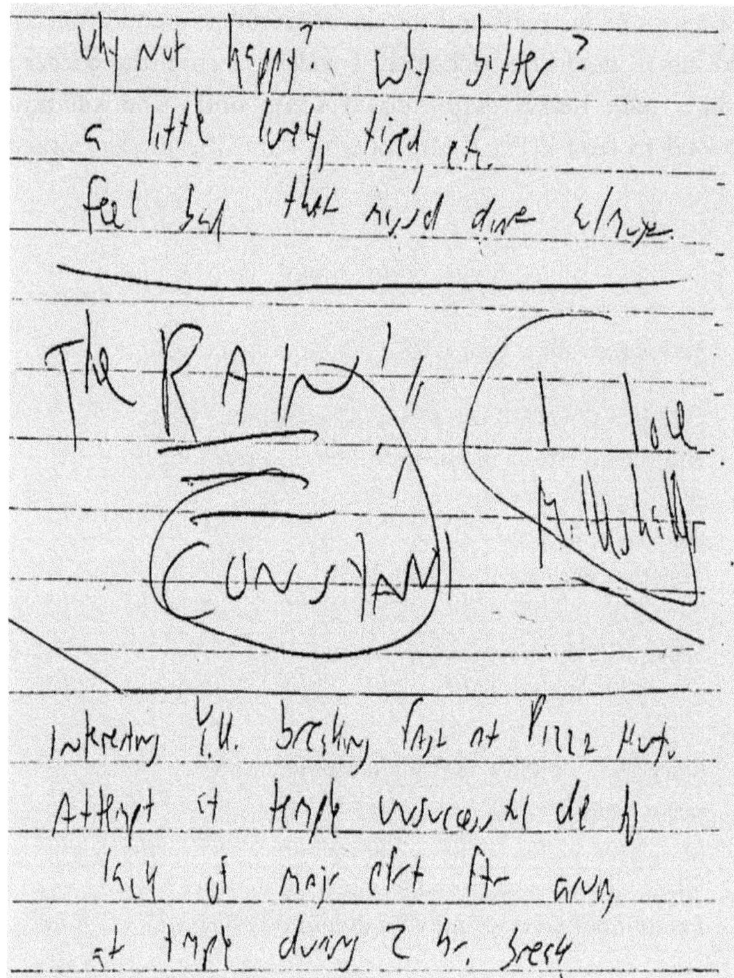

Why not happy? Why bitter?
A little lonely, tired, etc.
Feel bad that I missed date with *la mujer*.
<u>THE RAIN!!! CONSTANT!!!</u>
<u>I love milkshakes.</u>
Interesting Yom Kippur, breaking fast at Pizza Hut.
Attempt at temple unsuccessful due to lack of major effort after arriving at temple during 2 hr. break.

Faced with temptation and worsening conditions, I chose Pizza Hut. My *fast* became a *feast*—five hours before sundown. I ordered a milkshake and a pizza and lasciviously devoured both. After I finished, I felt guilt—and then an epiphany—that this sequence was a microcosm of my life! Instead of persevering through difficult conditions, I would always become distracted and move on to "the next big thing." And the next big thing was getting shadier and shadier, culminating with offshore gambling—illegal and jailable in the U.S. I called Cedric that night and told him I wouldn't be needing his money, since I had decided to abandon the offshore sportsbook venture. He said he was surprised, unaccustomed to people turning down $75,000! But he also sounded relieved, as if he might have been regretting his hasty decision to commit to the venture. After I called Uncle Buddy and told him I was out, I felt a similar relief.

With no job waiting for me in the U.S., and Costa Rica's beauty and low cost of living, I decided to stay for two more months. My goal was to become fluent in Spanish, one of the rare skills that I had learned in school and had actually retained. (Thanks to a few romances and my Ecuador experience, I was now quite expressive.) I researched some of the Spanish language schools in San Jose, where I could attend classes on weekdays from 8 a.m. until noon and receive living accommodations in a Costa Rican household, all for a great price. It was a chance to be immersed in Spanish 24/7, a sure path to fluency. The school I chose was full of excellent teachers and interesting students from all over the world, including England, Germany, Belgium, Australia, and Texas, all there to learn Spanish and enjoy the beautiful country. The positive, carefree vibe reminded me of my time in Israel, five years ago, where I had loved the academic atmosphere, the great conversations, and the weekend travel with fellow students. Far away from New York, I felt more spiritual, more confident around girls, and I rarely considered marijuana—while at home those days, I rarely didn't consider it.

Spanish guitar lessons Mon, Tues, 1 hour (probably a waste)

-Spanish in AM

Girls:

-Girl from internet café, Silvana: bad face, hot body, she might have hairy armpits

-Ina—German girl, cool, great body, so-so face

-Rafaela—the cutest, young British girl, gone for a week, doesn't seem interested, so not worth thinking about.

-Cindy is too domineering

-RIGHT NOW YOU HAVE QUANTITY, NOT QUALITY

After class, I would sometimes go to an Internet café in downtown San Jose, where I would eat lunch and go online. I instant messaged one afternoon with my sister.

Fredda: Hey sucky! just wanted to say a quick hello.. but I'm leaving in two minutes… so.. hello… and I guess goodbye!

Mitch: hola.. wait one minute!!

Mitch: r u there?

Fredda: aqui

Mitch: I have been thinking a lot about pursuing an old dream I had when I get back.

Fredda: what dream? To build a house in back of mom and dad's and live there?

Mitch: trying to open up a tiny bar in nyc, on the upper west side, where they can have simple acoustic music, couches, totally mellow…

Fredda: do you remember The Magic Garden show?

Mitch: yes….?

Fredda: ooooooooooooooooh! I like that dream! Perfect for you my little bro, I like that dream a lot…

Mitch: just a home base… it does not exist on the upper west side at all…. And it is fucking nyc!!!!

Fredda: that dream will help other's dreams! karmically it cannot go wrong!

Mitch: I had an awesome experience (not sexual) with this guy named Ray Tico. He is 73, and famous here for playing guitar

Fredda: can I learn bartending and do bartending once a week or so for extra money???

Mitch: You can run the bar — $5 an hour

Fredda: where did you meet Ray? And how was the beach?

Mitch: I requested a song called Cu-cu-ru, and he said that the king of England requested it when he was playing in Cuba in 1955!!! I am gonna play harmonica with him at this bar on Thursday. it was really cool… he said, "you have to play cause there is no tomorrow, because you have to play, because you love to play, and that is the only reason."

Mitch: I have never seen someone play like him… he was addressing every song to me, talking about me, it was slightly embarrassing and ridiculous but great…

Fredda: the problem with bars in New York City now, is that you can't dance at them anymore… most don't have cabaret licenses, and I miss dancing! But you are trying to achieve something different…

Mitch: the beach was awesome… I belted out lyrics at the beach in your honor, and thought of you

Fredda: YES!!!!!! I'm so happy!!!!! Did the vocals sound different at the beach? Clear? Cleansing?

Mitch: yes – and it was that day that I thought about the small bar. Do you think it is "not enough" since I have a Wharton degree, experience, etc., to just open a small bar? That is what mom will think

Fredda: that guy sounds so cool! You have a definite connection it sounds like… "because you love to play, and that is the only reason…" I love it! That is the way to live life… to follow your heart and be happy… to do what feels wonderful and what makes your heart sing….

Mitch: I met a new girl named Ana. Hot, 23 years old, long black hair. She looks like Catherine Zeta Jones. We are gonna visit that active volcano this weekend… should be interesting

Fredda: Mitch… you must do in life what is going to feel right for you… everyone else who loves you will fall into place and accept it… in the end… if you are smiling and laughing daily, you will bring happiness to all of our days too, and it will be contagious… if you pursue this bar, you will be exploring your inner spirit, your music and the music field in general. Your Wharton degree will be very important for you to open a business… it will not be going to waste, for you will need that sense on how to make the thing profitable… not fail… etc..

Mitch: I am thinking of a basement type of location, low rent, cheap to maintain… after this, who knows? I feel like I cannot just get a job, ya know? this is a great thing to do, I think

Mitch: you have to go, no? we can talk tomorrow… I think I am coming back on October 25.

Fredda: it will take a while to get off the ground… you probably should get a job for a few months to catch up on finances and then break off and open the bar… but I'm not sure about basement… remember dad's words, location, location, location… then again… basement like you say could be a start…

Fredda: I immediately thought about a weird beat-poetry night… a bunch of people like in the 60's or 50's… whenever… in a basement, wearing black, rapping about poetry man! Probably not what you had in mind!

Mitch: you are probably right… but maybe I can find an owner who wants to leave his bar and I can work there, and take it over, and make a deal with him, while being paid to work there… as long as we have a deal worked out

Fredda: I can do what I was going to do now…later… this conversation is the most stimulating moment of my week! Unless you have to go…

Mitch: Believe it or not, I already thought about what you said, regarding poetry, etc. even one night a week for an open mic situation, etc. I cannot believe there are not more open mic opportunities, ya know? bongo drums, we can get the guy from wetlands to give a speech…

Fredda: there's nothing wrong with working for a few months, so there is no rush in getting the business together… you know? I mean, get paid while you are doing your research…

Fredda: ha ha!!

Fredda: if you had a drum circle, oh my lord!!!!!

Mitch: you think it would fill up the bar? Do drum circle kinds of people buy drinks?

Fredda: the possibilities are endless!! It's all about how YOU envision it, and what will make you money and keep on bringing life into your days… keep up your creativity Mitch…

Mitch: I am sick of changing my mind every day, but it has taken me into different places… but I really feel like I have to get something established… and this seems like something I could love, without too much stress after a year or so if it worked…

Fredda: dad had two TV's out again and was watching baseball on one and football on the other!! He cracks me up!

Inspired by Ray Tico, I got the courage to schedule my first live show, a solo acoustic performance at a bohemian bar in the historic neighborhood of Barrio Amon. My supportive classmates and new friends attended my show. I wasn't the manager, I was the artist—and I vowed that night to never manage again. I played my few originals plus some Bruce Springsteen songs from his album *The Ghost of Tom Joad,* including "Dry Lightning" and "The Line." This album is a tribute to the Latin American migrant laborers who risk their lives on a daily basis to cross the U.S. border, just to provide food for their families. Springsteen summed it up when he said, "Hunger is a powerful thing." It felt good to be playing those songs in Costa Rica. I was feeling a strong connection to the Latin American people.

Ray Tico

When Ray Tico sings,
the people in the audience,
Don't got problems..
Without solutions.
He travels 'round the world,
Playing guitar not making money,
But understanding his freedom..
In society.

Chorus:
His name is Ray, Ray, Tico
He's the reason why,
I sing tonight

Ray, Ray Tico
Where are you?
Are you still playing tonight?

I was feeling real bad,
had a nightmare last night.
"I finally accepted a path..
To my mediocrity."
I asked Ray what to do,
He said, "You know what you gotta do.
You got to play guitar...
'Cause you got to."

(Chorus)

El comprende el mundo,
Hace lo que quiere,
Y toca la guitarra y canta....
Como un ave.
Estaba en Costa Rica
Y pensando en mi vida.
Quiero ser suave, tranquilo....
Como en mis suenos.

He went to Cuba
And the King of England
Requested the Song,
"Cu-cu-ru-cu-cu"
He sang the rhythm
And when he was finished,
The king sat down in his chair,
He was crying.

(Chorus)

When my two months in Costa Rica ended, I returned to New York City, energized and clean. The New Millennium approached. For this occasion, Andy Metternich and his new girlfriend, (who was sweet but never as cool as Annie), and former Ixchel staffer Jarrett and his girlfriend, had rented a house in Lubec, Maine. This is the easternmost point of the United States, where they planned to catch the first rays of the first sunrise of the New Millennium—before anyone else in America. It sounded appealing, and there was room in the Lubec house for one more couple—but I didn't have a date. I called Ana from Costa Rica, the girl I had dated during my last few weeks there, and invited her to visit me in America and be my Lubec date for the new millennium. She applied for a tourist visa and was successful.

We weren't a serious couple in Costa Rica, but from the moment that Ana got off the plane in America, we were inseparable. Something clicked here that had not clicked there. Ana didn't speak English, so I was the only one in Maine who could communicate with her, which Andy and Jarrett noted was becoming my *modus operandi*. Ana was unassuming, accepting, and appreciative of everything. On our first day in Maine, we all went to the grocery store, and Ana requested only potato chips and grape soda, which everyone found cute. Andy, Jarrett and I were high all week, and we attended some local Lubec millennium events, like their well-advertised "Polar Bear Swim." Everyone in town gathered to watch a hundred psycho hicks run across the beach into the freezing ocean waters, and then right back out. The entire event took thirty seconds, after which the crowd seemed lost, looking for direction. An uncomfortable silence ensued, and someone yelled out to the organizers, "What do we do now?!"

The vibe between Ana and me in Lubec was new and romantic, while the other two couples were having big issues. (Neither of the two would last long after the start of the millennium.) On New Millennium's Eve, the guys partied extra hard. Our thoughts rolled to spiritual places, and big words flowed. I proclaimed to the room that Ana and I were in love, and she would soon be moving to America to marry me. Everybody congratulated us, and we toasted the moment and The New Millennium. Around 4 a.m., Ana and I fell asleep, intertwined amorously in a single bed, before the first rays of the Millennium's first sunrise hit Maine, which we had chased from Costa Rica and New York. After such a romantic week, we didn't care.

We all left the next day. On the ten-hour ride back to New York City, Andy reminded me, in English, that I was engaged. I didn't agree, but I couldn't fully disagree either, since details from the previous night were murky. He and I shared a joint and began reminiscing about some funny experiences we had over the years, such as the time we drove to another hick town, this one in upstate New York, to play golf. To prepare for the match we got high, as usual, but a rainstorm developed while we were driving, and the course was temporarily closed. To kill time before it reopened, we wanted to find a KFC, and if the storm persisted, a movie theater. We spotted a few locals who looked like they might know where things were, and I pulled up next to them and lowered Andy's window so he could inquire. Face to face with these toothless characters, reminiscent of the movie *Deliverance*, Andy froze up: All he could manage to say was, "Do you know where there's any rednecks or chickens around here?" (We burst out laughing, and I sped away for safety.)

Another poultry-related incident we recalled was the time he and I were hanging out at West 80th, after getting high, and we decided to order-in chicken wings from Blondie's. Andy always wanted his wings super-well done. He had emphasized this in past orders, but never received them quite well-done enough. This time, he wasn't going to be denied: As I was placing the order, *after* I emphasized that the wings be extremely well done, Andy grabbed the phone out of my hand and yelled into the receiver, "BURN THE

SHIT OUT OF 'EM!! BRING 'EM TO HELL AND BACK!!" Thirty minutes later, we received exactly what we requested: A platter of something that resembled twenty black smoldering coals: inedible, unidentifiable, and tragically unreturnable. (But on what grounds could we complain?) After we related this story, Andy's soon-to-be ex-girlfriend asked passive-aggressively, "Andy, do you realize that every story you have starts with you guys getting stoned? Do you have *any* stories that happened when you were sober?" It got quiet for a minute. Then he lit up another and we continued south.

Chapter 14

My Nucleus

"Cien Fuegos"

BEFORE ANA RETURNED to Costa Rica, I backtracked on my Lubec proclamations and clarified that we were *not* engaged. But we were a couple, and now viewed our relationship as exclusive. I invited her to visit me toward the end of February, and we both looked forward to it. The vision I had in Costa Rica, to open a small bar in Manhattan that focused on acoustic music, was back on my mind. It seemed simple and right, like Ray Tico's lifestyle and words. I started looking for locations. But in the meantime, I needed a job. My dad spotted an ad in the New York Times employment section that seemed to be written for me: The owners of a company called Incubator Solutions were looking for a business plan writer who could package up their portfolio of fledgling Internet-based companies. With my Wharton degree, TB&A success, and my experience as my dad's writing partner on countless documents—plus the comforting pledge of his continued assistance—I was confident going into my interview.

Two Wall Street-looking guys named Dick and Aaron, a few years older than I, interviewed me in their office on the 66th floor of Manhattan's Chrysler Building. Dick excused himself after ten minutes, but I stayed with Aaron for two more hours. He told me about each of their incubator's "eggs," the six companies they had already seed-funded and for which they were seeking additional financing. I knew what Aaron wanted from me: Six perfect business plans. I told him I could deliver, and looked him in the eye and made my usual pledge: "I won't let you down." Those words never failed! He offered me the job on the spot, with a starting annual salary of $100,000 and a promise of future equity if things went well.

The following week I reported for duty. I got along well with Aaron; Dick showed up only once a week but called the office every hour. (I heard there was a legal issue that kept him behind the scenes, but I didn't know the details.) I didn't like how Dick spoke to me on the phone, his tone condescending. And when he did come to the office, wearing a slick expensive suit and shiny shoes, his aura made me cringe. He seemed evil, down to the bone, and I couldn't look him in the eye. I perceived him to be a "civilized hyena." There was bad karma at Incubator Solutions, all caused by Dick—and we soon clashed. He was upset that Aaron had granted me a salary of $100,000, and he asked me to accept a reduction until they acquired second-round financing. He had a reputation for raising money successfully with relentless, hyena-like tactics, and I think he viewed my taking a salary reduction as a form of raising money. Following my own gut (and the advice of my dad), I refused, which upset Dick—and he wouldn't stop asking, and needling, which upset *me*. Even though we were in a business environment, I was prepared to pull a Vickers—I was ready for a physical confrontation with Dick if he didn't back off. I tried to convey this message of credibility with my eyes, not my words.

I asked my dad, "Why does Aaron keep Dick around? His vibe is killing the company!" He said it must be that Dick knew how to raise money, the most important skill in business, by far. Then he recounted a few of his own business experiences in which one partner was honorable and the other wasn't—and things never ended well. I viewed Incubator Solutions as a textbook case of an

Internet company destined to crash, but I stayed there because my salary was good, very good. And Dick and Aaron, for all their flaws, were skilled at raising money—and my six business plans were developing nicely. They had a good chance to secure that coveted second-round financing, which would prolong my stay and increase my salary. To avoid the toxic Dick, who now came to the office more often, I received Aaron's permission to work from home. I also made sure that my six business plans were saved cryptically and in piecemeal on separate computers, so my services would be needed until their final delivery.

February, 2000 (Translated from Spanish)

Hello Ana, my love,

How are you? There are so many emotions running through my head! My music, my life, my work. What strong feelings. I had a very difficult conversation with one of the people I work for in the new company. We were speaking about my salary, and I was very surprised when he told me how much he thought I should earn. I couldn't believe how much he told me - it was a very low number! And he said to me: "You think you deserve more? Why? The ideas are mine. The money we have is mine. The company is mine." And I said, "If you think of me like an employee, and not a partner, then we have a big problem with this relationship." And he said to me: "When you have a company of your own, you are going to understand what I said. And now, if you can't accept the number or a number closer that I am saying for your salary, I am going to come to your apartment in order to get your materials, and we can end it now. And I said: "You can do what you want. But I'm not giving you the files until we settle everything."

It's incredible, Ana. In my past, I would have said, "What is the best you can pay me," and whatever he then said, I would have accepted it. But now I have much more confidence in myself, my ideas, and my ability to earn a lot of money. And I am not going to accept a person trying to make me do what he wants, and doing it with force. That's crazy, right?????????

Ayyyyy!!! All of my feelings are so strong, Ana. This is a period of my life that is very important. I have to do what my mind is telling me, and what Ray Tico said, and be the type of man I have to be. And during this time, and many conversations, arguments, emotions, it's very crazy. But I am not afraid. I have confidence, but it's difficult to stay relaxed and tranquil in these times. But I am learning a lot, and trying to stay positive.

Estaba en Costa Rica
Y pensando en mi vida..
Quiero ser suave, tranquilo,
Como en mis suenos.

I love you, my love. You give me security. And don't worry, because I am happy.

Mitchell

I finally convinced Andy Metternich to play a live show with me in New York City, and I invited my sister's friend Dawn to join us. Dawn was skinny and blonde—and quirky—with a sultry, feline femininity. She believed in molecular time travel, interplanetary life, and the fusion of alternate universes, swearing she was once abducted by aliens. Since meeting her a few years earlier, I had occasionally fantasized about an earthly fusion of our own molecules, and I sensed the feelings were mutual. When I learned later that Dawn sang and played the flute, I invited her to jam with Andy and me. We had a lot of fun, it sounded good, and Dawn agreed to play the show with us.

During the rehearsals, the vibe was sometimes awkward. Andy was constantly proclaiming how bad we were, (his usual shtick), and that we were going to make fools of ourselves in public. This irritated me, because it had taken me years to convince him to play this one small show, and he was still saying how much we sucked. I snapped at him, "If we are so bad, why the hell did you agree to play the show?" He answered, "To be honest, I still don't want to play it, but you asked so many times that I finally felt bad enough for you to say yes." I said, "If you don't want to play it, you can drop out now." And he did! He picked up his guitar and left my apartment. It wasn't as dramatic as the Jamaican Tea Incident, but it was tense, and happening in front of Dawn—who remained felinely silent.

Suddenly it was Dawn and me, alone in my apartment. Neither of us were single, and we refrained from all physical contact—which made the vibe in the room more stirring. We played music, talked, and scribbled philosophical thoughts and sentences. I anticipated our creative and meaningful get-togethers a great deal, and they started happening with increased frequency.

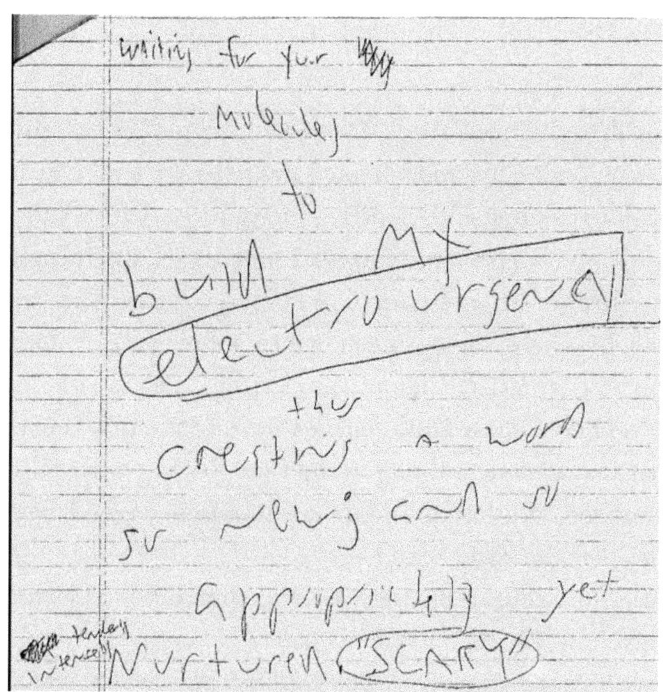

Waiting for your molecules to build my electrourgency—
thus creating a world so new;
and so appropriately yet tenderly, intensely nurtured.
"SCARY"

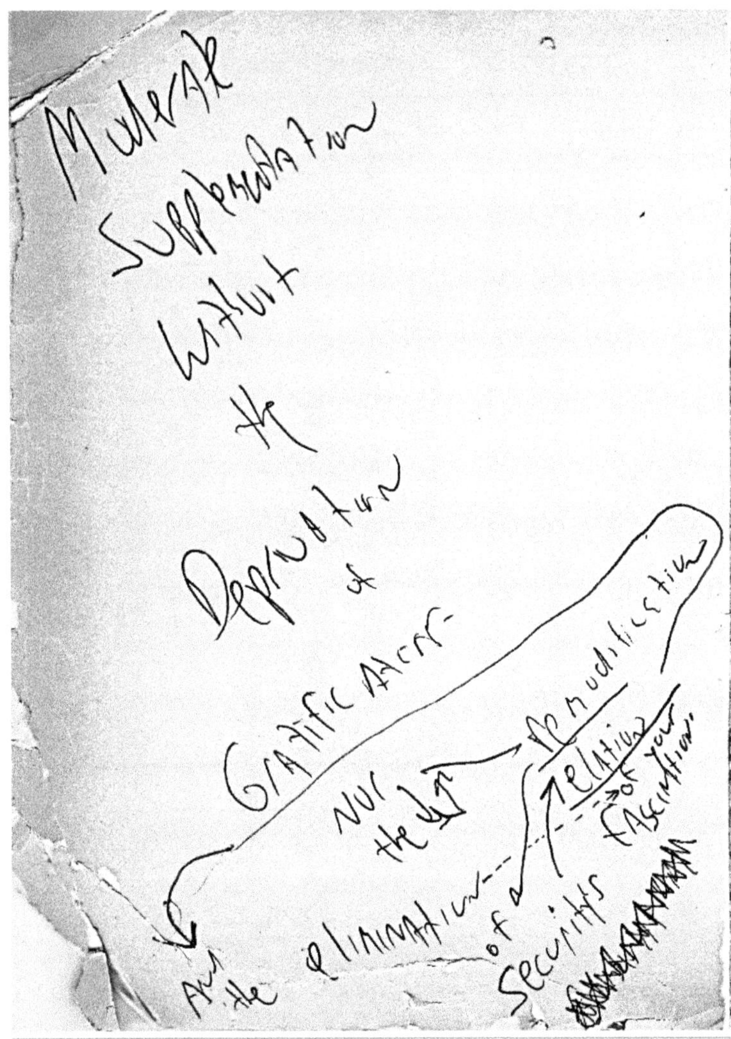

Moderate Supplementation
Without the Deprivation of Gratification-
nor the remodification of security's elation
and the elimination of your fascination.

Evaporation of the condensation mitigated your elumination.
There was an infiltration of my hallucinations that caused a
diffusion of my delusional fusion—
to your inspiration our love ameliorated.
<u>And we love with patience here.</u>

A few weeks before the show, Ana came to visit. Dawn and I paused our rehearsals, while Ana and I enjoyed a great week in New York City. It was her first time there. She loved its huge buildings, like the World Trade Center and the Empire State Building, and appreciated its smallest things, like the $10 rooster stuffed animal that I gave her at the airport. The Lubec fire was still burning.

Before the week was over, I invited Ana to come back to New York in June for an extended stay—between one month and six months. (The duration depended on the stamp she would receive when she passed through U.S. immigration, a seemingly random determination based on the agent's mood or preference that day.) I had no problem with this commitment; it felt right. On Ana's last morning at West 80th, she was showering before leaving for the airport, and I picked up her passport to see her picture. I looked at it once, and then again in disbelief: It said she was 29 years old—not 23! She had lied about her age when we met. This posed a big problem, not just because she lied, impossibly out of her angelic character, but also because I *wanted* her to be 23. 23 meant less pressure on me to get married and have kids, which Ana had already communicated as her number one desire. (Her urgency in this area had struck me as odd, but now it made more sense.)

There was no time to fight, and I didn't want to hear any apologies. We drove to the airport in silence, and then she was off. I wasn't sure if I would ever see her again. She called me multiple times that week from Costa Rica, crying and swearing that she had planned to tell me each day but never found the right moment—her fear and embarrassment had gotten in the way. She also said that if I really loved her, age shouldn't matter. I believed her that she was planning to tell me the truth, and it felt chauvinistic for me, 28, to have a problem dating a girl who was 29. My anger was also hypocritical: Five years earlier, I had lied about my own age to Amparo. That relationship had not lasted long enough for my convenient dishonesty to matter, but it was the same lie.

According to my own *authentic meter*, I should have forgiven Ana. But there were heavier thoughts on my mind which were harder to get past: Over the years, I had developed confidence in my ability to judge people's characters. I had a keen sense of who was good, who was bad, who could be trusted, and who couldn't. These intuitions rarely let me down; and when they did, it rattled me. Two years earlier, in the Jamaican Tea Incident, I was overcome with feelings of shock and betrayal—by Andy *and* my intuitions. (The Andy I knew would never have done that!) But I later attributed his actions to his mental state that week, which bordered on depression, and was worsened by the gluttony and inebriation of our Jamaican experience. I forgave him, like a father forgives his son for a random act of selfishness—but I never forgot how I felt that night. "Age-gate" with Ana felt exponentially worse: She was the least likely of anyone I had *ever* met to deceive. She was the innocent white angel from Costa Rica, who requested grape soda and potato chips. Her betrayal of me meant a betrayal of my own intuition. Still, I had a feeling I would forgive Ana, but I told her I didn't want to speak for a while and put our relationship on hold. This (convenient) respite gave me the moral permission to merge molecularly with Dawn—who had also just become single, and also from a lie.

My Nucleus

I've traded heartache,
To walk alone in the sun.
Or in the night-time,
When my day is done.

I've been with women,
And a couple of girls.
I lived with feelings,
That re-created my world.

Chorus:
But it's you now,
You said only for a while.
You're inside my nucleus,
With your radiant style.

I've tailored passion,
From an insolent dream.
Created sadness,
From a smile's release.

I've been forsaken,
Just got it going again.
I have forsaken,
I don't know what they did.

(Chorus)

Bridge:
I wanna live in the past through the visions of your many lives.
Appear on the horizons of the pleasures that you recognize.
See the things I see again through your eyes.
Prove to you that I am cosmic
Not just for a while

I wasn't foolin,
I been around for a while.
You say you've lived other lives, I swear,
This is my only time.

A star-eyed illusion,
They leave you nothing to gain.
Don't mind their intrusions
They make me shake my head.

(Chorus)

On the night of our live show, as we arrived at the Orange Bear, I felt the sudden urge to defecate, fast—and multi-tasked in the bathroom by smoking a joint to calm me. The lights in the bathroom were motion-activated, and faulty, turning off every thirty seconds and leaving me in pitch darkness. I sat on the toilet, joint in my mouth, waving my arms in the air to keep the lights on. The lock on the door was also faulty, and three girls walked right in on my embarrassing display, and then right out, laughing.

When *I* emerged, I asked the club's house drummer, Kent Carter, to sit in with Dawn and me for the set. He was a cool guy, and his sparse drumming style enhanced the vibe without overpowering it. Andy came to the show too, and I invited him on stage to play the set with us anyway. He accepted, which made the night feel much better. We also earned $10, which I told my dad made me a professional musician.

My mind racing, I emailed Kent a few days later.

> Kent,
>
> How are you? Thanks for the other night…
>
> I want to do an impromptu recording of a couple of my songs – a 2-hour live recorded session at a studio in NYC that I can burn to a cd. I will have everything arranged.
>
> I will definitely pay you to play – I just want to pound out three very mellow songs to have a disc this week.
>
> If you get this email on time and are available Sunday morning early, please let me know as soon as possible. Or just let me know when you might be able to do something like this. As I said, I will definitely pay you.
>
> Mitch

Kent slowed me down and explained that a recording session had to be planned properly. He connected me with a few of his musician friends, one of whom had an apartment recording studio with a decent set-up. This is where we recorded my four-song demo. It felt good to be back in a real music studio—this time as the artist. (My vow in Costa Rica to never manage again was paying off already.) My sister's friend helped me design the CD cover, and she asked me what I planned to use for my band's name. With Darwin on my mind, I replied, "Mitch Winston and the Band of Natural Selection."

CLOSE YOUR EYES AND LOOK FOR THE COSMIC TRUTH.
SEARCH FOR IT WITH EMPTY HANDS.
LIVE BY WHAT YOU NOW REALIZE.

Gregory Laurence and I had recently started going to the same all-night clubs in New York City that I once negatively judged Fredda and my ex-Danielle for enjoying—mind-blowing social scenes where trance and house music engulfed nonstop, from late at night until the next day, and amazing crowds rolled in and out. We decided to take a trip to Ibiza, Spain, after Greg had researched its club scene and heard it was decent too. (That was the understatement of the New Millennium.) Our goal was to experience these clubs in all-out fashion, which we accomplished. The hash in Spain was also excellent, which we bought off the streets from persistent vagrants who wouldn't take no for an answer—and smoked all day. The week wasn't just a party; it was spiritual and meaningful for our friendship too. We listened to the Jackie Wilson album, *Reet Petite,* over and over—which *still* wasn't enough. We also listened to my new four-song demo, which I loved, and Greg liked too. (But I also used headphones, accepting that even Greg, my most supportive friend, shouldn't have to hear it fifteen times a day.) Inspired by our hilltop view of Ibiza and that smooth Spanish hash, I wrote some notes.

Blue Pad - 5/24/2000

This pad will one day be full of great things.

One day I will be playing in front of 25,000 people, singing, "You couldn't even begin, to relate to my passions within, but you remember that I seldomly tried to explain."

How crazy what just happened with Dick. He questioned my integrity, my convictions! He said Aaron is "fired up" over the fact that I said I was taking my company Amex card to Spain!!

That is ridiculous – I helped with – blah blah blah

It just reaffirms my complete knowledge that I should look elsewhere.

Money, professionalism, etc. Why waste time here?

Money issues – you should look immediately for something interesting

But Dick and Aaron have access to capital, etc.

You need to get close to some of Dick and Aaron's investors.

You are so much better than Dick, Aaron, businesswise.

Look for something awesome - $ - Music =

Work for someone who pays me but I don't have to come to the office every day.

Look for deals – get hired by someone with $ - with independence to really pursue music.

YOU ARE WASTING TIME!!

Dick, Aaron, Incubator Solutions = all three don't fit w/Ana!!)

I said, "go fuck yourself" to Dick/Aaron.

I have to keep following my dreams and persevere

I like golf.

I need to go to the gym!!

I deal well with people

I can build relationships while having freedom.

But if I had to work for someone–totally professional, $135k

Incubator Solutions are all bad people – bad karma

I don't believe in these people!!

Fuck them!!

Spring into motion – by 6/15, new situation

Keep dreaming – seriously!!!!

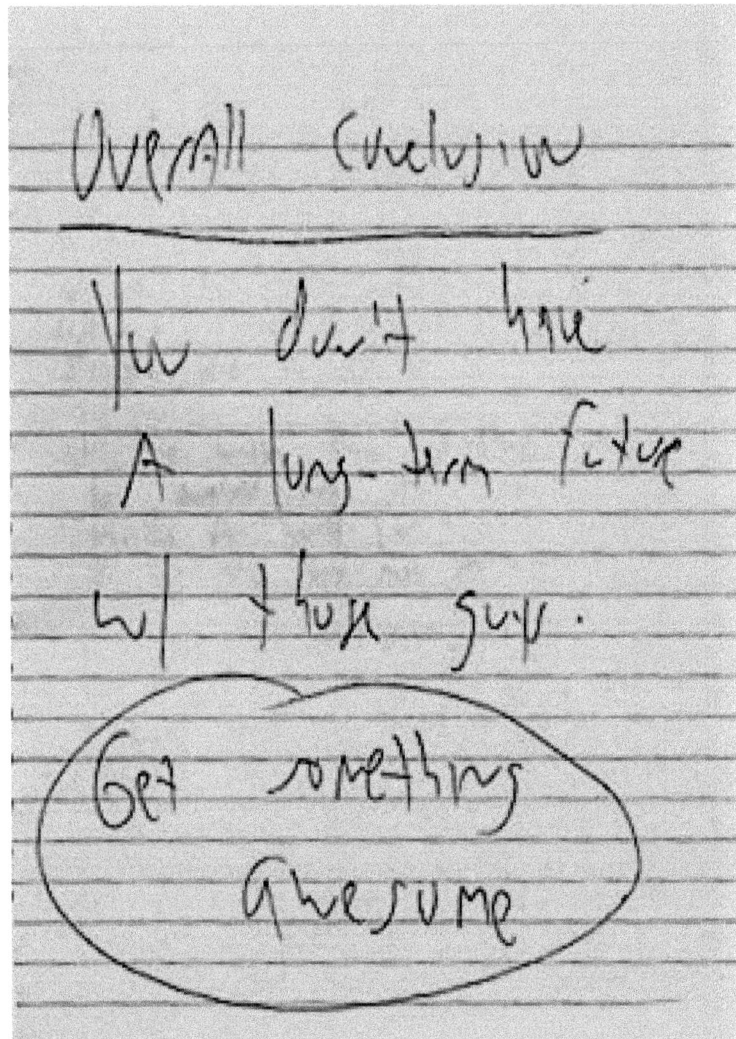

<u>Overall Conclusion</u>
You don't have a long-term future with those guys.
<u>Get something awesome</u>

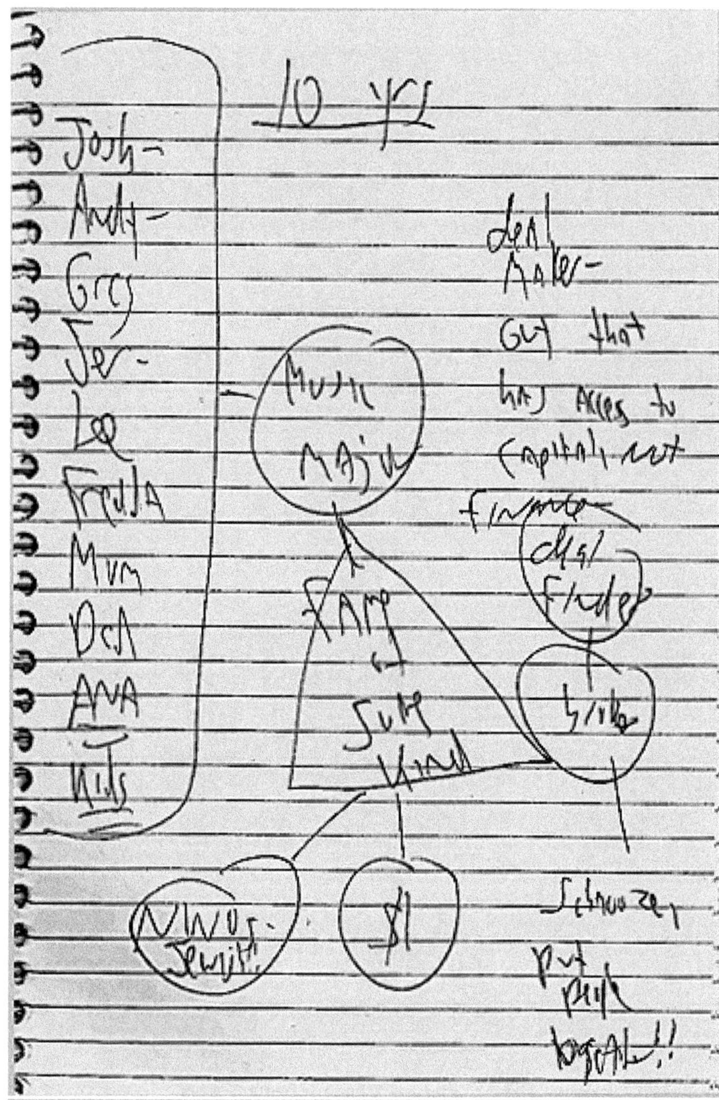

10-Years
Deal maker, guy that has access to capital, not finance.
Deal finder. Broker. Schmoozer, Put people together!!
Music Major. Fame of some kind. Ninos-Jewish! $
Josh-Andy-Greg-Jer-Lee-Fredda-Mom-Dad-Ana-Kids

The New York City club scene was even better than Ibiza's. With the right DJ at the right space, such as Danny Tenaglia at *Vinyl* on Friday nights, one could get lost in the atmosphere for hours on end, immersed in a heightened world of intense stimulation and sexy adventure. I enjoyed wandering around the club alone, and Greg and I would often get separated and meet up again. Once, after we had gotten separated for longer than usual, I met two petite brunette standouts, Veronique and Michelle, and I wanted to find Greg so they wouldn't think I had come alone. I spotted him leaning against a speaker, looking a bit less lively and more disheveled than usual. But when he saw us, his energy was back. He sprang up and made a beeline in my direction, his reddish-blond mane flailing in his wake. Instead of slowing down when he got closer, he lost his balance and slammed into me, almost knocking us down. We stayed on our feet, but I was afraid he had made us look bad. I privately barked into his ear, bitch-like, "Dude, what are you doing?! Relax!" Thankfully, he didn't hear a word I said. He beamed back triumphantly, *yelling* into my ear, "DUDE, I'M ON FIRE!! I RULE THIS PLACE!" Maybe he did.

If things were going well in the club, I would circle around from room to room, my eyes glowing but not appearing too high. I was filled with pleasure bubbles and felt an internal euphoria, a cool, sexy, spiritual vibe. I was approached by beautiful people from all over the world, singles and couples of every gender and preference—with the next move up to me. But I was gone, circling again, searching for better. I was playing an exhilarating yet inauthentic game of cat-and-mouse, because the result of my search, regardless of what I found, was more circling. A rare connection could halt my fiendish circling and satisfy me. Such trysts could last the rest of the night, the weekend, or a lifetime. Regardless of duration, they were the most stimulating and satisfying experiences of my life. This serendipity was elusive, though. Greg and I joked about the number of times you could circle around the club until your mystery was gone, your luster was tarnished, and you bore the indelible *scarlet letter* of a "fiendish circler." We estimated this took about four or five laps, and with each lap your chances of success dwindled. Right before being downgraded to a circler, you must downshift into "Bargain-Basement Mode," lower your standards, and accept *any* female companionship that presented itself. The key was not to wait too long before downshifting, because after too many laps, even the bargain-basement candidates would no longer be available to a "fiendish circler" like you.

Too much circling—and downshifting too late—were *my* most common club failings. And when all luster was gone, it was time to leave the club. Greg and I would sometimes walk from the club in the West 20s all the way to my apartment on West 80th, where we would catch our breath, recap the night, and inhale large amounts of marijuana. Unlike Greg, who was able to let go of the night and go to sleep, I needed physical contact before granting myself this permission. It was imperative, a necessary elixir before my body would permit my mind—and my mind would permit my body—to sleep. I sought the attention of prostitutes who advertised in The Village Voice, which led me into some unknown, potentially dangerous situations. I was relying on luck for my own safety, but I didn't care. (If I would have just gone into my bedroom and tried hard, I could have lived out my weirdest, wildest erotic fantasies—safely and for free—and satisfied my search for stimulation without leaving home. Not all fantasies and needs have to be fulfilled in person, and even Toby Tyler's "bed-fucking" technique may have come in handy.) But I was a heat seeking missile, an unstoppable object moving toward an irresistible force. I could not be deflected. On too many weekend mornings, around 10 a.m., while normal people headed for brunch carrying *The New York Times* and pushing baby strollers, I was in a cab heading *somewhere*, my heart racing—as emotionally stimulated and erotically charged as a human could be.

On one such occasion, I visited the Lower East Side apartment of a bubbly young Asian woman who barely spoke English, and she answered her door with a lollipop and a smile. She said her name was Cookie, giggling and laughing as we entered her dimly-lit room, the aroma of oils and candles soothing my nerves and slowing down my racing heart. We sat on her bed, and she held my hand. We had a connection, and our bond was solidified by the softest, most sensual love-making I had ever experienced. We came together, at the same perfect instant, and while looking into her eyes I almost said, "Cookie, I love you." But before I could, she pushed me off her with both palms and ushered me off the bed, on with my clothes, and toward the door—while clapping and chanting, "OKAY, OKAY, GOODBYE!! YOU A BIG MAN, YOU A BIG STRONG MAN!! OKAY, BYE-BYE! GO NOW!!" In two minutes, I was in a taxi headed right back to West 80th.

Back at West 80th a month later, around 7:00 a.m.—after another club night of unrequited circling and poorly-timed downshifting—I convinced a reluctant Greg to join my shenanigans. We chipped in $250 each and invited a duo of female escorts to my apartment. Two-and-a-half hours later, we were both feeling shaky, the girls had still not arrived, and even I was ready to cancel it and crash. When I tried, their *driver* said we would have to pay anyway, due to this late notice, and he would soon be over to collect—so I cancelled the cancellation. The girls arrived at 10 a.m. showing signs of a long night, reeking of cigarettes, perfume and (most unfortunately) cologne. And they were *not* the two girls whose pictures were shown in the ad! But they were *here*, and we had already paid $500, so we decided to make the best of it.

Greg and his girl sat on the pink couch in my living room, side-by-side in awkward silence. I went into the bedroom with mine, who proceeded to give me the most uninspired hand-job in the history of man. Her rapid hand motions mimicked the disinterested shaking of a bottle of orange juice, while her eyes and mind wandered way off. I wanted to finish fast, so the girls could leave and we could sleep, but we were getting nowhere. I politely pleaded, "Can you please pretend for a few seconds that you have some interest here?" She answered, "No, I can't. I hate my job, I hate my fucking life, and I hate doing this shit." Her eloquence ended matters; I felt too guilty to continue and told her we were done. She went into the bathroom, and I redressed and went into the living room and sat down next to Greg and his girl, who were still sitting in silence. (Greg whispered to me that he had felt sorry for his girl too, and hadn't touched her.) Ten minutes later, my girl emerged from the bathroom and proudly announced to everyone, "The pussy is clean again!!" (At first her comment didn't make sense, since *I* hadn't touched her—but when it did, I was glad I hadn't.) We waited on the couch together for thirty more painful minutes, and then they were gone. It was now 11:00 a.m., and Greg and I were strung out, depressed, and $500 poorer. It was all my fault, and I apologized to Greg for the expensive bullshit—both economically and spiritually—that I caused.

I preferred going to clubs on Fridays, because if Friday night lasted into Saturday, I would have all day Sunday to recover, regroup, and organize myself for the upcoming week. On these "Comedown Sundays," staying in my apartment alone and sleeping on and off was a guaranteed prescription for depression, worsened by the fact that no sunlight reached my apartment. I would force myself to get up and get out, grab a huge iced coffee, and walk alone to either Central or Riverside Park. On one of those walks I met a group of Quaker women engaged in silent companionship, journeying around Central Park, together, without uttering a word. I asked them who they were and what they were doing, and received my answer on a pre-prepared note, which also invited me on a future walk. (After my recent foolishness, some forced silence sounded appealing; but I never followed up.) I continued alone to The Meadow and sat down near a cute tan-skinned mom wearing loose faded jeans and a white tee-shirt. She was with her eight-year-old daughter. The mom said hello, and we hung out and talked for a few hours—mostly about music—and I played Frisbee with her daughter. I appreciated the normalcy of this daytime interaction.

Then I would head home to my dark apartment, where post-club depression had patiently waited; it was time to stop fighting it. I would try to think positive thoughts and fall asleep early, both proving difficult. These difficult nights were when I most thought about Ana, and the acceptance and companionship she was ready to provide. Again she was the pure white angel, cleansed by my own dirtiness. But she was still in Costa Rica, waiting for my call. I hadn't forgiven her—I hadn't even contacted her.

Cien Fuegos

**I crawled into bed last night,
You were already sleeping.
And I thanked the Lord as I watched you,
Silently dreaming.
For my health and my friends and my family,
for You beside me.
And for Helping me to be the man that
You Needed to Guide me…
To Guide me.**

**Chorus:
The fire in your eyes, Cien Fuegos.
The message that you left him on the table, you said goodbye.
The burning of your shaky spirt, holding you down.
The burning of your shaky spirit, holding you down.**

**I was hoping that wherever you are…
You're feeling good now.
And your laying in my flowers as we gaze
into the midnight sky.
But I know I'm gonna love you
as much tomorrow,
As the tightness in my grip,
when I held you in my arms last night…
Last night.**

Chapter 15

Changing of the Guard

"Stars of David"

IT HAD BEEN an eventful six months since the start of the New Millennium, and the timing felt right to *take it down a thousand* and make a mature commitment. I forgave Ana for "Age-gate"—and we revived her plans to come to New York in late June. Passing through U.S. customs, she received a six-month stamp. We agreed she would stay for this duration, and if things went well, forever. I enrolled Ana in English classes and a weekly *Introduction to Judaism* class designed for people contemplating conversion. (We attended that class as a couple.) All was pardoned; we were both having a great time and building something.

When I brought Ana to Armonk for the first time, I had high hopes for an immediate parental connection. I had already briefed my parents on the situation, and proudly told them that Ana had begun her conversion to Judaism. But the visit was surprisingly uncomfortable, with unspoken displeasure and disappointment emanating from my parents, which only I noticed. Ana seemed to be having a wonderful time. After the weekend, my mom and dad privately voiced their opinions to me: I was "suddenly living with Ana," a quiet girl who didn't know English, whom I had nothing in common with, and whom they knew nothing about. They thought I had "settled" and acted too fast. I told them I had never met a girl so kind, so accepting, and with such great values—all the attributes of a great wife. I explained to them that Ana's quietness was due to the language barrier, which would soon be gone; and I was confident they would soon get to know and love the real Ana. I didn't like this strange new feeling of parental conflict, which took its toll on my dad's countenance and made him look older.

Gregory was still working for Cedric Kushner and living in Amagansett. He got along well with Ana; like my sister had been, Greg was instantly supportive of the relationship. A few weeks later, Ana and I visited Greg, along with another couple Greg was friends with, Marcy and Yanni, who weren't getting along with each other. We spent most of the night outdoors, talking and philosophizing as we looked up at the star-filled Amagansett skies. With spiritual thoughts rolling through my mind more than ever, I took notes.

Fear of dying crossing the street.
When you die, your thoughts either die,
or continue in others' thoughts.
Will people be more spiritual when I die because of me?
I can die or get cancer today.

Marcy became spiritual.
Marcy said she is seeing lights all around me. Silver lights
I don't know who I am, or anyone else, when I die
Spirit is what? Self-confidence developed.

Don't regret things that you did.
But don't continue with assuming.
Stop looking down on others!

Youth very important.
People are either good or bad.
Birthday is meaningless. Conception is everything.
Can't love something you don't know.
Out there = in here.
10 is not equal to 11.
Haggard girls = Bitter guys.

Everyone who is smart shares the same worst fear–
losing your health.

Physical resources beget leisure.

Charismatic = able to draw a following.
You're an orator

Poor on the streets: How can they be positive?

Are wild animals ever really happy? Do they know who's who?
Survival: It's not why we are here, but what keeps us here.
Cockroaches.
Helping = Figuring out how to stop wars, make people positive
Lavender Sing/Estoy Aqui

Yanni to Marcy: Ever since I was born, I was open to death.
Yanni to Marcy: I understand you, even when you lose control.
Yanni to Marcy: Do you hear anything I'm saying?
Marcy to Yanni: No.
Bad vibes now
You are strong
Your aura is making them both go inside

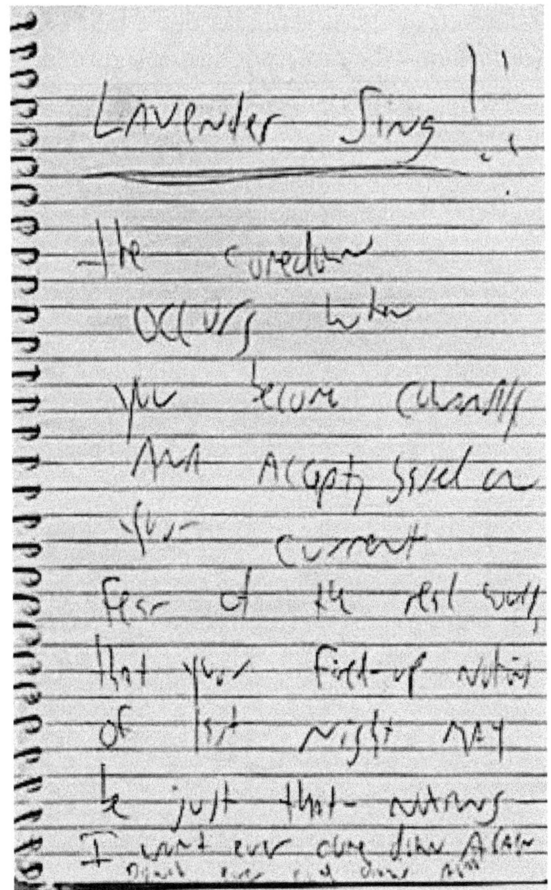

<u>Lavender Sing!!</u>
The comedown occurs when you become cowardly and accept, based on your current fear of the real world, that your fired-up notions of last night may be just that – notions.
I won't ever come down again.
Don't ever come down again.

<u>July 12, 2000, *Daily News*: The cover says, **“EXPLOSION!!”**</u> But it should mention the cause was gas or something, not terrorism. The potential cause is buried because they want you to think terrorism-it sells papers!

How do you think the soldiers in Israel feel?

You think they want to be killing? Fighting?

If something can rest, what can we infer about it?

If I try to outrun you, baby, I’ll slow down first.

If I try to deceive you, I’ll be deceived first.

If I try to understand you, it’s me I’ll understand first.

To combat drugs: Find <u>intense</u> stimulation elsewhere!

To save boxing, have them wear helmets and play boxing!

<u>Fight your enemy for charity</u>
PPV!! (Pay per view!!)
That’s fucked up!

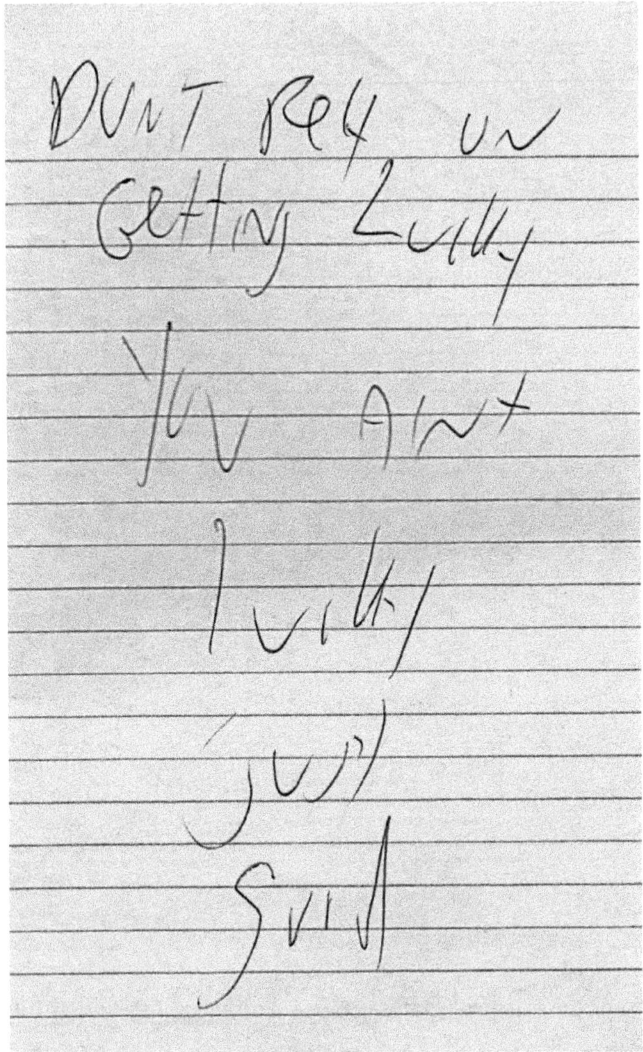

Don't rely on getting lucky.
You aint lucky
just good

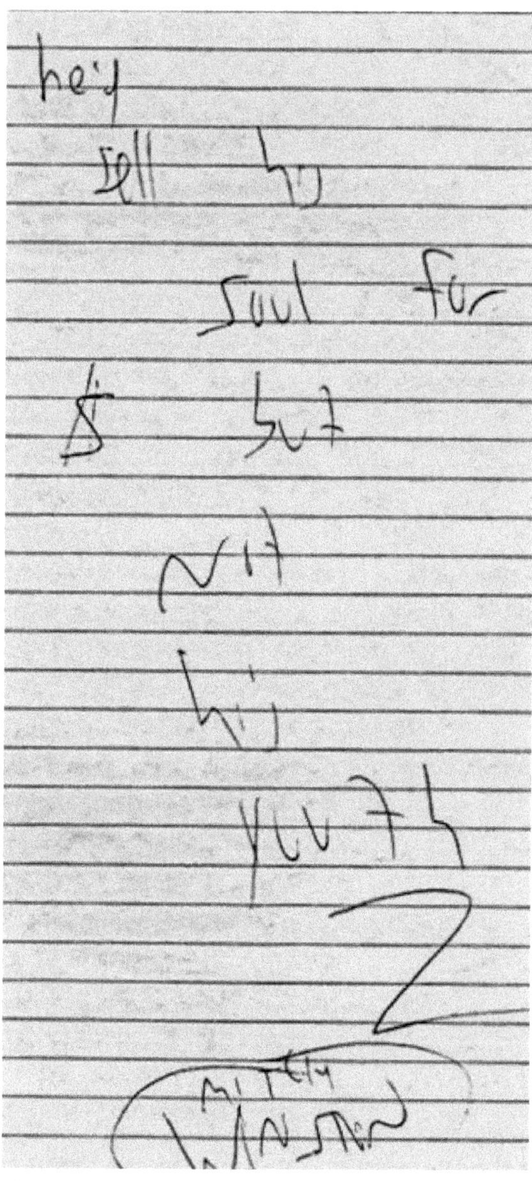

He'd sell his soul for $ but not his youth
Mitch Winston

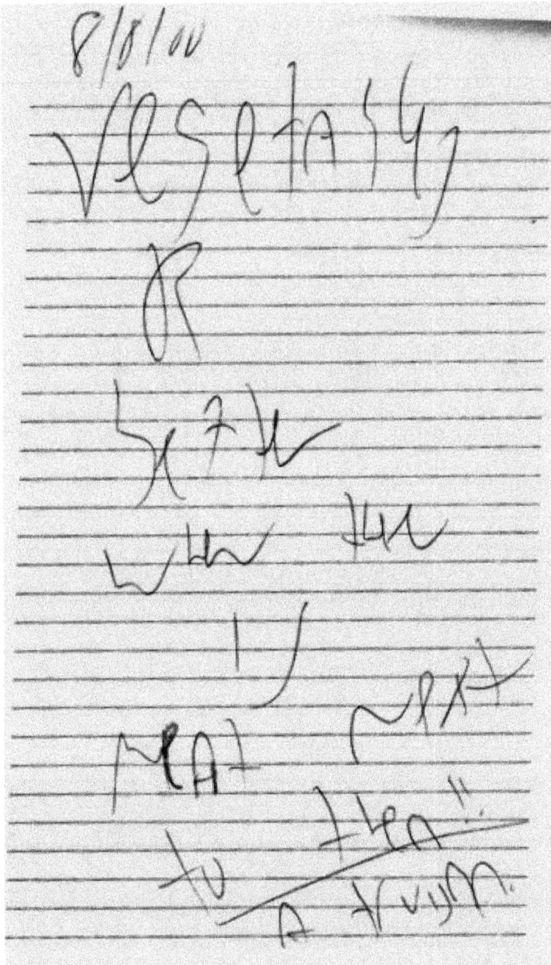

8/8/00
Vegetables are better
when there is meat next to them!!
A truism.

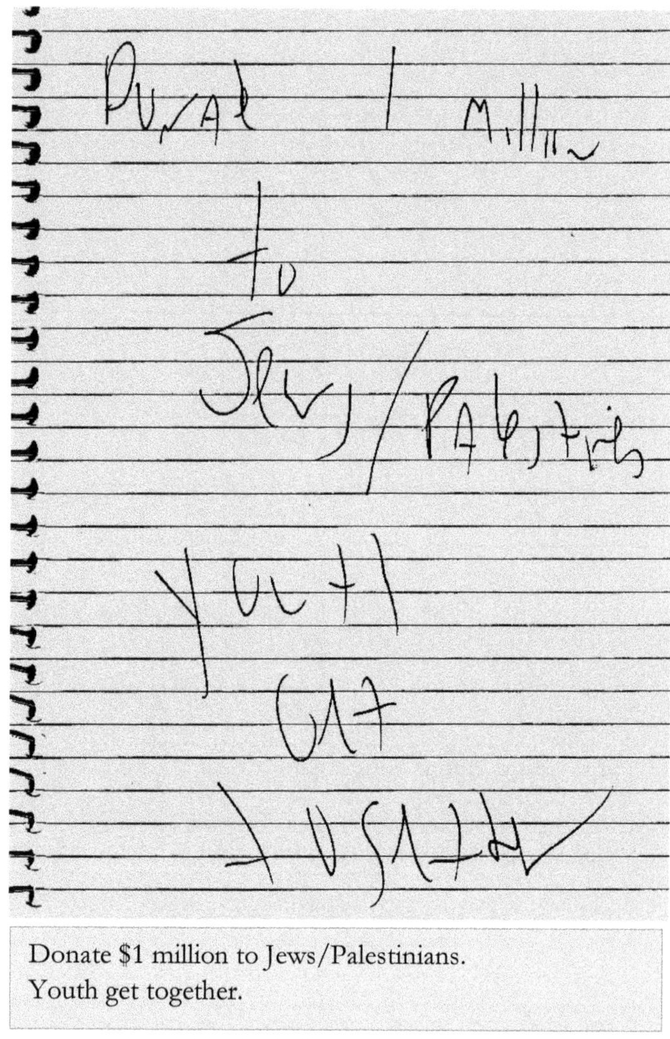

Donate $1 million to Jews/Palestinians.
Youth get together.

During that weekend at Greg's, I was inspired to call my mom—to tell her again how much I loved Ana, and that I knew she would soon love Ana too. My mom replied that she was even more miserable and confused about my relationship with Ana than before. The severity of her displeasure threw me: While I knew she had a way to go before she would accept and love Ana, I hadn't realized how far that was. I was therefore relieved when she handed the phone to my dad, who had always been the voice of reason, the buffer between my mom and me. (Over the years, he had assisted my various lobbying efforts with my mom, like securing her long-withheld permission to let me get a skateboard, or calming her down when I decided to spend more time in Israel.) But on the Ana issue they were one, united in their displeasure. My dad offered me no comfort here, a first for him. It was hard to hear.

I suspected my parents' displeasure was due to the abrupt manner in which I brought Ana into our lives, magnified by their not understanding the legitimacy of her conversion to Judaism. One close friend found it "funny" that after my rabbinical odyssey and orthodox commitments, I was now living with a girl who wasn't Jewish. I pointed out that Ana was converting, but he downplayed the validity of her process and questioned her motives. This made me feel hypocritical, and I decided to call Rabbi Price of the UTJ. It had been three years since we last spoke, but he came right to the phone, warm and gracious, as welcoming as always. I told him about my new relationship with Ana and her desire to convert to Judaism—leaving out that we were living together. Unlike those less educated, Rabbi Price made no assumptions. He asked to meet with Ana in person, one-on-one. He knew only a little Spanish, and she knew only a little English. But he looked into her heart to see if she was genuine—and saw that she was.

After their meeting, I joined them in his study. Rabbi Price offered to guide Ana's conversion process through classes and private tutoring, and when the time came, to officiate her conversion ceremony. Rabbi Price pointed out that when one completes their conversion to Judaism, they are as much a Jew as any other Jew. Moreover, he said it was considered an insult to ask a Jew if he or she was born a Jew or converted, because this question implied that there were two levels of Jews—a fallacy. A Jew is a Jew! I was very glad I had involved Rabbi Price in this process. Ana was in good hands. As we concluded the meeting, I asked Rabbi Price how many years Ana's conversion would take, and he caught my reference. He replied with a smile that his only guarantee, G-d willing, was that it would happen *before* I became a rabbi.

About a month later, after attending a Bruce Springsteen concert at Madison Square Garden with Andy Metternich, we were rolling down Broadway. The vibe that night was extra good. I noticed a tall young black man with the gleam in his eye, wearing a gold Star of David necklace outside his shirt. He was hanging out with a few others outside a reggae club. We made eye contact, and I said to him, "Nice Star of David," and then flashed him mine. He nodded a half-smile, and then I introduced himself. He said he was Khani Jones, twenty-one years old, from Jamaica. I asked him what he did for a living, and he told me he wrote and sang reggae music. I told him I had recently managed a singer and a fighter. Andy was eager to keep walking, but I felt there was a reason for Khani and me to talk more. I asked for his number, which he gave me on a self-designed business card.

I called Khani a few weeks later. He didn't want to share anything personal over the phone, and he had reservations about meeting in public too. His supreme caution seemed odd to me, verging on paranoia. Instead of giving up, I invited him to my apartment, which he accepted. When Khani came over, he told me that I was the first white person he had ever interacted with socially, and he didn't trust white people.

Khani's Bible school and peer group in America were made up of black separatists who were staunchly opposed to blacks mingling with whites. They had taught Khani that whites were descendants of Edom, or *Edomites* ("devils who couldn't be trusted, the great deceivers of man"). These separatists, whose street preaching Khani could regurgitate verbatim and cite biblical sources for, would not have approved of our meeting. But in the privacy of West 80th, we talked for hours about society, politics, race, and religion. Khani was intelligent and full of integrity. He told me he had grown up in a part of Jamaica where gang warfare was prevalent; but as a young kid, he and his best friend had tried to avoid joining gangs. For this transgression, his best friend was killed, right in front of him, while Khani's life was inexplicably spared.

Hours passed, we were still talking, and I was still riveted. We decided to meet again at my apartment one week later. This time, Khani brought his Bible and showed me "proof" that I, being a white man, *really* was an Edomite, a cunning deceiver of mankind. I joked that there was no point in arguing his accusation, because by definition, whether it were true or false, I would deny it! (And if I agreed with him, would that make it untrue?) Khani had been schooled on how to defend biblical passages and fragments which implied that the only way the black man could survive was through total separation from the white man. But Khani's willingness to come to my apartment and the openness he displayed there suggested that he wasn't convinced of that. Since his dad wasn't in the picture, I felt like a potential father figure to Khani, meant to teach him certain things about society—while knowing he could teach me some things too.

With my other friends, I was the one who *gave* the advice, not took it. I respected their opinions, but they rarely offered me fresh insight into my own feelings, which I analyzed myself and seldom tried to explain. Khani's wisdom came from a fresh perspective. His view of me was new and unbiased, and I was comfortable telling him personal things. I told him about my parents, how much they meant to me, and how frustrating it was that they were disappointed with my decision to be with Ana, whom they were misreading and misjudging. I told him that I had noticed my dad getting older more rapidly, perhaps aided by this rare conflict, and shared a saying I once got from a fortune cookie: "If youth only knew, if old age only could." Khani told me that *his* mother, a righteous and hard-working lady whom he lived with in the Bronx, was a caregiver for the elderly; so aging was a subject he also contemplated. He shared a proverb too, sometimes credited to Bob Marley, with a similar yet more somber message: "Once a man, twice a baby." That expression stayed with me, due to its sad simplicity, and the smooth eloquence in which Khani delivered the words.

When I first met Khani I was open to a spiritual encounter, perhaps looking for one. Bringing people together "across so-called enemy lines" was on my mind. These feelings were heightened by the amazing vibe I experienced at the Springsteen concert, namely the tangible love affair between The Boss and his audience. Khani was spiritual too, but focused on his goal to write and perform reggae music—when I mentioned my talent management experience that night, this had piqued *his* interest. At West 80th, he played me a cassette of him singing original lyrics over a hard reggae beat, which he had recorded at his friend's apartment. I was excited to hear how he sounded, but the sonic quality was poor and too hard to judge. Without hesitating, Khani pulled out a sheet of handwritten lyrics and sang for me *a cappella*. I marveled at his courage to *just sing* for me in my apartment, soberly and fearlessly, something I could not have done. And I liked what I heard: Khani's vocal style comfortably (and uniquely) stayed up in the falsetto; and his rapid pacing of socially conscious lyrics, peppered with extra wisdom from his Jamaican accent, reminded me of "It's All Right, Ma, I'm only Bleeding." I thought Khani could become the "Bob Dylan of reggae."

Race and religion were our main topics of conversation, and Khani and I met regularly in my apartment and studied more scripture from the Bible. Over time, the biblical passages Khani chose spoke less to why we were different and more to why we were the same, viewed by G-d as equals. One day he brought over the New Testament and showed me this passage: "…for He maketh His sun to rise on the evil and on the good, and sendeth rain on the just and on the unjust" (*King James Bible*, Matthew 5:45).

I had never read one word from the New Testament, and I felt Jewish guilt for looking at this one passage. But I also felt evolved to be studying it, with Khani—permitting it to teach me something—regardless of my religion. To me the passage meant, "If G-d doesn't discriminate, how can man?" Khani told me that this passage permitted him to follow his own intuitions, not those of his teachers, and to consider that my intentions for approaching him and pursuing a friendship were righteous.

While studying this passage, the pride I had in being Jewish remained strong as ever, and I never downplayed the fact that our Stars of David brought us together. But Khani and I had "crossed so-called enemy lines" by shedding the separatism often implied by race and religion. This was the direction I was most interested in.

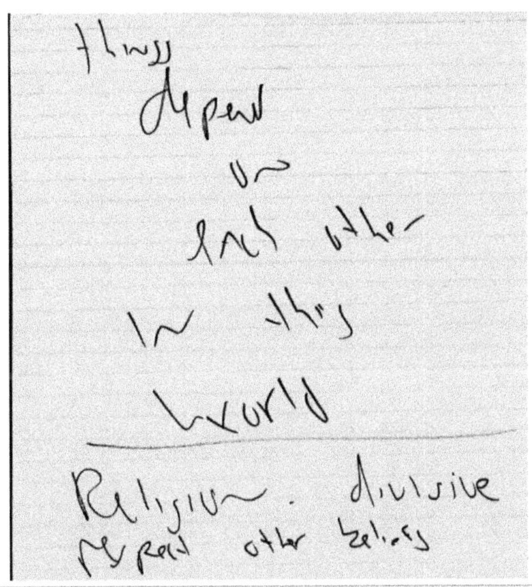

Things depend on each other in this world
Religion – divisive
respect other beliefs

I recalled my experiences managing The Robin, the imposing heavyweight who showed mercy, and The Cardinal, the talented troubadour with dirty sneakers on my pink pillows. Those ventures lacked spirituality and friendship, and were hindered by my need for secrecy. I remembered my vow in Costa Rica, to never manage again, which paid off instantly and led to the recording of my own demo. But my respect and affection for Khani and our spiritual connection changed the equation. The summer of 2000 was a turning point in my New York City experience. Ana and I had settled into a groove at West 80th, while I did my best to ignore the disapproval of my parents. Andy left my faulty nest and moved to Las Vegas to pursue a promising career opportunity, his timely exodus from Manhattan both safe and wise. I asked Khani Jones if he wanted me to be his manager. He said yes—Kid Lightning was resurrected.

Chapter 16

Dream Team Scores Big

"Dayenu!"

I ASKED KHANI one day if he had a girlfriend. He smiled and said no with a Jamaican expression, "There's no romance without finance!" I liked how his words sounded, as usual, and I also knew they were true for our business relationship—I needed to raise money to manage Khani's musical career. I didn't want to manage him in the usual way. I came up with the idea of doing it in front of rolling video cameras that were set up to capture every move we made. This would yield a marketable television program that would show how the "crossing of so-called enemy lines" could lead to wealth and success. At the same time, the program would highlight Khani's personality and attract interest in his music. To videotape our journey, we needed an interesting home base where much of our interaction would take place. While in Costa Rica, I had thought about buying a bar, which now felt like a great fit: It could fill that locational need while providing a strong profit center. And my West 80th apartment would be our office, where we could also film our progress.

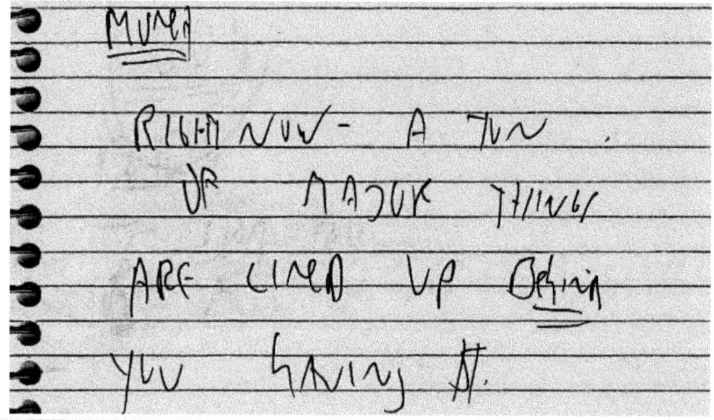

MONEY
RIGHT NOW –
A TON OF MAJOR THINGS ARE LINED UP BEHIND YOU HAVING $.

President, student body (3)
Rabbi – scholarship
Ced's best guy by far
Greg and I are superheroes from G-d
Buy a bar/studio and always be filming
100 reasons to give us 250k
Costa Rica - hero
$$ from DeLeon
Black people like us
We like black people
Don't drink, smoke weed!
Pot is magical.
Youth must get together.
Show: Celebration of the appreciation of life
Get a website!!
Words and Music and the Wave of Peace.
It's a great fucking investment!

Gregory Laurence, whom Khani felt comfortable with and whose tenure with Cedric Kushner was winding down, was interested in my ideas. It seemed he was meant to be a part of this, but I didn't need his help managing Khani, and couldn't envision him running a bar. We shared a spiritual connection, which felt strongest when I would visit him in Amagansett at the house he had rented for the past three years. Located one hundred miles east of Manhattan, it was situated on two acres of land that abutted a majestic golf course; there was something about Amagansett that got our spiritual juices flowing. Then Greg's role came to me: Forget buying a bar in New York City—we would buy that Amagansett house instead! There we could come together spiritually, assess our progress, and plan our next moves, all in front of the rolling cameras. Greg would continue to live there, manage the property, and oversee summer rentals in the lucrative Hamptons market, another profit center for Kid Lightning.

My dad agreed that it would be a smart money-raising tactic to package the purchase of the Amagansett house with the management of Khani Jones, because if our quest for a record deal failed, we would still be holding a tangible piece of real estate. He analogized that many major department store chains had survived plummeting sales and erratic market conditions—able to evolve and retool over decades because they owned the real estate upon which their stores sat.

Greg loved the idea of buying and running the Amagansett property, and we got serious about it. As a favor, my dad asked a friend of his to conduct an informal inspection of the house. After looking it over, he reported that it was in bad shape structurally and in need of major renovation, which would cost at least $150,000. This was discouraging at first, but my dad suggested that the house's poor condition might not be a problem, but rather an opportunity: The fact that the owner was letting his own house deteriorate could be a sign he was struggling financially and willing to sell cheap. Greg pointed out that even if the owner were willing to sell the house at a discount, we had no money to buy it! But I explained to him my East 26th Street strategy, in which the investor's money came *after* I gained contractual control of the property at "freakishly" good terms. Greg provided the owner's contact information, and we submitted an offer of $500,000, hoping to accomplish this.

To try to raise the money we needed for Khani Jones and the Amagansett house, Greg and I decided to first approach Lou Shafer, our good friend and still the head of HBO Boxing. I was eager to try out the hyena-like tactics of Dick and Aaron, who never took no for an answer and refused to leave an investor meeting without a check—Lou Shafer would be my first prey. Greg set up the meeting, and Lou invited us to his Long Island home the following Sunday to tell him what we had in mind.

The night before the big meeting, Greg and I went out. We were feeling great, and since our appointment with Lou wasn't until late afternoon, we rolled into a club. The vibe was spectacular, as usual, and we were charged up, absolutely positive that Lou was going to invest in Kid Lightning the next day. At one point that night, Greg and I were jumping up and down on the dance floor, face to face, yelling, "WE'RE GETTING THE MONEY FROM LOU!! WE'RE GETTING IT TOMORROW!! THE FUCKING MONEY IS OURS TOMORROW!!"

The next afternoon, we drove to Lou's house in Greg's car. I was feeling nervous, and physically shaky from the night before, so I smoked a joint in the driveway. That settled me down and restored my confidence. Lou was friendly and happy we stopped by, and invited us to sit down and talk. I took the lead and explained Kid Lightning Enterprises (KLE) and its various components: Khani Jones (the "Bob Dylan of reggae"); the West 80th apartment (our cheap Manhattan office); Greg's Amagansett house (our spiritual center out east); my plan to build a business and spiritual empire in front of the rolling video cameras; and the marketable TV program that would result from all this. I told Lou that I hoped this TV show might inspire others to "cross so-called enemy lines" and work together, as Khani and I had done, and that the key to everything was the circular, mutualistic nature of each component—each also an independent profit center.

I was presenting my ideas in rapid-fire pace, and probably rambling. It was now time to converge on my prey. I asked Lou for a $25,000 check—immediately—as a sign of his good faith and to cement our future partnership. I explained that this would help us package each KLE sector for future funding. Lou politely said that he would never write a check to *anyone* on the spot, but he was interested. He asked me to write a business plan with financial projections and then get back to him.

We had piqued his interest and received our marching orders, which made it a successful meeting, and I should have stopped there—*Dayenu!* Lou wanted to change the subject and socialize, and Greg's stare conveyed the same message. Instead I leaned harder on Lou, *my* prey, offering him 10% of everything, "for just $25,000," but he had to give us the check *today*. It was a huge discount, I explained, but again he said no—we would talk after the business plan and financial projections were ready. Hyena-like, I was about to ask again, until he cut me off: "STOP!! NOW!! I love you guys, I really do, and I like the ideas! But there's no fucking way I'm giving you a check today, so calm down, shut up, and smoke a joint with me, which I'm sure you brought with you." We followed that part of his advice, Greg rolling his usual perfect one. The awkwardness I caused was gone, all friendships intact. My business dealings with Lou Shafer never went beyond that meeting.

A few months passed. I was still working at Incubator Solutions, and nothing was happening with the Khani project. I was trading time for money while my spiritual ideas stalled, something I had vowed never to do again. Khani and I had yet to sign our three-year management contract because I didn't want the clock to start ticking until I had the capital to make moves. I told Khani that I was in the process of raising money and we would soon be ready to roll, but it was a promise of convenience, meant to buy time. Khani remained patient and optimistic, appreciative of my efforts to help him.

The energy at Incubator Solutions deteriorated by the week. I vented to my dad over how frustrated I was with Dick, so drenched in duplicity that it was hard to be near him, and that I doubted he and Aaron would ever make me a partner. (Moreover, Dick was going through legal problems, and an equity association with him would be unwise anyway.) And further, the six fledgling companies for which I was writing business plans were run by inexperienced people with low integrity, whose concepts were neither original nor impressive. Finally, I explained how frivolous Dick and Aaron were with their investor's money, spending it on expensive office space and unnecessary perks, while carrying too many people on their payroll. I painted the full picture to my dad: Incubator Solutions was rampant with gluttony and bad karma—a house of cards, ready to fall. My dad was shocked by this information. He couldn't believe that those two guys had an investor and we didn't.

Just as I had been trying to raise money for Kid Lightning, my dad had been trying to get funding for his real estate company, SCS Real Estate Development. It would be the first time in his real estate career that he would be the owner and the developer, instead of an employee, broker, or consultant. He had always managed to make a living and support the family, along with my mom. But on multiple occasions throughout his career, he had been promised equity and partnership opportunities—and those promises had been broken. He said he could relate all too well to my stories about low-integrity people in strong financial positions. He repeated that the only reason those people had power was because they knew how to raise money. If one can raise money, he explained, one can do as he wishes in business! So my dad and I, the Dream Team, were in the same frustrating boat as always, with hungry eyes and great concepts—but no capital.

I told my father that Dick and Aaron's investor, a man in his mid-50s named Victor DeLeon, once came to the office while I was there—and didn't seem too happy. We had made brief eye-contact, and it seemed as if he wanted to ask me some questions about what was really going on at Incubator Solutions. But Dick and Aaron hadn't introduced us, so talking to him would have looked suspicious.

The brother of a well-known sports legend, Victor DeLeon was self-made. He had earned a few hundred million dollars by first opening one mall kiosk, and then more kiosks. Eventually, those led to a major retail chain of a thousand full-size stores, which he then liquidated. As soon as I mentioned the name Victor DeLeon to my dad, his eyes lit up: He already knew him! While working as Director of Leasing for a company that owned shopping malls, my dad had worked directly with Victor DeLeon on multiple occasions, and had leased him many of his stores. They had enjoyed a cordial and successful relationship for years, and every location my dad provided DeLeon had resulted in a successful store. My dad's emphasis on "Location, Location, Location," and his uncanny ability to find the best ones, had earned him DeLeon's gratitude and praise. My dad went to his files and showed me specific positive correspondence between him and DeLeon.

The Dream Team formed a plan: We would leverage my dad's pre-existing relationship with DeLeon, and my inside position at Incubator Solutions, to benefit *our* two fledgling companies. My dad would confidentially call DeLeon, rekindle their relationship, and mention that his son Mitch was an employee at Incubator Solutions. He would then explain *our* two companies, and if DeLeon showed interest, request a meeting to discuss their potential financing.

From my childhood bedroom in Armonk, I listened in as my dad dialed Victor DeLeon from the other room. DeLeon came right to the phone; he remembered my dad. My dad told him that his son Mitch worked for Incubator Solutions, and DeLeon expressed frustration over being "left in the dark" about the company's financial status. Then my dad explained what he and I were working on, and DeLeon showed preliminary interest in *our* two companies. They scheduled a meeting for the three of us, three weeks later in Delaware, where DeLeon was based. My dad had followed the plan and conducted the phone call masterfully!

It was time for the Dream Team to spring into action and write up two business plans, polished documents that Victor DeLeon could not refuse. My dad suggested that I simplify my proposal and focus only on Khani Jones and the Amagansett house—with concrete financial projections—while omitting the spirituality and the "crossing of so-called enemy lines." "Focus, focus, focus!" he said, and I followed his advice. Working together, we wrote up two excellent documents, "taking pains" with each and every draft. The process seemed easier than it had been six years ago for the *Building of Champions* proposal. I wasn't sure if this was because my dad had become less vigilant or I had become a better writing partner; I hoped it was the latter.

When we met with Victor DeLeon, his wife Rena was also in attendance. We presented our two companies, and the conversation flowed. Victor expressed more interest in my dad's real estate company, which was closer to his expertise. Rena, on the other hand, was more interested in my entertainment company. I tried to follow my dad's advice, to stick to the numbers and not emphasize the spiritual stuff, but it became unavoidable when she asked how I had met Khani. Her eyes lit up when I told her the story about meeting Khani after the Springsteen concert (thanks to our gold Stars of David), the spiritual connection we made "crossing so-called enemy lines," and the subsequent personal growth we had each experienced. I felt a connection to Rena DeLeon that could be further developed. Surprisingly, Victor DeLeon never asked about Incubator Solutions or anything related to Dick and Aaron. I was relieved, since I didn't have a pretty picture to paint of that situation, and I didn't want to sabotage them—although I would have if necessary.

After an hour, Rena excused herself from the meeting, and my dad and I remained at the table with Victor DeLeon for two more hours. Then it was time to wrap up. Before the meeting, my dad and I had hoped that DeLeon would show preliminary interest in our two companies. Any offer to meet again (or a similar follow-up opportunity) would have been sufficient for us—*Dayenu.* I wasn't going to re-invoke Dick's hyena-like money-raising tactics, which I now accepted were not my style. It wasn't necessary anyway: DeLeon pulled out his checkbook and cut two checks, each for $100,000—one for my dad's company and one for mine! He asked if this was enough to "get us by" for a few months until we could reach formal equity deals, which he tentatively agreed would total a $250,000 commitment to each company, for a 25% stake in each.

My dad and I kept our cool, shook hands with Victor DeLeon, and calmly walked to our car. The instant we were out of earshot, we started screaming and hugging and shouting for joy: HOLY CRAP!! THE DREAM TEAM WAS IN BUSINESS!! The money was in our hands and we'd done it together. For the first time in our lives, and at the exact same moment, we had gone from "frustrated with big ideas" to "funded business owners—true entrepreneurs." It would not have happened if we hadn't worked together.

On the way back to New York, we stopped off to celebrate, sharing our usual Twix bar and two hot chocolates. We got a photo of us standing together—in the same hemisphere—holding up the two checks. I didn't take notice of the sign hanging behind us until years later.

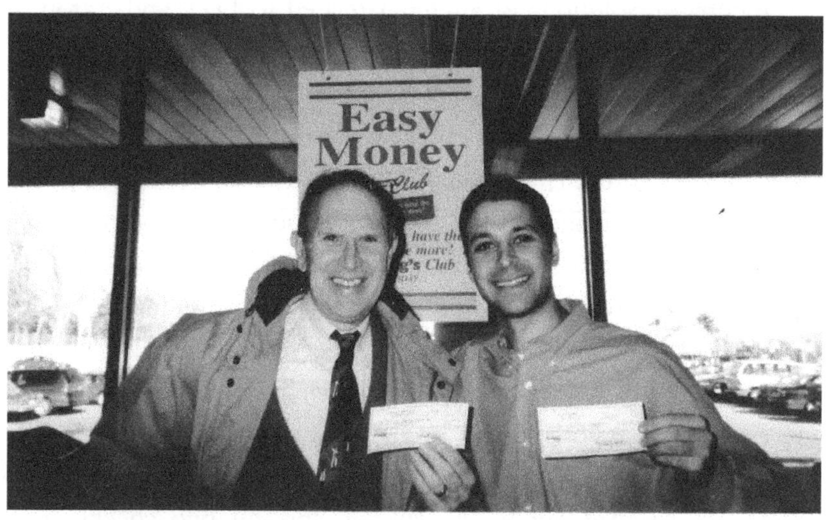
Easy
Money

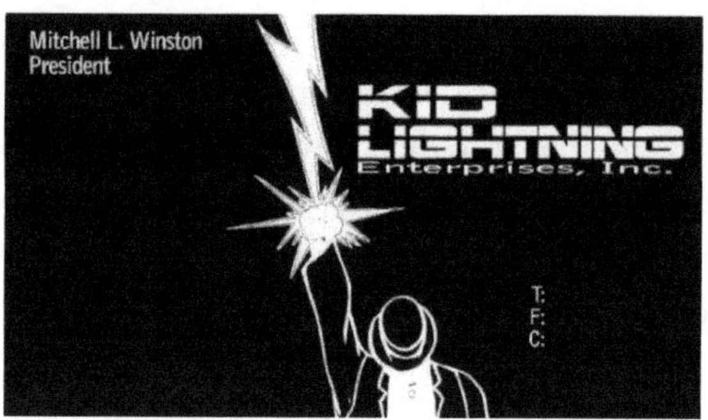
Mitchell L. Winston
President
KID
LIGHTNING
Enterprises, Inc.
T:
F:
C:

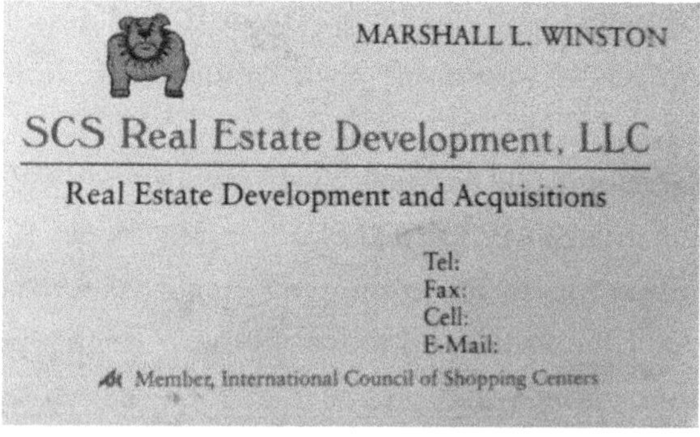
MARSHALL L. WINSTON
SCS Real Estate Development, LLC
Real Estate Development and Acquisitions
Tel:
Fax:
Cell:
E-Mail:
Member, International Council of Shopping Centers

Chapter 17

The Cat Will Run

"Focus, Focus, Focus!"

THE RIPPLE EFFECT of the Dream Team's accomplishment was gratifying. I gave Dick and Aaron official notice—without much elaboration—that I was leaving Incubator Solutions. (I told them I was going to work with my dad.) Then I told Khani we were in business. The *Fredda-ship*, still docked at East 26th Street, had been looking for a more creative career position. I hired her to become my full-time assistant, ten years after there was too much money in her register at The Candy Man.

> January 5, 2001
> From: Klight (Mitch)
> To: TwinkieGirl (Fredda)
>
> How sweet it is. I am totally relieved and am sure that we made the right decision with you coming on board full-time. This project is a dream of mine, and I feel that it is going to work. With you involved, we have a great chance of putting this together much better!!!
>
> Michael has lighting experience, and it is worth it to pay him to come by on Monday, like $50 or so, to help us set up the apartment lighting-wise, and have him give us advice on the camera also. Even

for the whole day, for $100, would be totally worth it. And we will promise him additional work as things develop. Can you see if he can come?

Also, we have to buy a kick ass speakerphone to record "the other side" of important phone conversations.

I love you. I know we are going to work together. You are also my best friend (tied with dad, with mom and I having a different type of relationship). My vision of bringing "all of my people" together to work on something special and spiritual is coming together faster than ever. My reading of the bible is giving me inspiration, as had my true realization that I must be completely free of pot smoking during this entire project.

Fredda – this project literally has the chance of making all of my dreams come true at the same time. I will elaborate later. I have never been happier than I am now. Clean and sharp mentally and physically, happy with all of my family relationships, Ana, friendships, business contacts, etc. My belief in G-d is growing in such a real way that it is filling me with confidence.

Also, important: please realize that the money I will spend on this project could not be used more wisely in my eyes, and your pay is a business expense that I have to incur, and can afford.

I love you!!! I am pumped!!!!! I will fully update you on Sunday! No backing out now!

-Mitch

Big fuck-up #1: I took $17,500 of the $100,000 I had received from DeLeon and paid off my remaining credit card debts, the balance of which I had carried since the night The Queen Pigeon went down. My justification was that I would be working full-time for Kid Lightning, without drawing a salary. Plus, my sister and I would be operating out of my apartment, instead of an expensive office, which would save us a lot in overhead.

To properly manage Khani and perform other Kid Lightning duties, I needed respectable transportation. A classified ad in *New York Newsday* listed a 1985 Jaguar XJ6 with low mileage, which the original owner was selling for $6,000. It was a sweet deal for my lifelong dream car, and I was excited about it. Before I went to see it, I mentioned it to my dad, who advised me to pass on it. He explained what I already knew, that old Jaguars were unreliable and expensive to repair. I lied to my dad like I had before Costa Rica—that I was only going there to "do research."

Big fuck-up #2: I withdrew another $5,500 from the Kid Lightning account before Ana and I boarded the train to Long Island. The seller, a Harvard professor and well-known Darwinist, had told me on the phone that the car was a head-turner. He hadn't lied: "The Cat" was as gorgeous as I had imagined, with a cream-colored exterior, its smooth, healthy skin, and leather seats of burgundy, its fresh flowing blood. I offered $5,000 cash. The Darwinist said that someone else was coming to see it that afternoon—I could wait and hope, or take it now for $500 more. I pulled out the $5,500 and handed it over. The cat was mine.

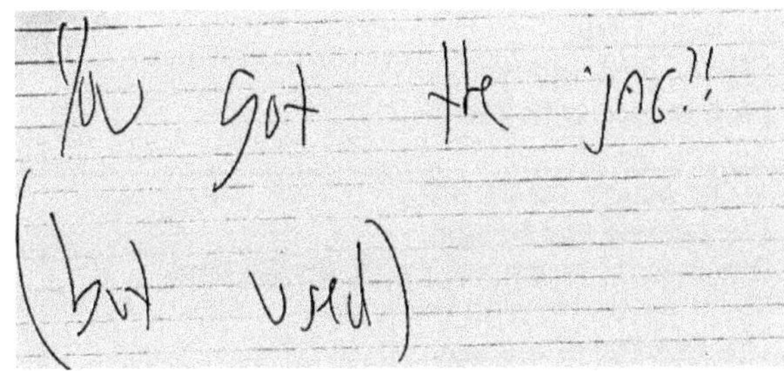

On our ride back to the city in my 1985 Jag, Ana laughed at how easily I had caved in and accepted the higher price, even though I had told her on the train I would hold firm at $5,000. I felt cool when I replied that I didn't want to take the train back to the city. The following weekend we drove the cat to Armonk, and I surprised my parents with it. When my dad first saw it he smiled and admitted it was beautiful. It was hard not to. But after his brief initial admiration, he told me privately that he was very disappointed that I bought it. Almost six months after Ana's arrival, there was still tension between my parents and me. Even with the Dream Team's recent business success, it had not waned. My dad made a troubling comparison between the abrupt, impulsive way that I had introduced Ana to him and my mom, and the similarly impulsive way that I had purchased the Jaguar. He still loved analogies; this one hurt.

The Cat Will Run

Come, my darlin',
Let's ride to the end,
Across the silver lining in the sand.
I'm not talkin', about the dying.
I'm sure you won't complain.
The skies are opening now, but there 'aint no rain.

Chorus:
Poco a Poco
Little by Little
I fell in love with you
I fell in love with you.

To the ocean, my darlin',
The cat will run tonight.
It leaves its streaming fears, on the land.
Silent partners, with the water,
The sanctity of the sea.
It doesn't know who we are,
or where we're gonna be.

(Chorus)

(Chorus)

Using that $23,000 to pay old debts and buy the Jaguar was impulsive and foolish—and bordered on illegal accounting—I had commingled personal and company funds; DeLeon had nothing to do with those old debts; and our accounting books reflected my actions. The proper way would have been to pay myself a salary, deposit it monthly into my personal bank account, and pay these from that account when enough money had built up. Since I was entitled to a salary, all I would have needed was patience—but that was never my forte.

Big fuck-up #3: Shortly after these mistakes, I could have come clean to DeLeon and apologized to him, explained how clearing my old debts had cleared my mind too, and made me a better executive for Kid Lightning. Then I could have fixed our accounting books and classified the $23,000 as a loan I owed the company. Five years earlier, when I came clean with Nygil Cox, he had said, "The truth frees you." And it did—my reward was a life-changing affordable apartment on West 80th. Here was my second chance for the truth to free me, when honesty and integrity would again be rewarded, all my sins forgiven—if I just came clean. As usual, guilt and fear got in the way: I carried on with the business of Kid Lightning and kept the $23,000 a secret.

My first official Kid Lightning task was to draft and execute the three-year management contract between Kid Lightning and Khani Jones. Lee Deerman, now an attorney with his dad's firm in Beverly Hills, again helped me tailor the agreement. I thought a quick signing would be a formality, a camera-worthy ceremonial demonstration of mutual trust between Khani and me. It would represent the perfect start to our spiritual journey, enabling us to sidestep the paperwork and "get on with the music," like Eddie Wilson once said. Then we could focus on the important stuff, namely our main goal of securing a record deal for Khani. I was wrong! Khani had studied the contract like he studied the Bible. (I had barely read it.) He copied every legal term and ambiguous word in the margins, and insisted on adding each's definition, in layman's terms, to the document.

This dragged on for hours. I tried to explain to Khani that even with a perfect contract, a dishonest person could still easily screw the other over. It was all about trust, I said, and unless one of us planned to sue the other, the management contract was a formality. Khani countered that the management contract laid out each of our responsibilities in the artist-manager relationship; and even though we trusted each other, it was better to have a specific, ironclad contract with no ambiguity. I couldn't disagree, but my frustration grew as the hours wore on.

This meticulous exercise spanned the entire day, with Fredda videotaping everything, multiple tapes filling up and being changed. I felt embarrassed, annoyed, and then resentful toward Khani for not displaying the trust I thought he had in me. Though I kept smiling, I was pinching my leg hard under the table to relieve my stress. Soon the day was over and the document was not close to being signed. I had no choice but to schedule Khani to return to West 80th the following day to resume. I cringed at wasting another day, and maybe another, dissecting a standard management deal! This was far from the spiritual journey of friendship and brotherhood I had wanted the cameras to capture. Later that evening, after getting high, I thought more about Khani and his tedious "document methodology." My perception of his behavior softened; I decided that his careful examination of the contract showed how seriously he took his career and the opportunity I was presenting.

It took two more days and numerous revisions by The Deerman, but we got the contract executed. When Khani and I shook hands on camera, I said to him, "I hope this is the last time that you and I are ever on the opposite side of a negotiating table!" This was a conciliatory quote my dad had once used after a tedious mediation of his own.

Now we could get on with the music. We agreed that the best opening strategy was to build a kickass reggae band with Khani as the front man and band leader. The band would prepare and rehearse Khani's four best songs and record a professional demo to shop to the record labels. Securing a major label record deal, with Khani's music in every store, was our clearly stated goal. We placed an ad in *The Village Voice* and auditioned musicians, cameras always rolling.

> Reggae front man on a mission needs a band immediately to satisfy record label and TV interest. If you are a hot Reggae musician that is willing to dedicate yourself totally to rising to the top, call now. Drums/percussion/bass/guitar/keyboards needed. Professionals only. Call Kid Lightning Enterprises (212) 721-XX59

This step also proved more tedious than I had expected. Most of the musicians who answered our *Village Voice* ad were older and more experienced than Khani. To "test the musicians," Khani's method was to choose a particular riff, sing it to them *a cappella*, note by note, and ask them to regurgitate it on their particular instrument. This left no room for creativity, and wasn't a good way to determine anything. Many of these seasoned musicians didn't appreciate a twenty-one-year-old novice, who didn't play an instrument, pointing at theirs and telling them what notes to play. (Khani pointed at their fretboards and piano keys because he hadn't yet learned music terminology, and this was his only way to ask the player to go higher or lower, or play a chord instead of a note, etc.) I feared we were losing the musicians' inspirations and killing the vibe before we learned what they could really do; but I remained silent and observed the situation.

From the musicians' perspective, Khani's auditioning style was disrespectful. They felt he was pulling rank, that he was the artist and they were workers looking for jobs. This wasn't the case—Khani did respect them. He hadn't yet learned proper studio communication, and had yet to develop a softer (more political) vibe around other artists. This, and the willingness to trust others would come with experience and maturity. But we needed to find the right musicians now, and my strategy of staying silent in the background was not working. I began to intervene more and act like a buffer to help smooth out the communication between Khani and these musicians. I wanted to ensure that everyone, including Khani, felt respected. I had long ago developed the ability to do this, and was successful at it again.

When we honed in on a few musicians that looked good, we grouped them into a makeshift band, and they tried a few of Khani's songs. A few of the more experienced musicians pointed out that Khani's songs sounded similar to one another, and they offered ideas on how each could be differentiated. Khani wasn't willing to yield control of his songs' arrangements, and he rejected their suggestions. This was a touchier subject, because they weren't *my* songs, so I remained silent—even though I agreed inwardly that they needed some development. Khani confided to me later that he agreed that his songs needed development, but if he had accepted these musicians' ideas, he would have had to grant them ownership percentages in each. I wasn't sure if that was accurate. He said he would fix the songs himself, but I also wasn't sure he had the songwriting experience to do that. I was sure we were stagnating.

A fortunate breakthrough occurred when an experienced bass player named Shawinza, about 40 years old and with a fantastic afro a la Jimi Hendrix, answered our ad. He told me his funk band was playing a show that night on the Lower East Side, and my sister and I went downtown to check it out. Shawinza was a flashy player with an awesome stage vibe. He played the bass behind his back, upside down, and with his elbows; we were impressed. After the set, we spoke privately, and I confided to Shawinza that we were having difficulty finding the right musicians and communicating with them properly in the rehearsal studio. I also mentioned we were having some issues regarding the arrangement and readiness of Khani's songs. Shawinza said that he was not only a bass player but also a producer and a composer. With his assistance, he assured us, our problems would be solved. I invited him to my apartment later that week to meet Khani, talk about music, and find out if they could work together—to get us moving again.

Their first meeting at West 80th again reminded me of *Eddie and the Cruisers*, when Eddie had crossed his two fingers and said to the Wordman, "We need each other. Words and music." With cameras rolling throughout, Khani sang his songs *a cappella* for Shawinza. Shawinza liked Khani's vocal style and songs; he said both were unique. He suggested that the verses and choruses needed to be differentiated; Khani needed to use more of his vocal range, not just his falsetto; and the pacing had to change from one song to the next. Shawinza said he could help Khani do this. Khani showed maturity by accepting Shawinza's constructive criticism, thereby demonstrating trust, and putting aside ego for the good of the music. We scheduled a few more such sessions, with me paying Shawinza each time, and the two succeeded at their task. Then we made an additional agreement with Shawinza to lead the band rehearsals, to ensure healthy studio communication between Khani and the musicians. We also contracted with Shawinza to be the producer for Khani's upcoming four-song recording session, for which he would be paid for his time and collect a standard producer's royalty. We were putting a great deal of faith in Shawinza, and it seemed to be working: We soon had four great songs and a tight band that was ready to lay them down.

I searched for a professional recording studio in New York City and chose *Dan Wise's House of Love.* Dan Wise was cool and charismatic, a master in his studio and fun to work with. Both Khani and I liked and trusted him from the beginning. His equipment was top-of-the-line, highlighted by a gigantic Neve soundboard, which The Kinks had once recorded on. It made me proud to see Khani in this professional environment, surrounded by great musicians, engineers, and producers.

The sessions started well, except that certain musicians showed up late every day, which annoyed both Khani and me. The first day was dedicated to Shawinza on bass, along with the drummer, laying down the rhythm sections for the four songs, while Khani recorded rough vocal takes to ensure he was comfortable with the tempos. On the second day, when the other musicians got involved and built on the tracks, I noticed Shawinza trying to control things *too much*, brushing off Khani's suggestions and leaving him frustrated. Yes, Shawinza was the producer, but the songs were Khani's, which to me made Khani the co-producer in the studio. Due to my inexperience, I had failed to define their producer-artist in-studio relationship in advance, and Khani's opinions were increasingly ignored.

Shawinza thought he had more autonomy than we had planned to give him; this was a general form of entitlement that Khani and I would soon get used to: We would often put a lot of faith in a particular hired gun early on, and I would be effusive in gratitude and appreciation for that hired gun's service, partly to counter the tendency I perceived for people to misread Khani's stoic manner. My overly-appreciative style with these hired guns made *them* feel too much like the owners—but Khani and I were the owners, the ones at financial risk. (Even though I laid out the money, all Kid Lightning expenses relating to Khani's music would be reimbursed by him after we (hopefully) secured his record deal.) Over time, we would improve at this, with me getting a bit harder and Khani getting a bit softer. But the *Shawinza Studio Takeover* was our first taste of this entitlement, and it was manifesting at the worst possible time—in the midst of our crucial and expensive recording session. I needed to fix the balance of power that had shifted away from Khani, but I also couldn't afford to lose Shawinza's inspiration.

Shawinza, while vital to the process, didn't like giving up control. He was showing himself to be more emotional and volatile than I had expected, even childlike at times, demonstrating a willingness to walk out on the project if Khani "thought he could do it better." When Khani pointed at his bass to suggest a higher register for a bass line, Shawinza barked back sarcastically, "Why don't you play it yourself!" It was a touchy situation, mid-session, which required experience. Dan Wise approached me that evening because he had noticed the same thing we did—Shawinza taking over and ignoring Khani's inputs. Once again, I felt like the perfect buffer, authorizing and encouraging Dan to step in when necessary to put Shawinza in check. Dan was able to do that smoothly, without Shawinza losing pride, because he was the studio owner and a seasoned professional, close to Shawinza's age, and Shawinza perceived him as an equal. After this subtle tweak, the sessions found their groove. And when it was time to lay down the final vocals, Khani delivered too. We ended up with an original, professional four-song recording we were proud, of—and a solid band ready to support it live. During these sessions, I had some downtime. I scribbled some notes, brainstorming again about bringing people together "across so-called enemy lines," and possible names for our budding television show.

Khani is fucking reggae!!!
Dan/Shawinza/Khani – full album
Make it a TV show
KID LIGHTNING AND KHANI JONES!!
10 Grand – my album?
KID LIGHTNING, KHANI JONES, WAVE OF PEACE!
Can he bring it all together?
Plot: Mitch records an album, Khani records an album, Mitch pursues and tries to balance Wave of Peace, DeLeon.

Mitch will never take salary from Wave of Peace!!!

It was time for Khani and his band to play some live shows, create a buzz, and build momentum, so we could approach the record labels—or better yet—they could approach us. But then Khani and Shawinza had a disagreement over who owned what percentage of each of the four songs they had worked on. Again from inexperience, I thought we had handled this in advance: Shawinza was paid for his private sessions with Khani and the band rehearsals; he had signed a waiver for the video footage we captured; he had agreed to a standard producer's royalty for the recordings; and he was paid for his time in the studio. I had also made it clear to Khani, from the beginning of our management relationship, that I had no desire to gain ownership in his songs—since they were, and always would be, *his* songs. Hence, I had not bothered to learn about publishing rights or their ramifications on the producer-artist relationship.

Khani accepted that Shawinza had earned an ownership percentage in each of the four songs, but not nearly as much as Shawinza was requesting. I agreed with Khani and thought Shawinza was being greedy. The three of us met multiple times at Bar 7A in the East Village, cameras rolling, as I again tried to be the perfect buffer. But this time things went nowhere; they were too far apart in their numbers, and the relationship was deteriorating by the second. During these tedious meetings and discussions, I re-invoked my new habit of pinching my leg—hard—under the table, to relieve my frustration over this waste of time. Dealing with this legal stuff was by far my least favorite aspect of managing Khani, since it had nothing to do with the spirit of why I signed him, and couldn't lead to any financial gain for Kid Lightning. But when Shawinza hired a lawyer, Khani needed one too. I found him a good one, which meant an expensive one. This publishing issue had become a costly, time-consuming process, halting all the momentum we had gained from the recording. We couldn't do anything else until it got resolved.

When the two men finally came to agreement, I was relieved: We were ready to sidestep the legal shit and (finally) "Get on with the music." But instead, this publishing conflict made Khani determined to copyright every song he ever wrote, even the incomplete ones and the ones we were not dealing with, and to consider and reconsider every possible legal loophole in the copyright process. Again, I knew that this would have no bearing on Kid Lightning's earnings because I was not involved with Khani's publishing rights. But I also knew that he would not be happy or effective as an artist until this got done—and he was also my friend who needed my help. Together we completed the process; the bruises on my legs were a testament to its frustrating tediousness.

This was a microcosm of how much Khani's life philosophy differed from mine. I always assumed that "things would work out in the end," and so I never worried too much about paperwork. Khani's philosophy was to dot all the I's and cross all the T's to *prevent* issues, such as the ones we had encountered with Shawinza. He cited several incidents in the history of music in which artists had been cheated out of their own songs and left with nothing, while others had gotten rich off them. He explained in great depth what I already knew—and had demonstrated as a manager by never requesting any publishing royalties from him—that the songs are a songwriter's asset and greatest security. As usual, Khani's facts and logic were accurate, based on thorough research. But in those moments, I wished he were less wordy and less pedagogical: Instead of pursuing a record deal and building a buzz, we were stuck in my dark apartment, filling out copyright forms. I wasn't in the mood for a lesson or a lecture. I was missing the spiritual stuff, the "coming together across enemy lines" stuff, and the music—the only reasons I got involved with Khani in the first place. It all felt miles away.

Later in life I came to better understand Khani's motives for this meticulous document methodology—his intense focus on the fine print: I never thought of myself as someone who *also* had to read the fine print. I was the one who got away with stuff, relied on getting lucky, and was afforded endless chances to try, fail, and try again—my next opportunity always on the horizon. I likened Khani's document methodology to some of my dad's advice, to "Focus, focus, focus," or "Take pains, Mitch, take pains." But that was never *my* style. I would skim through important documents like contracts and medical forms, while Khani and my dad actually read them. Perhaps they had lived in environments where opportunities were fewer, and therefore more precious, conditions which necessitated more caution and attention to detail. I always assumed that I was entitled to endless opportunities, and everything would work out in the end. That would have dire consequences one day, in both business and areas far more important than business—health. I would regret that my style had been so unlike theirs. And worst of all, my dad would bear the brunt.

Chapter 18

The Wave of Peace

"Pay-per-view peace negotiations"

Yellow Pad, April, 2001

Say to DeLeon I need $5 million – after you cut the trailer!!

Trailer: About a guy, a little crazy, but wants to start a wave of peace. And very damn interesting and talented, wants to change the world

Has Khani and his own music.

Which is also damn good and interesting

Has the power to get huge

Hundreds of millions of dollars!!

He physically doesn't have a guarantee, but his message does – only if he promotes it heavily and totally boldly

Doesn't know if his music is good or not

Wishes it is, goes through tremendous musical angst and ecstasy… Is he delusional? Or is it true?

Khani, DeLeon, Judaism, Ana, immigration,

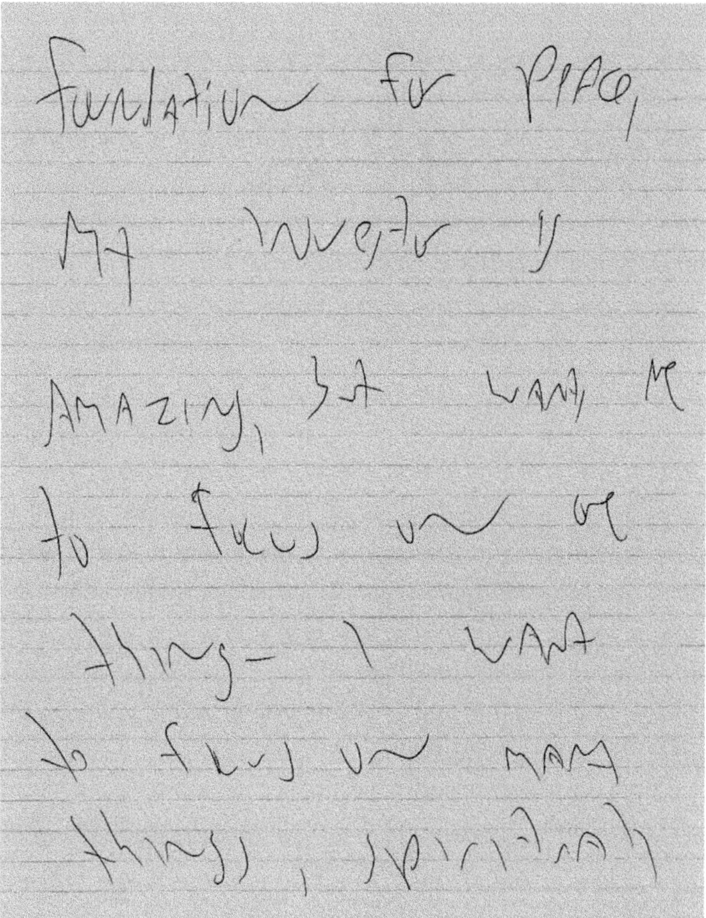

Foundation for peace,
my investor is amazing,
but wants me to focus on one thing –
I want to focus on many things, spirituality

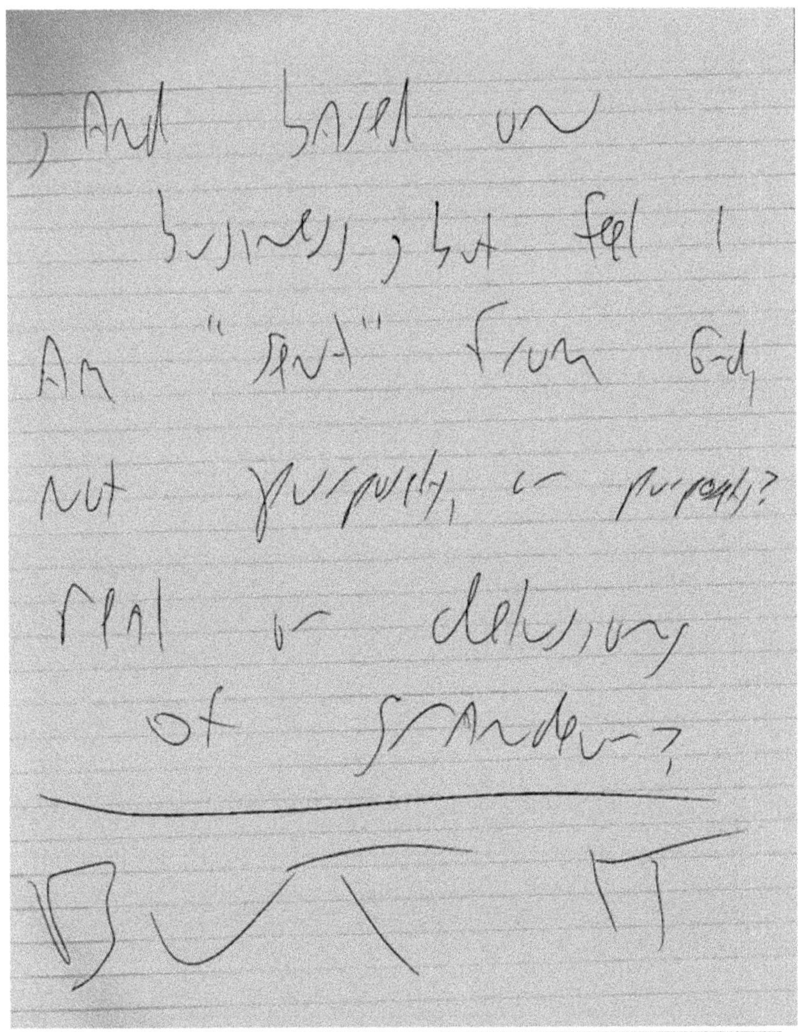

, and based on business,
but I feel I am “sent” from G-d,
not purposely, or purposely?
Real or delusions of grandeur?
BUT IT

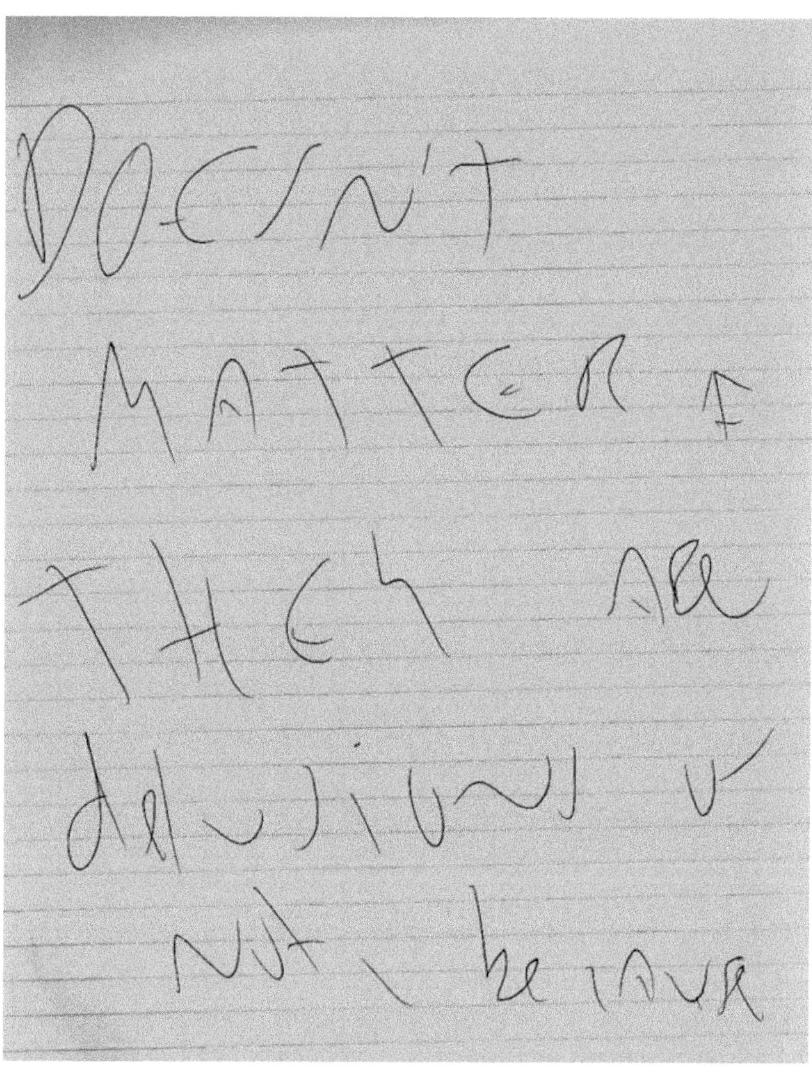

DOESN'T MATTER IF THEY ARE DELUSIONS OR NOT, BECAUSE

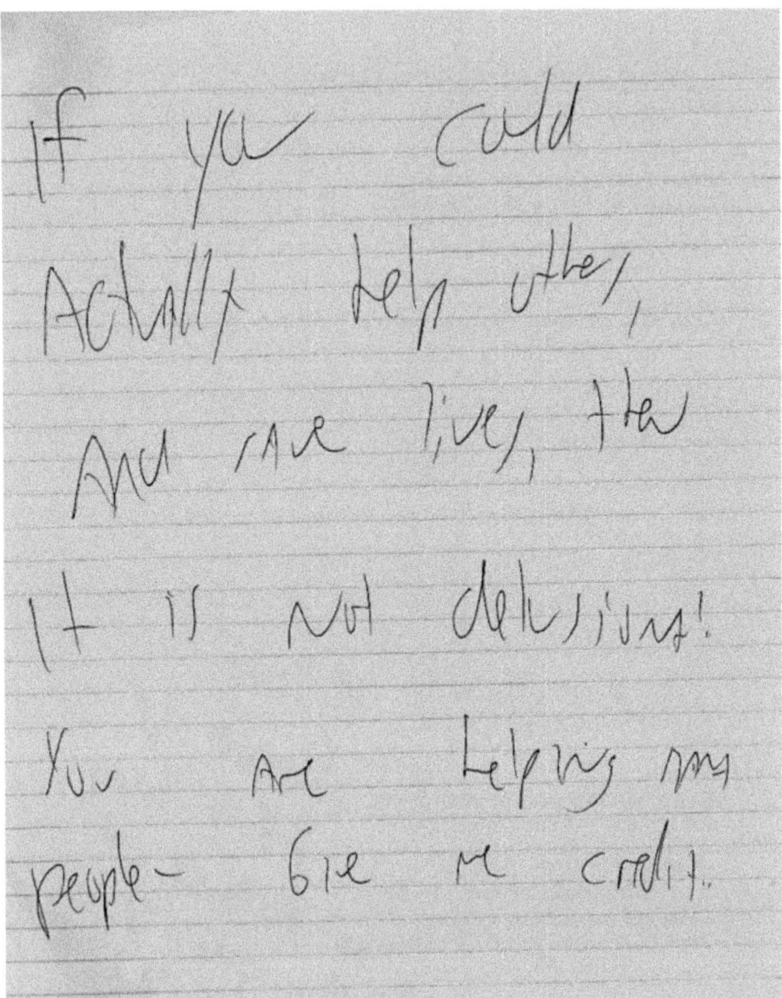
If you could
Actually help others,
And save lives, then
It is not delusional!
You are helping many
people – Give me credit..

If you could actually help others,
and save lives,
then it is not delusional!
You are helping many people –
Give me credit…

Arabs can reproduce with Jews, so must be same G-d.

Killing someone is taking away the excitement of a Knicks Game 7 against the Bulls

MAY 25, 2001. Television was reporting the news: During a Jewish wedding in Israel near a Palestinian neighborhood, the wedding hall collapsed. The dance floor fell in, swallowing a large number of guests—killing many and trapping others in the rubble. The vast majority of people who first heard this story, myself included, assumed that the collapse had been caused by terrorism. I waited to hear about the suicide bomber who had blown himself up at the wedding, destroying himself, the building, and the guests. I remember thinking, "THOSE FUCKING TERRORISTS!! THEY HAVE NO APPRECIATION FOR THE SANCTITY OF LIFE!"

Yes, terrorism was surging, and the Arab-Israeli conflict was on the minds of many. But terrorism was not the culprit this time. There had been a longstanding and undetected structural flaw in the building, which gave way during the wedding, and caused the collapse. After the collapse, many Palestinians came to the aid of the Jewish guests caught in the rubble. Arabs, risking their own safety, to help Jews! This story—and my preconceived notions about it—were eye-opening. I felt it was a message from G-d, telling me to "bring people together across so-called enemy lines."

Wave of Peace

I went on the line and I saw it again,
A bomb blew up on a crowd of ten.
It stole away a mother's dreams again,
But I knew you cared.

If you and I can make a life together,
We can't be coming from a different creator.
And even if we did I think they'd both agree,
You're stealing someone's only opportunity.
That's not fair!

Chorus:
Do you think you love your
father more than I do?
Do you think I think
the same about you?
Love's like a wave,
it crosses enemy lines.
We gotta stop the killing
and find….the time!

Maybe I can lend you a bigger hand.
Maybe economics will help understand.
People are starvin' they aint fighting for land.
The politicians only wanna be elected again!

But how can you take a life away?
You're parting a mother from her daughter today.
You take everything that she has away
And all that she's gonna be….
That's not fair!

(Chorus)

Why can't we start it together my friend?
We'll form a wave of peace and begin to mend
Who says you have to be my enemy?
If I help you and you help me!!

The floor fell in on a wedding today
At least they were sharing their love I say.
The enemy offered to help that day.
I'll never forget the 25th of May.

(Chorus)

Why can't we start it together my friend?
We'll form a wave of peace and begin to mend
Who says you have to be my enemy,
If I help you and you help me!!

When the wedding hall collapsed on May 25th, Ana and I were visiting Greg in Amagansett. Thoughts of bringing Arabs and Jews together, building empires, and buying houses were dominating my mind. I took some notes that night.

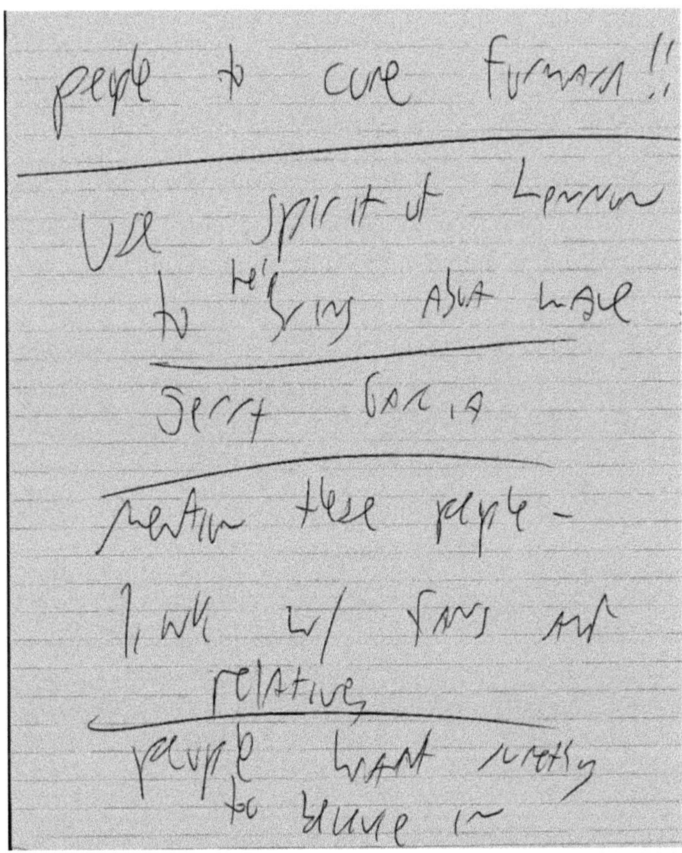

People to come forward!!
Use spirit of Lennon
to help bring about wave
Jerry Garcia
Mention these people -
link with fans and relatives
people want something to believe in

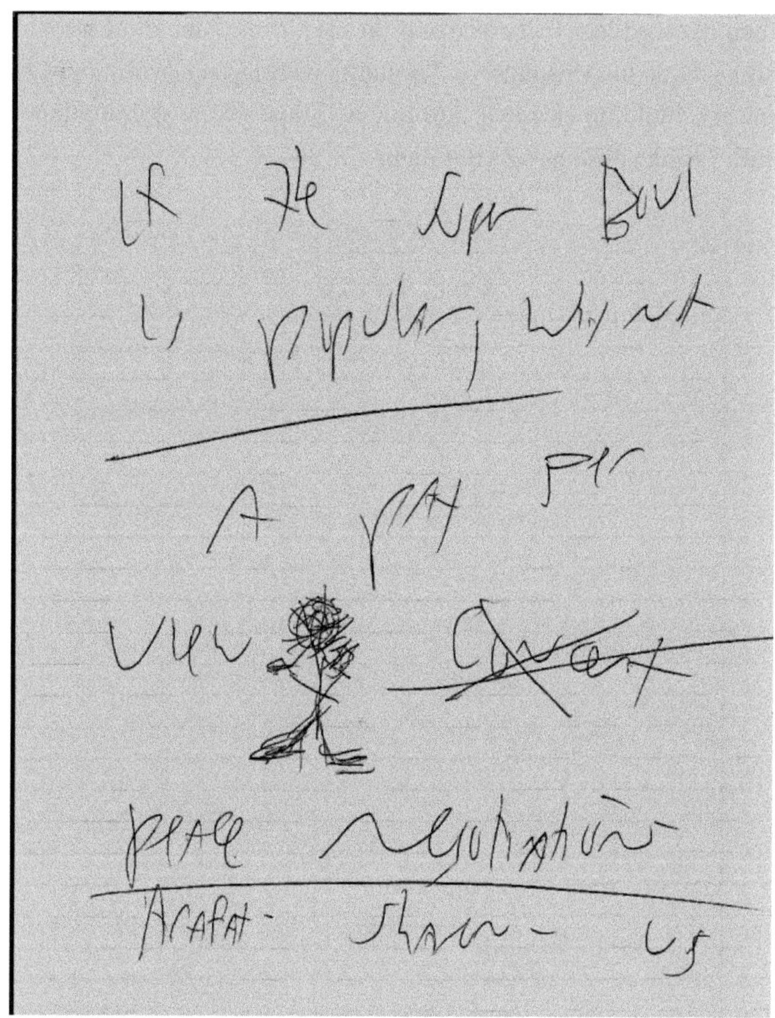

If the Super Bowl is popular, why not a
Pay-Per-View Peace Negotiation—
Arafat – Sharon – U.S.

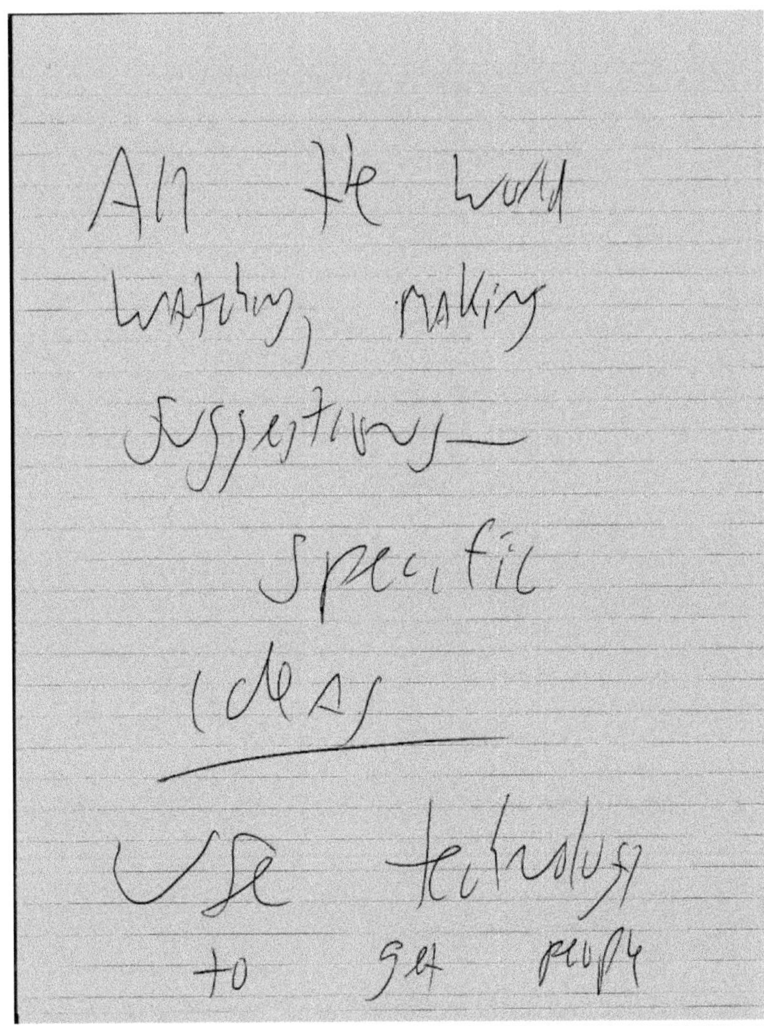

All the world watching, making suggestions-
<u>Specific Ideas</u>
Use technology to get people

involved, and even more importantly,
<u>to get the answers</u>
these thoughts are flowing through me like messages from G-d,
I know I can help the world.
I know I can create a Wave of Peace.
I feel connected to Abraham, Isaac, Jacob-

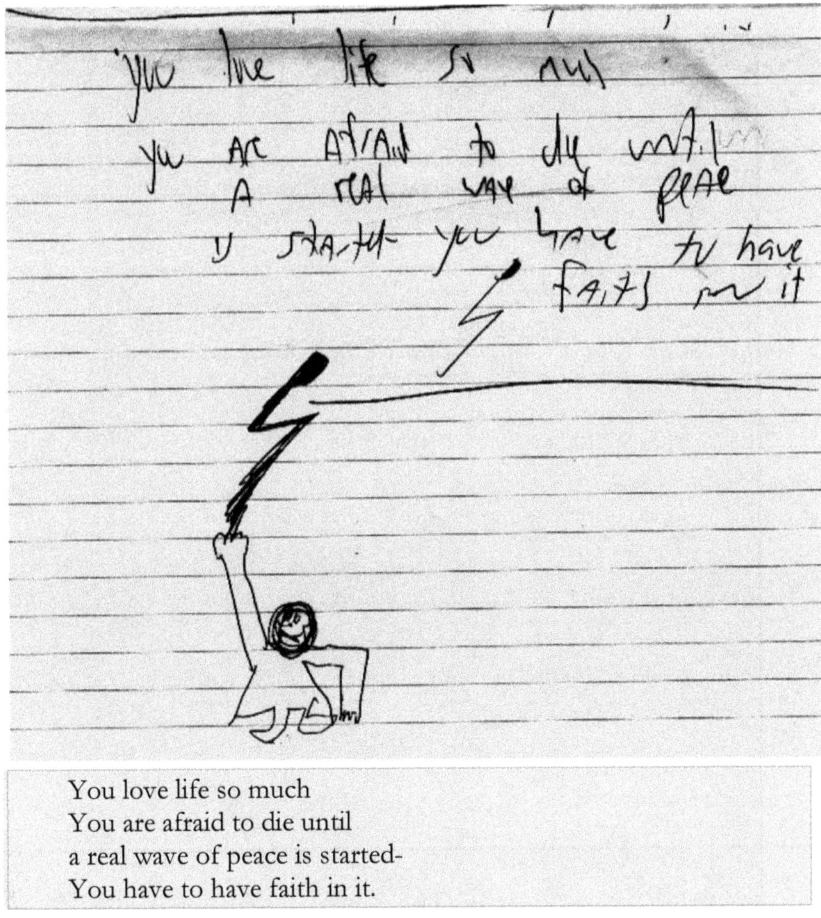

You love life so much
You are afraid to die until
a real wave of peace is started-
You have to have faith in it.

Long since we had offered $500,000 to buy it, we still hadn't heard back from the owner of Greg's Amagansett house. Greg viewed his silence as a rejection, because our offer was so low. I was never one for implied rejection, whether it was pursuing a girl or a house: Until hearing something concrete, I would remain optimistic that I could gain control at "freakishly" good terms.

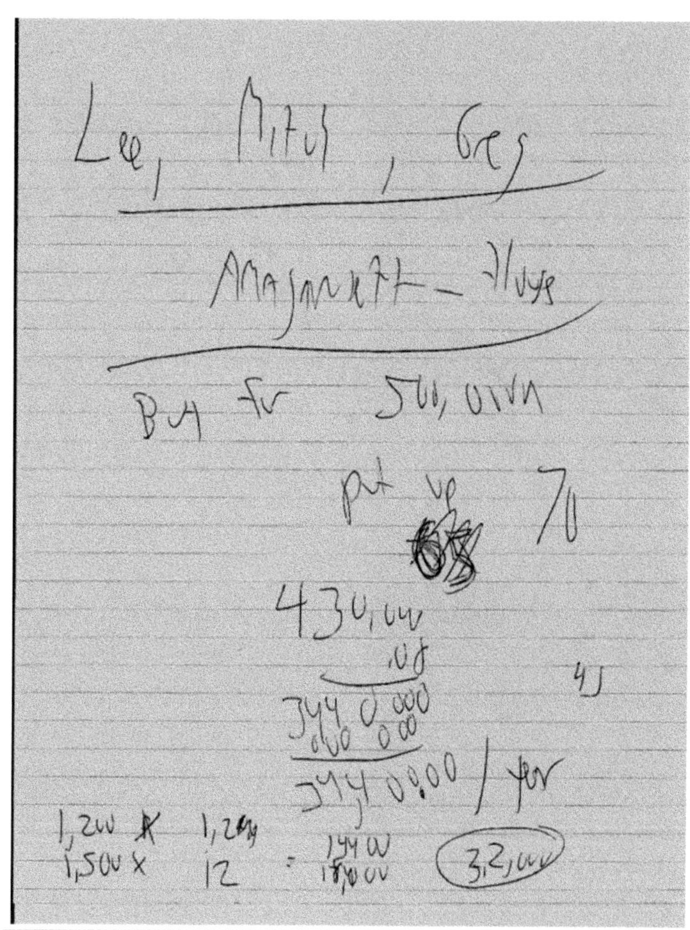

Lee, Mitch, Greg
Amagansett House
Buy for 500,000

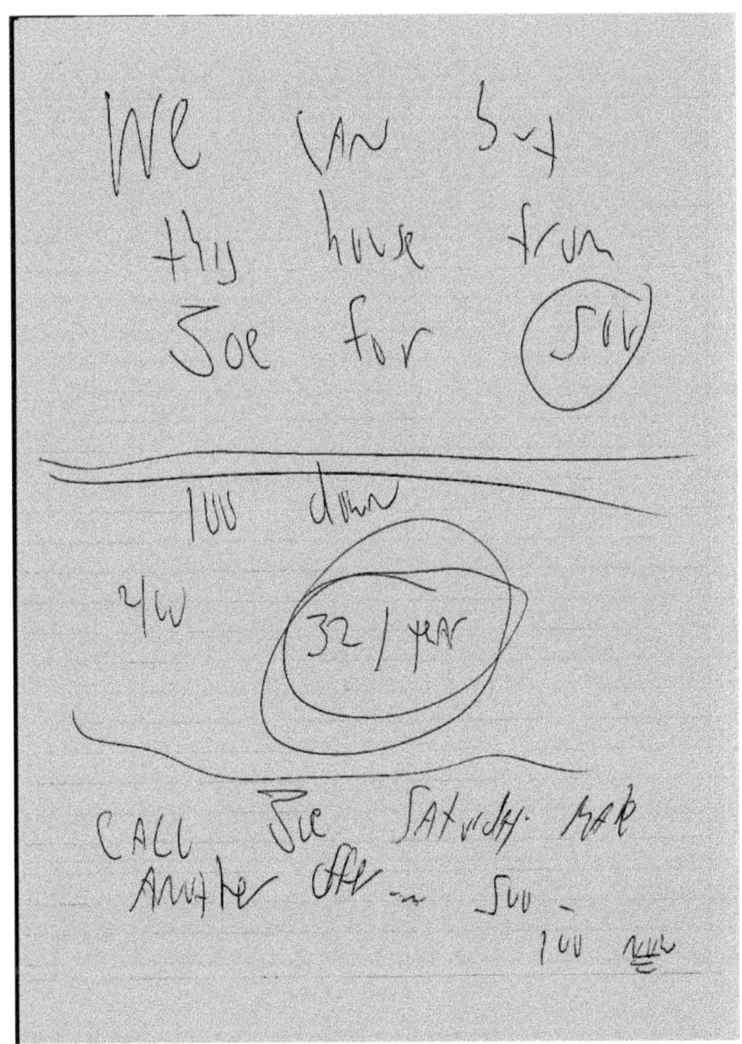

We can buy this house from Joe for $500k
100 down, 32k/year
Call Joe Saturday –
make another offer…
<u>NOW</u>

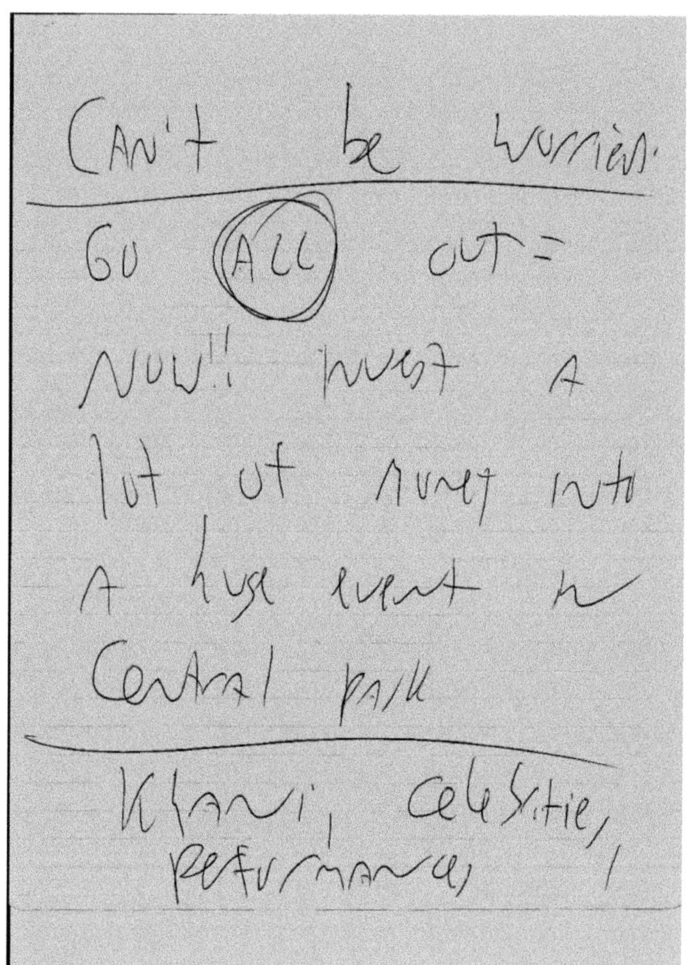

Can't be worried
GO ALL OUT -- NOW!!
Invest a lot of money into a huge event in
Central Park
Khani, celebrities, performances

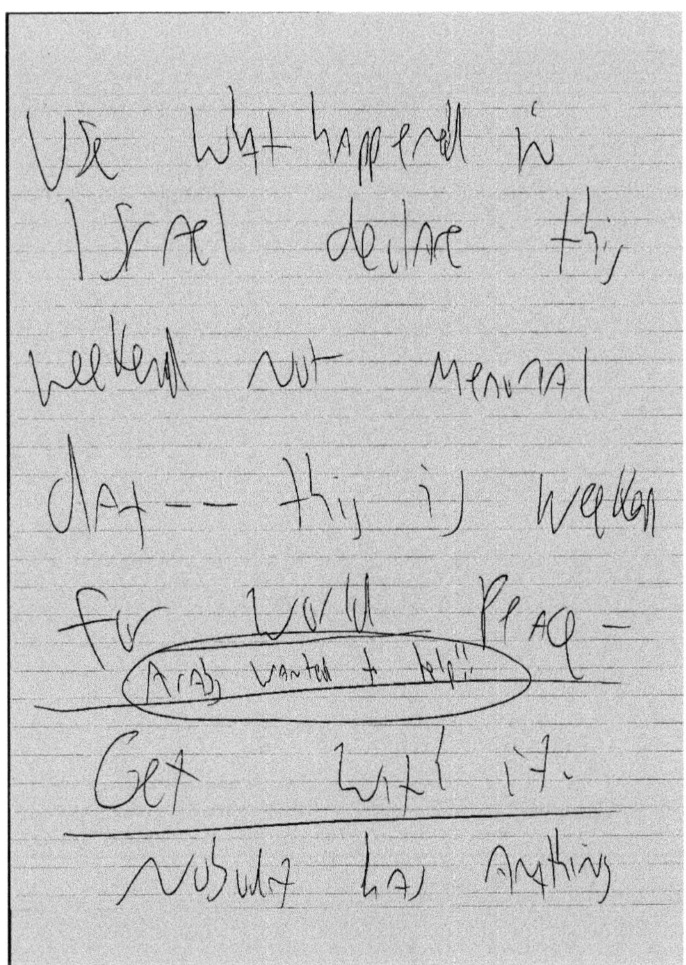

Use what happened in Israel
declare this weekend not Memorial Day --
this is weekend for World Peace -
<u>ARABS WANTED TO HELP!!</u>
Get with it
Nobody has anything

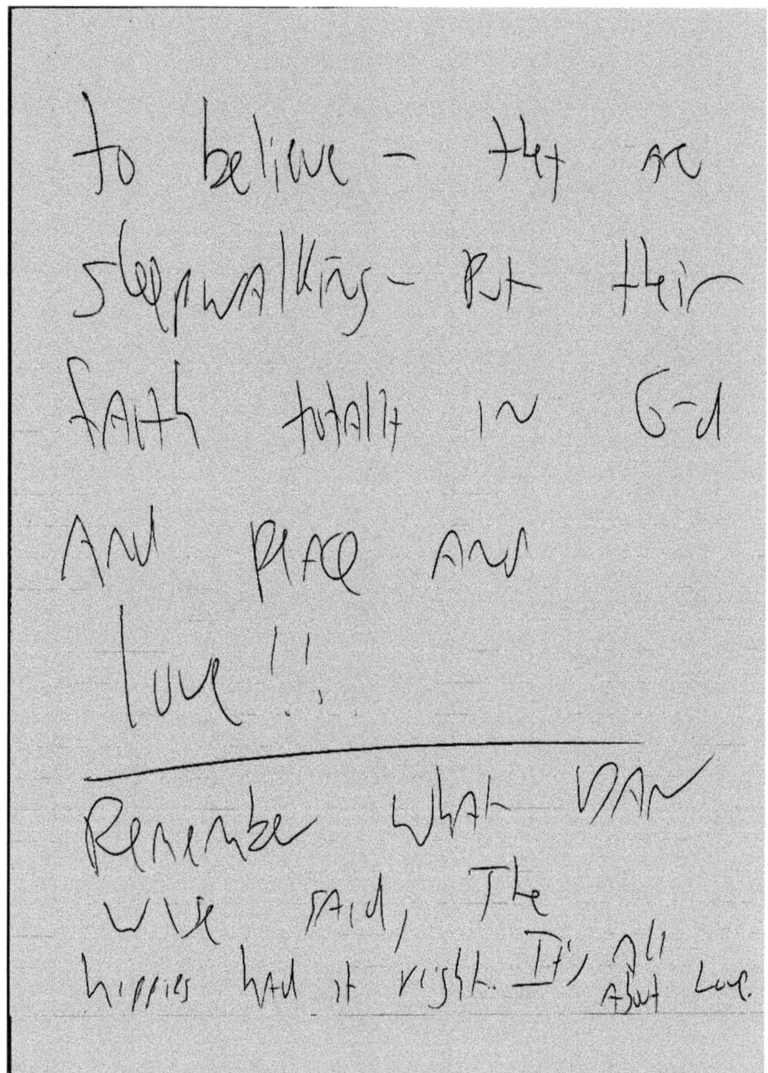
to believe - they are
sleepwalking - put their
faith totally in G-d
and peace and
love!!

Remember what Dan
Wise said, The
hippies had it right. It's all about love.

(Nobody has anything) to believe -
they are sleepwalking -
put their faith totally in G-d and peace and love!!
Remember what Dan Wise said,
The hippies had it right.
It's all about love.

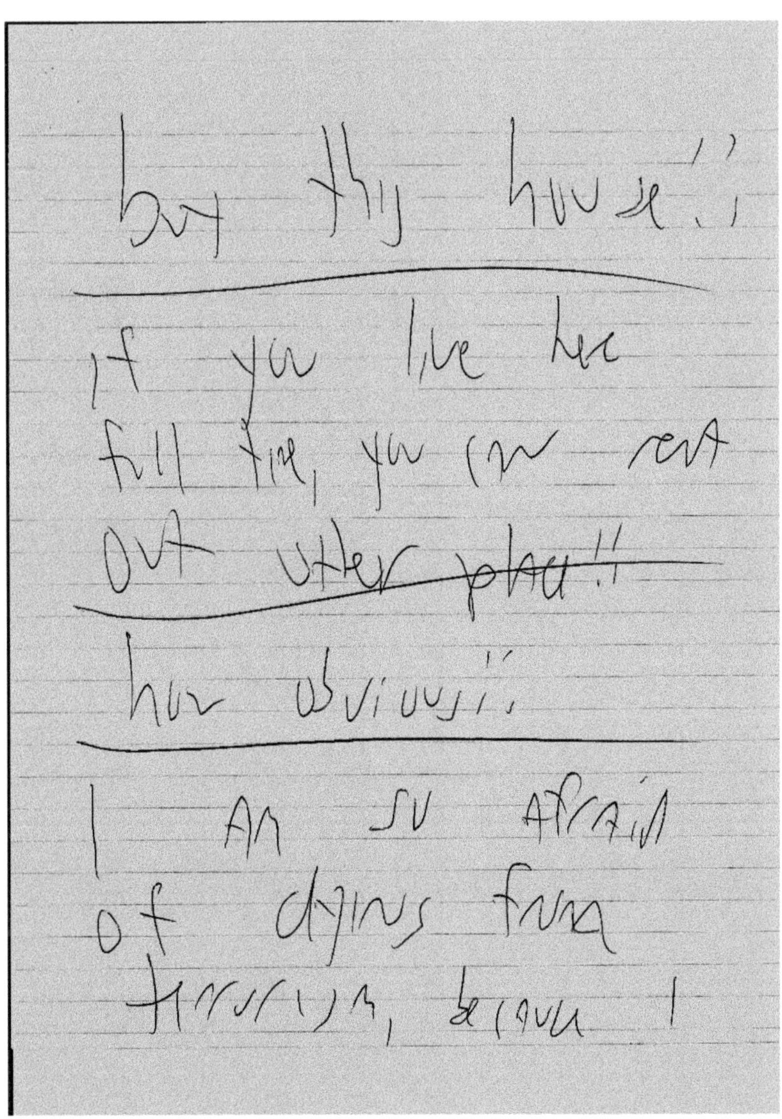

<u>buy this house!!</u>
If you live here full time, you can rent out other place!!
How obvious!!
I am so afraid of dying from terrorism, because I

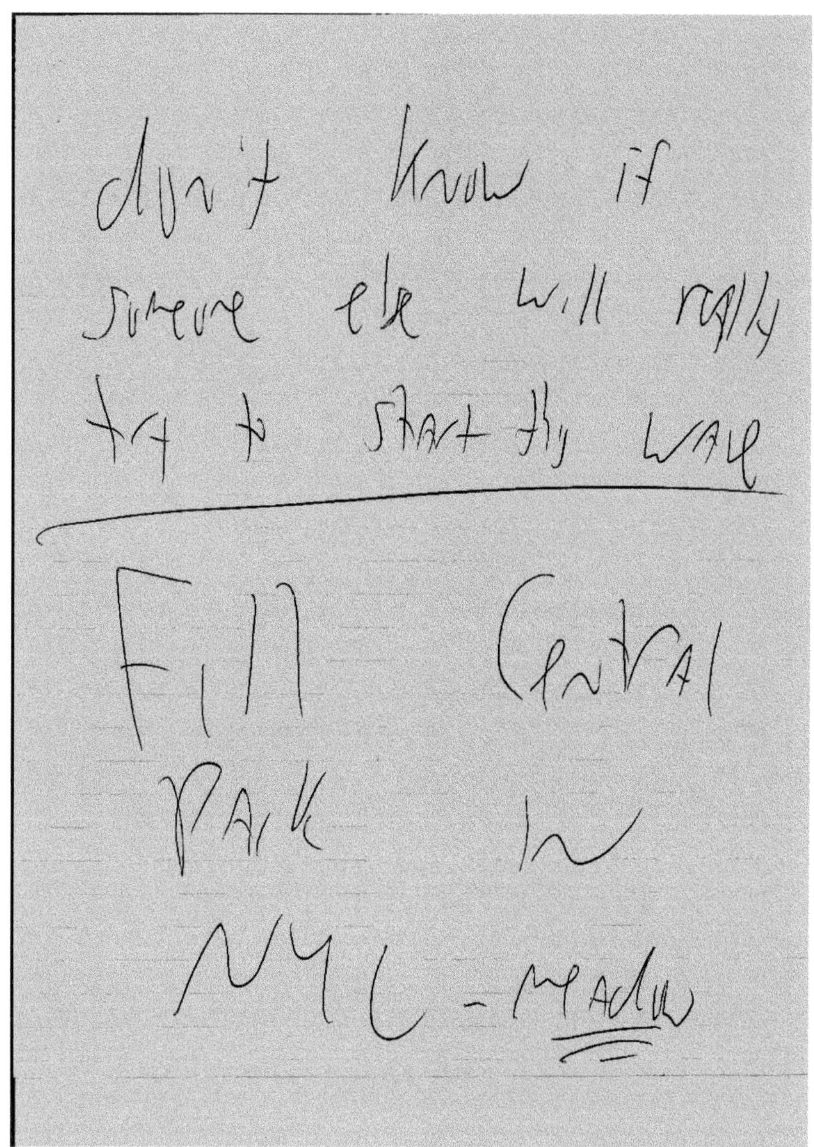

don't know if
someone else will really
try to start this wave

Fill Central
Park in
NYC - Meadow

Don't know if someone else will really try to start this wave
Fill Central Park in NYC - Meadow

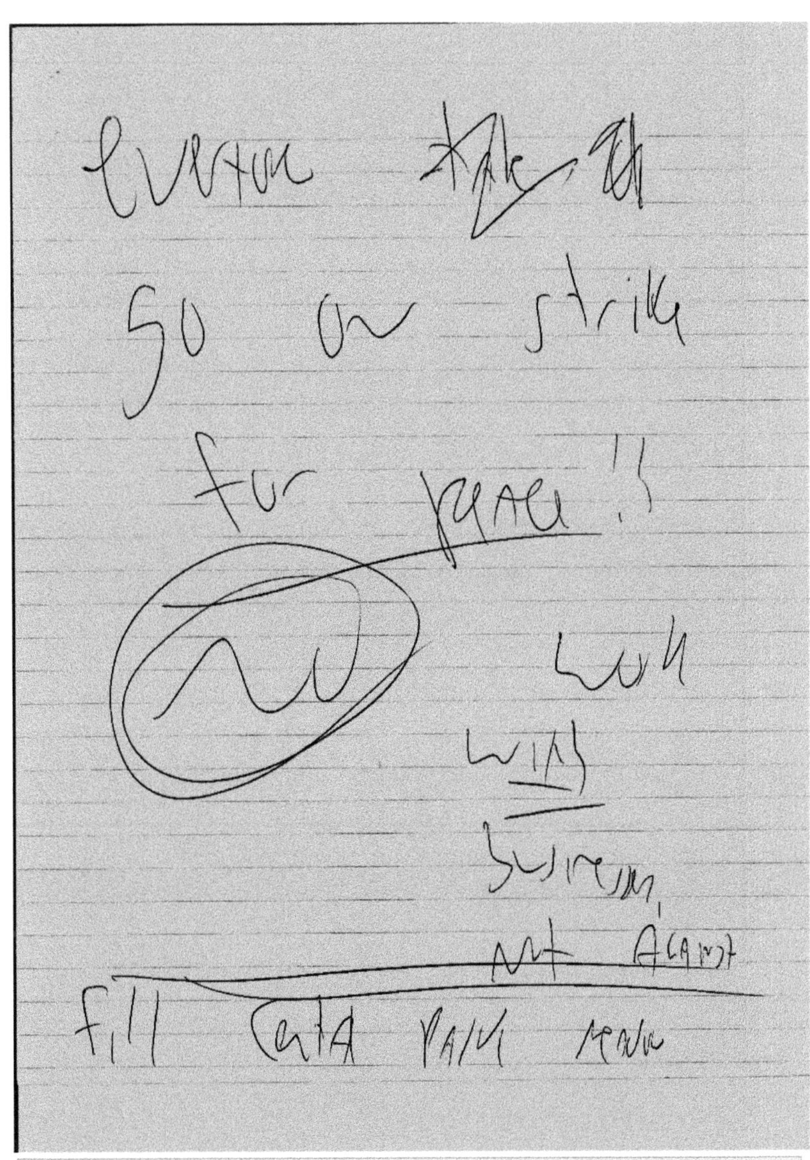

Everyone go on strike for peace!!
NO
Work with businesses, not against
FILL CENTRAL PARK MEADOW

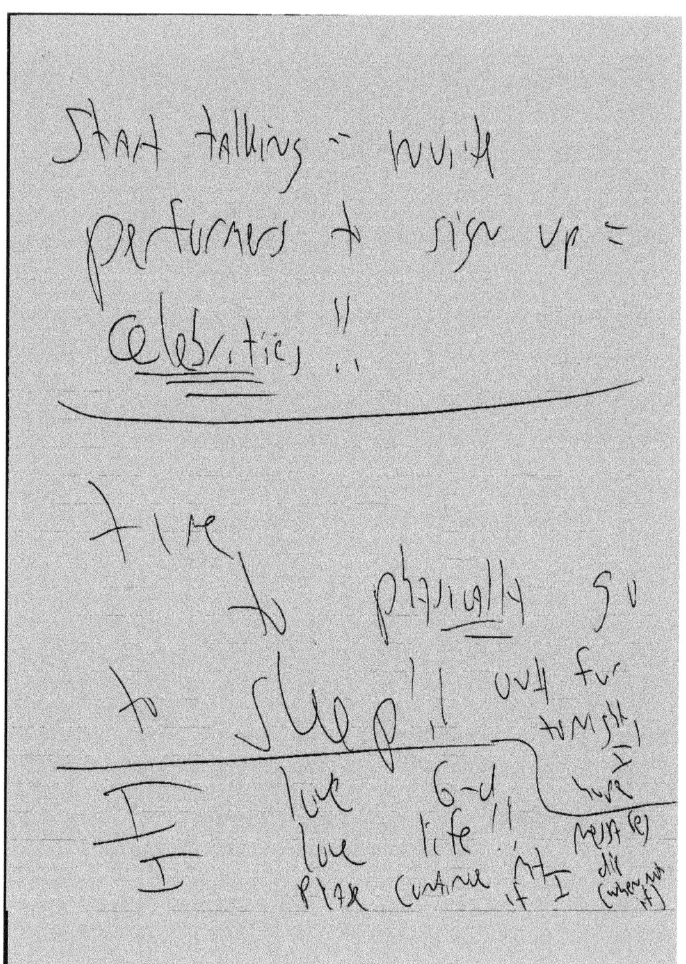

Start talking =
Invite performers to sign up =
Celebrities!!

Time to physically go to sleep!!
Only for tonight, I hope
I love G-d
I love life!!
Please continue my messages if I die (when, not if)

6/3/01 2:30 PM

Why am I capable of starting a wave of peace?

I truly understand how good life is, and I can express this very well through my G-d given gifts of perception and expression.

If you kill me (a terrorist),
look what you have taken away from humanity -
And therefore from yourself and your family.
From G-d?

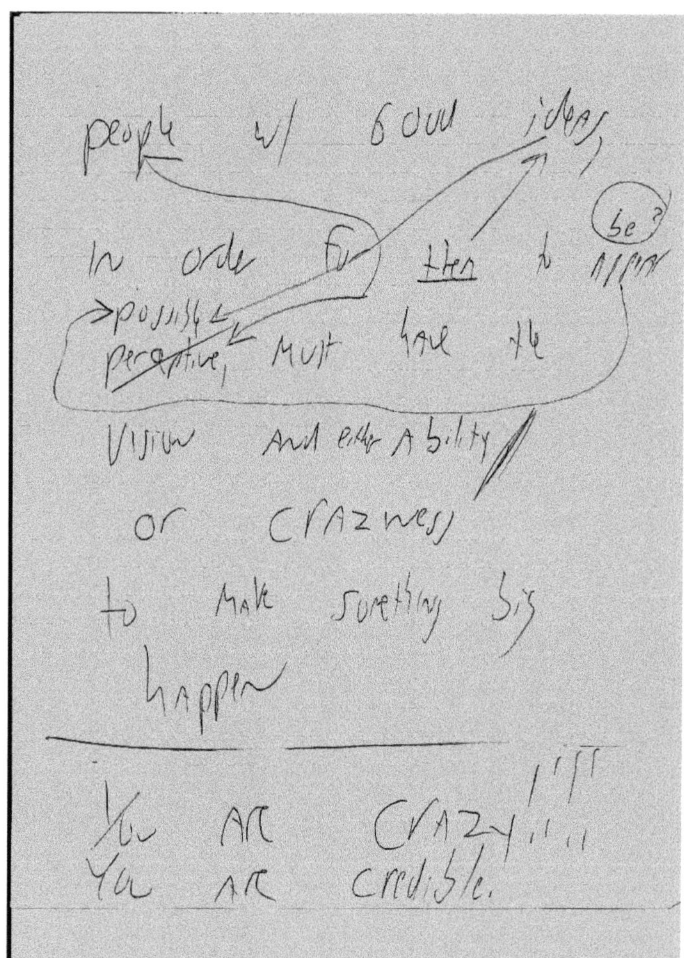

People with good ideas,
in order for them to appear possible,
must have the vision and either ability or craziness
<u>to make something big happen.</u>

YOU ARE CRAZY!!!!
YOU ARE CREDIBLE.

Saturday, July 07, 2001

Hey world! -

1:35 am just sitting here thinking about all the things I will attempt to accomplish, if nothing happens to me physically. But if something does, and I got something started that would outlive me, or last after my physical existence remains pleasant, or even existent, then I have lived the meaning of life, because I have truly realized my purpose here – to start a wave of peace that would change the world, and bring people together in a way that has never been imagined possible by a mere mortal.

~~Love,~~
Mitchell Winston
"I'm glad I know him." (G.L.)

CERTIFICATE OF INCORPORATION
OF
Wave of Peace Foundation, Inc

Under Section 402 of the Not-for-Profit Corporation Law

FIRST: The name of the corporation is Wave of Peace Foundation, Inc.

SECOND: The corporation is a corporation as defined in subparagraph (a)(5) of Section 102 (Definitions) of the Not-for-Profit Corporation Law.

THIRD: The purpose or purposes for which the corporation is formed are as follows:

The corporation will bring people of all cultures, races, and religions together through highly publicized entertainment events, conversation forums, concerts, and public gatherings. The objective will be to demonstrate to the world that nations who are supposed to be "enemies" can come together and organize events to benefit the entire community. Substantial funds will be donated to communities in need.

State of New York }
Department of State } *ss:*

I hereby certify that the annexed copy has been compared with the original document in the custody of the Secretary of State and that the same is a true copy of said original.

Witness my hand and seal of the Department of State on JUL 16 2001

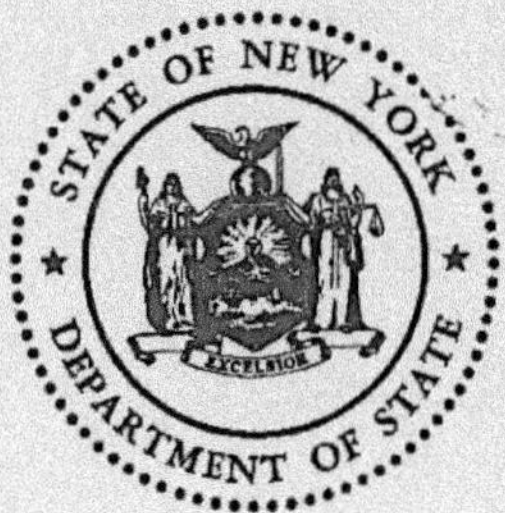

Special Deputy Secretary of State

DOS-1266 (7/00)

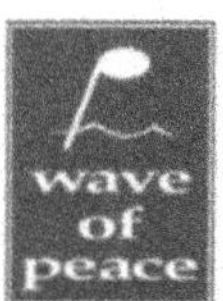

WAVE OF PEACE FOUNDATION, INC.

501(c)3, founded September 2001

MITCH WINSTON

PRESIDENT

Chapter 19

Eddie's Girl

"Ill-advised withdrawals"

IT WAS TIME for my dad and me to reconvene with Victor and Rena DeLeon. We had to show enough progress in both of our companies to cement the remainder of his $250,000 commitments to each. I was confident about Kid Lightning: The Khani project was healthy, his four song demo packaged up and ready to shop to record labels, and the video footage we were capturing would soon be edited into a pilot episode for a unique television program. We were on schedule to reach our stated goal of getting Khani a record deal and becoming a profitable company in the process. My dad's real estate development company was also showing progress. He had gained control of a few promising deals and formed an alliance with an Irish builder-investor named Finn, a great guy who became a close friend to both of us. This new relationship increased the size and diversity of deals that my dad's company could take on, which he knew would please DeLeon. This was what my dad wanted to "focus" on at the meeting.

My mind, however, was racing beyond Kid Lightning and Khani Jones, to the Arab-Israeli conflict and "bringing people together across so-called enemy lines." I was motivated to step things up in this area by the wedding hall collapse in Israel, which led to my official creation of The Wave of Peace Foundation—I wondered if I could get my foundation funded that same day in Delaware!

As my dad and I drove to the meeting, we planned our presentations. I reminded him of the keen interest Rena DeLeon had shown in my spiritual ideas of "bringing people together across so-called enemy lines." Based on the connection I felt with her in this area, I was contemplating asking the DeLeons for an *additional* $250,000 to fund The Wave of Peace Foundation. My dad was concerned with my thought process. He warned me that Victor DeLeon was not my friend—he was an investor who laid out $100,000 to help me build a profitable talent management company, and had not yet remitted the remaining $150,000 that he promised. My dad's point was that regardless of his wife's spirituality, Victor DeLeon was interested in Kid Lightning's bottom line—not world peace. My dad was telling me to "Focus, focus, focus!" on that during my presentation, or I risked blowing everything.

My dad's advice frustrated me but I followed it. I stuck to discussing Kid Lightning and Khani Jones, gave the DeLeons copies of Khani's four-song demo, and described the hundreds of hours of video footage we were collecting and the mutualistic nature of each Kid Lightning sector. Instead of talking about "saving the world," I focused my presentation on the "big revenues" that we would soon earn, especially when we would secure the record deal for Khani. My dad was right again. DeLeon provided each of our companies with the additional $150,000 he had promised, cementing his 25% stakes in each. The Dream Team was thrilled, since both of our companies were now guaranteed more time to exist and succeed. We were again a happy duo on our way back from Delaware, my dad again alluding to the Passover song, "*Dayenu*." If DeLeon had offered each of us the same $250,000, but had requested a 50% (or even 60%) stake in each company, it would have been sufficient for us—*Dayenu*. But with his $250,000 commitment for a 25% share in each, he had established each company's value at $1 million—*DAYENU!* My dad was glad I had followed his advice and focused on Kid Lightning's bottom line, not on "saving the world." But the vibe in the meeting had been so good that I wondered inwardly if I had missed a cosmic opportunity to get The Wave of Peace Foundation funded right on the spot—so the outcome of the meeting felt more like a *partial-Dayenu.* But when my dad actually started singing the song "*Dayenu*," his countenance cheerful and young, the gleam in *his* eye, I had to join in—it was now a full-*Dayenu* for me too.

Big fuck-up #3 (redux): During the meeting, DeLeon had asked me how much I had left in the Kid Lightning account from the first $100,000. When I gave my answer, I did not deduct my ill-advised withdrawal of $23,000 from six months ago, when I bought The Cat and paid those old debts. This lie of omission permanently closed the door on my "truth frees you" opportunity to come clean and admit my amateurish mistake. Big fuck-up #4: Then I overcompensated, probably from guilt, and proclaimed that I wouldn't be paying myself a salary until Kid Lightning earned "big revenues." This impulsive statement was almost as damaging as my ill-advised withdrawal, because it closed the door on the best option I had to correct my mistake: If I had just shut up, even without admitting my ill-advised withdrawal, I could have begun from that point to pay myself a monthly salary, which would have been reasonable, since Kid Lightning was now properly funded. In less than six months, when I built up $23,000 in my personal account, I could have reimbursed Kid Lightning—without DeLeon ever learning of the withdrawal.

With loose words, as usual, I had tried to *please in the present* without considering future consequences; and DeLeon was pleased with my proclamation. He graciously suggested that rather than working for free, I should "accrue my salary" and pay it to myself in a lump sum—*after* we earned those "big revenues" I promised.

DeLeon had reopened the door, slightly, for a potential last minute escape from the consequences of my ill-advised withdrawal. The "big revenues" would have to happen within ten months, before our 2001 taxes were due, when DeLeon would see our bank statements.

Given this time-limit, I knew these revenues could only come if I secured Khani a record deal, since Kid Lightning's other two sectors had not yet matured enough: The television program that would document our experience was still just a growing collection of videotapes, each one dated and filed away. With nothing edited, there was nothing to shop. (I had decided to hold off on this costly and tedious editing process until we achieved a "Hollywood ending," the securing of Khani's record deal, which would make the story marketable.) The other sector, securing the Amagansett house for Kid Lightning's spiritual home base and additional profit center, was also stymied; the owner had still not returned my calls or responded to my $500,000 offer. But by securing the record deal for Khani, his past expenses would be recouped, Kid Lightning's management commission would be earned, and I could reimburse the $23,000 to the company out of my accrued salary. So it all came down to *The Holy Grail*—the record deal—and the ten months I had to find it. I was concerned, but pumped up and motivated by the crisis I had created and the challenge to fix it—I operated best under these conditions.

Ana had lived with me in New York for almost a year, substantially overstaying the six-month stamp she had initially received from the U.S. immigration agent. In order to renew her legal status in America, she would have to return to Costa Rica for about a month, and then try to re-enter the U.S. It was becoming obvious that she was not a tourist, but rather someone who desired to live in the United States; soon we would have to make some "big decisions" and change her tourist visa to a more permanent one. This meant either getting engaged or married, which would allow her to stay in the U.S. indefinitely, and travel unfettered between Costa Rica and the United States. Ana was ready for those "big decisions" now, but I wasn't. I had promised Rabbi Price, perhaps conveniently, that I wouldn't get engaged to Ana until she was officially Jewish. This bought me time, which Ana could not argue with, because she was serious about her conversion. But since she had overstayed her initial six-month permission, we risked her being denied re-entrance back into the United States on her following attempt! And my sticking to this promise was a contradiction: We had previously lied to Rabbi Price that we were not already living together, which I had deemed both harmless and necessary to enable her conversion. So why was I unwilling to harmlessly lie to him again, since getting engaged to Ana now would guarantee her re-entrance into the United States This perceived hypocrisy, or change, albeit unspoken, was on both our minds as I drove Ana to the airport. Based on my research, the odds were very good that she would be granted permission to return after a month in Costa Rica, but there was no guarantee. It felt strange that I was okay with this risk.

The first Friday after Ana left, Gregory Laurence and I rolled into *Vinyl* around midnight. With Danny Tenaglia spinning, we expected an unbelievable club environment—we weren't disappointed. Five hours felt like five minutes, and it was 5 a.m. Greg and I had temporarily separated, and I was dancing in place, moving fluidly, exuding what I perceived as the perfect human vibe. I had halted my fiendish circling, those inauthentic cat-and-mouse charades, and allowed myself to chill in one spot, while thousands of pleasure bubbles again filled my mind and body. This exact moment was the most attractive I had ever felt, and a girl with supermodel looks approached me. She introduced herself as Edna, age twenty-three, a flight attendant for American Airlines. She was tall, with mesmerizing brown eyes, tan skin, and long brown hair. Her back had a beautiful sexy arch, her feet and toes were perfect, and her figure and movement were both harmonious and fluid. She was the perfect mix of my favorite features from all my past crushes. And even with this intense hotness, Edna emitted a naive innocence. She was the *beauty and the cutie*—and Ana's existence was suddenly an afterthought. I tried to focus on Edna's eyes, but mine wouldn't cooperate. I attempted to tell her that we had met at the exact moment I felt like my true best self—but the music was too loud for so many words. Instead I flashed my trusty gold Star of David and inexplicably blurted out, "My body is my temple." A few minutes later, Edna said she and her friends were leaving. Before I could wonder if I had scared her away by being "too abstract," she asked if I would like to meet her for coffee sometime. I didn't hesitate to take her number. Greg and I got home from *Vinyl* at 8 a.m. No further stimulation was necessary; I copied Edna's digits onto a second piece of paper, smoked some weed and went to sleep. Greg was impressed by my good behavior.

At noon, I arose wide awake and called Edna. She sounded tired but glad to hear from me. We made a plan to meet later that afternoon in Queens, where she lived with four other flight attendants. Wearing jeans and a white tee-shirt while driving my '85 Jag from Manhattan to Queens, I blasted my *Eddie and the Cruisers* soundtrack on cassette. When I arrived, I got out of the Jag, leaned against the hood, and waited stoically—like Eddie Wilson would have. And when Edna appeared, she carried the essence of Joann Carlino, Eddie's girl. Our vibe was mutual attraction and mutual confidence—no nerves, no charades—and still no thoughts of Ana.

We drove down the street, shared some French fries, and then walked through a park, where we held hands for the first time. Edna was of Mexican descent, but born in Texas, and her parents, who lived in Mexico, were conservative. Edna had left Mexico unmarried and come to the United States to be a flight attendant, which was not what her mom, a traditional woman, had envisioned for her. Edna had also previously been dating someone whom her parents had not approved of, which further fueled their rift, and wasn't helped by the fact that her parents, thousands of miles away, missed her a lot. Edna said that this was the first time in her life that she had experienced parental conflict, and there were tears in her eyes as she described it. I related well; I was experiencing parental conflict for the first time in my life too, and it hurt. She was opening up to me from her heart, and at that moment I had to mention Ana. I downplayed our relationship, disclosing only that I had begun dating Ana right around the millennium, she was often in Costa Rica visiting her family, and she was there now. I didn't mention that we had lived together (blissfully) for ten months, or that she was converting to Judaism and returning to New York in a month. I characterized our relationship as "tentative," although it had lately felt like the opposite—until I met Edna.

We spent the next two days together. Edna didn't speak as much as most girls I had known, but when she did, I understood her and felt her essence. When *I* spoke, she looked into my eyes and understood me. I was more attracted to her than I had ever been to anyone, and felt new levels of chemistry too. She told me she had recently won her state's beauty pageant and been crowned *Miss Nuevo Leon*, and then had gone on to become the second runner-up at the Miss Mexico Pageant. This was cool, since Edna wasn't the typical pageant girl I had seen over the years on television. (In fact, she seemed quite the opposite—but I still couldn't see how she didn't win the whole thing!) When I described my career to Edna, I mentioned that I managed Khani Jones, but I spoke most about *my* music and *my* foundation. (Eddie Wilson was the front man, the leader—not the manager.)

We continued to get together over the next three weeks. Every time I was with her, I felt cool, creative, and masculine. I was Eddie, and she was Joann—and when we made love, it was better than my movie fantasy. On those rare moments when I thought about Ana, her pending return, and the inevitable conflict that loomed, I put those thoughts aside, just like Eddie and Joann had done: "Eddie and I, we had a deal, we never talked about the future. We thought the present was so fine, why ruin it by planning ahead?" But this was an inauthentic analogy, because Eddie only had one girl. And he never lied.

A Friday evening phone call from Ana made me think more about my authenticity.

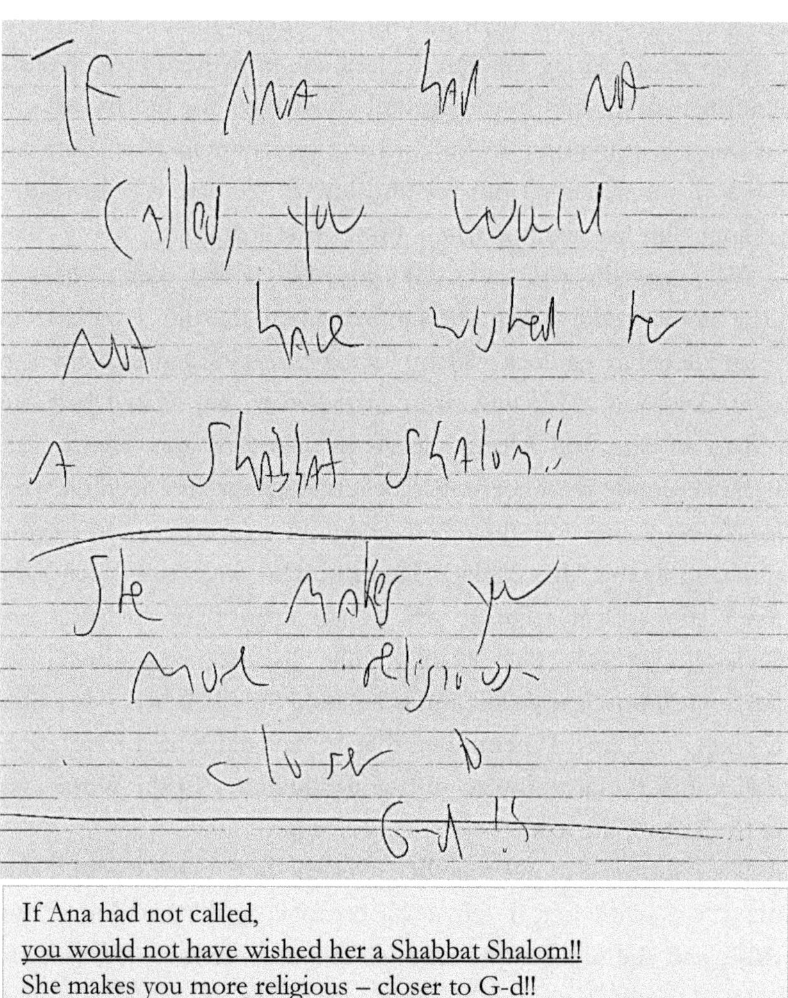

If Ana had not called,
you would not have wished her a Shabbat Shalom!!
She makes you more religious – closer to G-d!!

If you truly believe in G-d:
a) it is not okay to date more than one: D'rabbanan
or
b) it is okay to date more than one: D'raisa

Khani and I were still finding time to study the Bible together. During these days, we (conveniently) focused on the once-common practice of polygamy, noting that males in Biblical times were allowed to have more than one wife. I pointed out that in the Torah, accepted by Jews as the direct written word of G-d (called *D'raisa*), polygamy had been an accepted practice. Thousands of years later, due to societal issues, the major rabbis got together and outlawed polygamy. This change was not *D'raisa*, the word of G-d, but rather the word of the rabbis. I believed that since this was human interpretation, not G-d's, it carried no more weight than the interpretations made by Khani and me. We came to the conclusion that given full disclosure and substantial financial resources ("No romance without finance"), polygamy should be legal!

Khani had also studied this subject by himself, and I asked him, "When polygamy was practiced freely, thousands of years ago, why weren't the women allowed more than one husband? Why only the men?" He opined that if a polyandrous woman had become pregnant, there was no way to determine which husband was the father. Khani's logic made sense at the time, and I mentioned the conversation to Edna, partly in jest and partly to test her waters.

Edna said she couldn't imagine *any* scenario where polygamy could work, regardless of time period, and she also didn't think it was fair that only the men were allowed multiple spouses. Then our light conversation turned heavy, because Edna sensed a hidden agenda and asked me if I had something more to say. At that moment, I came clean: I admitted to her that my relationship with Ana was much more serious than I had previously described, and that she was converting to Judaism and coming back to New York in a week. While speaking, I woke up to the fact that I still had major feelings for Ana, and needed time to sort out the situation. I suggested to Edna that we not speak for a brief while. Edna suggested that we not speak *forever*, a policy she invoked by hanging up on me. But memories of touching her and dreams of touching her again dominated my fantasies—even as I made love to Ana, on her first night back.

2001 Notes on white handwritten pad

1) Don't investigate me, and I won't investigate you

2) You can always repent, but isn't it sad that you even have to? Or have to think about this?

And what does "have to" mean

Have to serve G-d?

Have to serve somebody?

3) Talk even less

4) Start treating yourself like a world leader

5) Deal with respect for yourself only

6) Apt. cleaned

7) Start following the bible as much as you believe it. Do you believe it? Yes.

YES.

8) This world is so crazy

9) If you don't win the Nobel Peace Prize, why?

10) Always forgive yourself for your errors, if you love G-d. Because he will be so happy he created a being so intelligent that with all we can do, we can also do this!!

11) Forgive others, but to what extent?

Forgive yourselves, but to what extent?

Who cares??

Is it that you are so tested by everything because everything is attracted to you?

It hurts that you can't sing now. Ahhh.

There is a reason why you lost your voice and you know it. Ahhh.

Chapter 20

Leverage

"Two trees go down in the city."

WE HAD BUILT UP a lot of video footage of the Kid Lightning-Khani Jones management experience, starting from when he and I had first come together "across so-called enemy lines." I was eager to create the television program, so I decided to use the formation of Khani's band and the completion of his four-song recording as the "Hollywood ending" we needed for the pilot episode to shop to the networks. We found a video editor (who seemed to like Fredda very much). He recommended we log the footage we had captured so far, pinpointing the best moments. This would save *him* from having to watch all the tapes, which would reduce editing costs and allow us to shape the story for him. Fredda and I would therefore have to watch every minute of every tape we had collected so far.

I did not enjoy the tedious, time-consuming process of reviewing the footage; nor did I like how I looked and sounded on the tapes: My posture slouched and my voice sounded whiny, even a bit feminine. Not enjoying the footage was a big letdown, given how much we had collected. During these sessions, I also watched a few (of the countless) tapes I continued to make weekly of myself alone in West 80th, philosophizing and playing guitar; and my reaction was the same—major disappointment. The playback, or reality, never looked or sounded as good as it felt when I got high and recorded—not even close.

While Fredda and I were logging the tapes, we discussed possible titles for the television program. We tried various permutations and combinations like "Kid Lightning and Khani Jones," "Kid Lightning, Khani Jones, and The Wave of Peace," or "Khani Jones and The Wave of Peace." I viewed Khani and me as spiritual partners in peace, who were setting a good example across so-called enemy lines, so I asked Khani which title he liked the most. He said that he didn't have any preference, and this led us to an important discussion: Khani said he had noticed that my peace aspirations and The Wave of Peace Foundation were creeping into the music sector more than before. He respectfully reminded me that the initial goal we had set together was still his goal—to get a record deal and become a reggae superstar. He felt his music was strong enough on its own to achieve that. He wasn't against my dreams of peace, and he was willing to help in the future, but he wanted to make sure I didn't get distracted from our quest for the record deal. His message reminded me of my dad's recent advice on our way to Delaware, to avoid the spiritual stuff until we made money. The two wise men were delivering the same message, "Focus, focus, focus! Get the record deal. We'll save the world later."

This conversation reminded me to do a better job of separating concerns; my management contract with Khani did not mention The Wave of Peace Foundation. I told Khani that I respected his forthrightness in pointing this out. Later that evening, after a few hits, I thought it over and saw that a tangible divergence had occurred between Khani and me. He was, and always would be my friend, even a brother. But he was not my "partner in peace." He wanted a conventional artist-manager relationship. Khani's goal for having this conversation, understandably, was to protect his career interests and keep things moving. My dad had given me the same advice, but his only goal had been to help *me*, his son. Yet they had reached the same conclusion: I should put my philanthropic and spiritual goals on hold and focus on securing that coveted record deal for Khani Jones. That would prove to Victor and Rena DeLeon that I, Kid Lightning, was a great judge of talent and a successful businessman. This tangible success would still allow me to "save the world"—but later.

My immediate, private reaction to each of their advice was damaged ego and pride. "Fuck that! They don't get it! They don't get me!" But that night I accepted they were right, that everything did depend on the record deal. I had to finish what I had started, to prove myself to my investor. That had to be my main focus. But it hurt to also accept that Khani Jones was no longer my "partner in peace." My search for that person would continue elsewhere, and at a later date. From then on, I did not include Khani Jones in any further discussions about The Wave of Peace Foundation.

Though refocused, we were in a familiar place: Khani's packaged-up music sounded great, but we were stymied due to my lack of contacts and influence in the music business. (I think my desire to avoid this reality is what had led me to manage Khani unconventionally to begin with.) But now I had to face this issue. I had already sent Khani's demo to my few music contacts, including the guy I had bribed off the street at CBGB's two years earlier. I had hoped for a quick, painless victory, but it didn't happen. Even though the critical feedback we received on Khani's four songs was positive, my limited contacts were not interested enough or capable enough to offer Khani a record deal.

Even while receiving these rejections, I noticed that my having an investor with a big name gave me status and made people more likely to listen to me and try to help. Learning to deal successfully with these people was a game of leverage, my new favorite business concept. The prize I dangled was Victor DeLeon's name and any potential association with him or his money, while not revealing how much he had already invested in Kid Lightning. (I suspected that most of them thought that DeLeon had invested more in Kid Lightning than he actually had. That was fine with me because it improved my position of leverage.) Over time, I got better at this game, which opened more doors and piqued more interest in Khani. But each time it was to no avail; these people were eventually unwilling or unable to help Khani get a major label record deal. The consensus was always that Khani was highly talented, but the reggae industry was too small. Introducing a brand new reggae artist into the market would be difficult, and would have limited upside potential.

I thought about my old boss and friend, Cedric Kushner. Before becoming a boxing promoter, he had been a major concert promoter, and he was still highly connected in the music business. I went to see Cedric, and he greeted me warmly. I explained to him that Khani Jones was the test case for my investor; I *had* to get Khani a major label record deal to prove I was a great judge of talent and a good businessman. That would help me secure at least a few million dollars in additional funding, which could help everyone, including Cedric. I told him that I didn't have the music industry contacts to secure this record deal. Then Cedric took over the meeting with his own brand of leverage: He wasn't interested in my vague promise of a future association with Victor DeLeon, or my pledge to work with him if I raised those millions in the future. Cedric was interested in some quick cash, as soon as possible, to tide him over until Christmas. At that time, he would receive an advance from HBO for the world title fight between his marquee fighter, "Sugar" Shane Mosley, and contender Vernon Forrest, on January 26, 2002. Cedric said he needed between $25,000 and $50,000 for personal expenses until then.

We came up with a possible deal: I would loan Cedric $25,000, and he would put me in touch with his top music contacts. These included Louis Levin (the manager of Michael Jackson and Michael

Bolton) and David Sonnenberg (the manager of Meat Loaf, The Fugees, and The Black Eyed Peas). Cedric would *also* lobby these people on Khani's behalf, because if any of these introductions resulted in a record deal, Cedric could keep the $25,000. Based on the confidence he had in his contacts, Cedric looked at this deal as an easy way to make $25,000. I liked it too, because if it didn't work out, I would get the $25,000 back around Christmas without having to tell DeLeon anything. If it did work out, I could classify Cedric's $25,000 payment as a consulting fee, which DeLeon would agree was money well spent to get Khani a record deal and make Kid Lightning a successful company. I told Cedric I would write up an agreement and send him a check in a few days.

At first it seemed like a perfect deal, but then I started having some misgivings. It was strange that *Cedric Kushner* needed *me* to loan him $25,000, an amount that should have been inconsequential to him. I told my dad about the proposal, expecting he would advise against it. But he endorsed it! He knew I trusted Cedric, and he did too. And he allayed my concerns about Cedric's need for cash by explaining that cash flow can be a tricky issue for *all* businesses, even successful ones. Since the HBO fight was officially on the calendar, prompt repayment seemed assured if we didn't find a record deal for Khani through Cedric's contacts. But my dad had one major recommendation for me: Cedric must pledge collateral for the loan before I give him the money.

Requesting collateral for this loan was an obvious move—Business 101—which I should have already made part of the deal. But since I had met Cedric, I had acted as his boxing groupie: I had appeased him, served him, and told him what he wanted to hear. And though I had not worked for him for two years, our interaction and friendship still had that same vibe. Even when I paid him a social visit, I always found myself answering his phones and bringing him treats from the fridge. I didn't have a problem with that—Cedric was my friend, and he was charming, world famous, and powerful. My reverence and self-deprecation around him were genuine. (Plus, I no longer had to act this way daily, just on the rare occasions when I saw him, which made it more tolerable.)

I thought that asking for collateral would disrupt this chemistry: It would brazenly declare that now *I* had some money and power, and *I* had rules too. And it would suggest to Cedric that I wasn't sure he would pay me back, even though I was sure he would. For these reasons, I admitted to my dad the next day that I was planning not to ask for collateral. I suggested that my demonstration of trust would help the spirit of our deal. My dad urged me to reconsider, and even offered me a diplomatic way to broach the subject. He suggested I tell Cedric that Victor DeLeon had to approve this loan, and only would if Cedric pledged collateral. This would sound plausible, since the two of them had never met or done business together. And with the collateral request coming from DeLeon, not me, Cedric could save face. (In truth, I had already decided *not* to tell Victor DeLeon about this loan, since I had previously boasted to him about my *own* list of contacts.)

I took my dad's advice and made the request to Cedric. He joked that he was insulted—and I think he really was. But he wanted the cash, and offered his gold, custom-designed Rolex, covered in diamonds and crusted with emeralds and rubies. It was gaudy and ostentatious, like his red limousine and pink sofas, but worth $90,000 according to Cedric, and I believed it. I wrote up a contract and we executed it, Cedric using his infamous signature that contained no real letters—he gave me the watch and I gave him the $25,000.

In the event that Kid Lightning Enterprises is entitled to sell the Rolex Watch pursuant to this Agreement, Kushner, through this Agreement, represents and transfers title and possession of the Rolex Watch to Kid Lightning Enterprises.

CEDRIC KUSHNER

By: MITCH WINSTON,
President of Kid Lightning Enterprises, LLC

Coupled with my ill-advised $23,000 withdrawal, there was now $48,000 out of the KLE account that DeLeon knew nothing about. But with access to Cedric's music industry contacts and his financial motivation to assist our efforts, Khani was now on his way to the coveted record deal, when everything would be good, and Kid Lightning Enterprises would be a healthy company—with clean books, a happy investor, and a bright future.

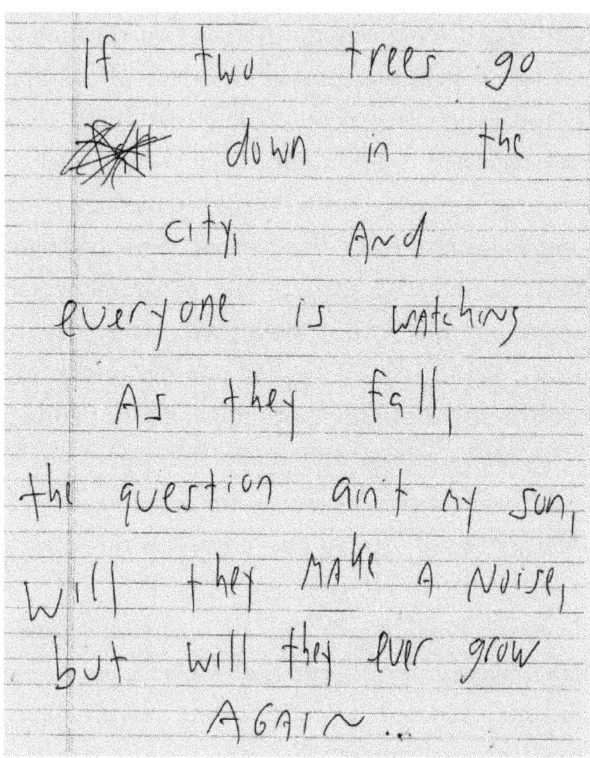

If two trees go
down in the
city, And
everyone is watching
As they fall,
the question ain't my son,
will they make a Noise,
but will they ever grow
Again..

On September 11, 2001, I was scheduled to travel to a studio in New Jersey to record my new song, "Wave of Peace," which I had written a few days after the May 25 wedding hall collapse in Israel. I had planned for this song to be the theme song for my new foundation, and I scheduled this day guilt-free, as a reward for the great deal I had recently inked with Cedric on Khani's behalf. As I was getting ready to leave my apartment, I got a call from Stevie D., the studio owner. He said, "I don't think we are going to be able to record today. People are flying planes into the World Trade Center." I turned on my television in time to see the second tower fall.

My initial reaction to the September 11 attacks was numbness; I found myself at the local grocery store in some form of survival mode, buying four gallons of water and three boxes of cereal. Ana's initial reaction angered me; she asserted that disasters happen every day, everywhere, but the United States always received the most sympathy and media attention. (I didn't argue with her because she hadn't yet comprehended the gravity of what had happened—and she wasn't alone in that regard.)

Three days later, while watching the news, we *both* cried: Every channel was showing stories about the dead and missing. Thousands of normal people were turned into trance-like nomadic wanderers, looking for loved ones, unable to stop looking—and forever lost themselves. We saw an interview with a mother who was holding up a picture of her fallen son, an innocent passenger on one of the planes. Her exhausted face epitomized agony and misery, the veins and blood vessels popping out like a roadmap. It suggested to me how my mom might have looked if I had perished that day too. With tears in her eyes and her English still a work in progress, Ana said, "That's not fair!!" Her simple words summed up what I and possibly many others were feeling: This attack was a robbery of infinite proportions; loved ones were stolen forever, and there was no way to get them back. That's not fair.

After Ana went to sleep, I thought about Edna—*the unresolved*—whom I hadn't heard from since our falling out. I remembered that Edna was a flight attendant for American Airlines, and she might have been on one of the planes that went down! I walked outside to call her, and her phone went straight to voicemail. I left a long frantic message, inquiring if she was alive, and apologizing for being such an asshole—while praying it wasn't too late. I called again later, to no avail, leaving another long message. The next morning I had some privacy; I went online to search the American Airlines victim list. "Edna Perez" was not there. She was alive! My journey from all-night panic to sudden euphoria confirmed that my feelings for her were real. She wasn't (just) a sexual fantasy, a risk I took, or a story I could forget. I had to see her again, or at least talk to her, regardless of any bad karma I might face. But based on my behavior, I didn't expect to hear back from her anytime soon. On that I was right.

Handwritten on white pad, after 9/11/2001

Dawn thinks you should be writing, but you are writing.

You're getting the nerve to stand up for what you believe in

You must tell DeLeon about everything!! Both can exist (Peace & Kid Lightning)

Mitch should be a leader now

Just call me and get together

Things are nuts?!!!

You really have to follow your dreams. You are learning how to do it!!!!

6,000 people – the youth need a voice. Let's get heard more – just get out there and set up a microphone.

Yellow Pages –

<u>Wave of Peace Foundation– Patron of Peace</u>

Make a cultural renaissance here in NYC

Mutual fund of peace organization

Have events, put out products, support local peace efforts

Arab/Israeli countries or here?

Do we give grants? Support other efforts – we stay lean

We are the SEAL OF APPROVAL on records, books

How do we get the masses to care if only Arabs/Jews

Pay-per-view debates!

With $ you can directly affect what gets created!!

Lectures - $$

Cultural renaissance for peace

9/11 –Tap into the pool of caring/talented people

Start a Mutual Fund for Peace?

Open mic for peace, etc. (4 acts!!)

Lost songs, lost art, of people who have been killed by terror!!! Where are they? Where is their art?

Product Distribution: Record label, Publishing, Art

Results: Artists vaulted who care, Money Donated

Cultural events, Concerts, Readings, Cocktail parties

Results: People come together who care, Money donated

Use resources of people and money and talent from here to

A. create a renaissance here

B. vault those who care

C. help over there!!

Less than a month later, my dad read in the newspaper that the IRS was granting expedited 501(c)(3) tax-exempt status to charitable foundations whose scopes related to promoting peace or helping the September 11 victims and families. This prestigious delineation would allow The Wave of Peace Foundation to offer tax deductions to potential donors. I decided to apply, since our motto was "bringing people together across so-called enemy lines." Under normal circumstances, this highly scrutinized application process required foundations to have a proven track record and financial history. But given the post-September 11 environment, The Wave of Peace Foundation was quickly granted 501(c)(3) status. This gave us instant prestige and credibility—and set us up to raise money.

Raising money required a business plan, which I started writing, enlisting my dad's usual assistance (of course). After he read my first draft, he said the document felt empty because the foundation hadn't done anything. Yes, we had achieved that prestigious 501(c)(3) status, but we were not an active entity. It was time to do something, to bring The Wave of Peace Foundation from idea mode to execution mode. Fredda designed the Village Voice ad, and we put out the call for the first Wave of Peace meeting. Our goal was to find like-minded people, "across so-called enemy lines," and brainstorm peace-ideas with them. I was also searching for my "partner in peace."

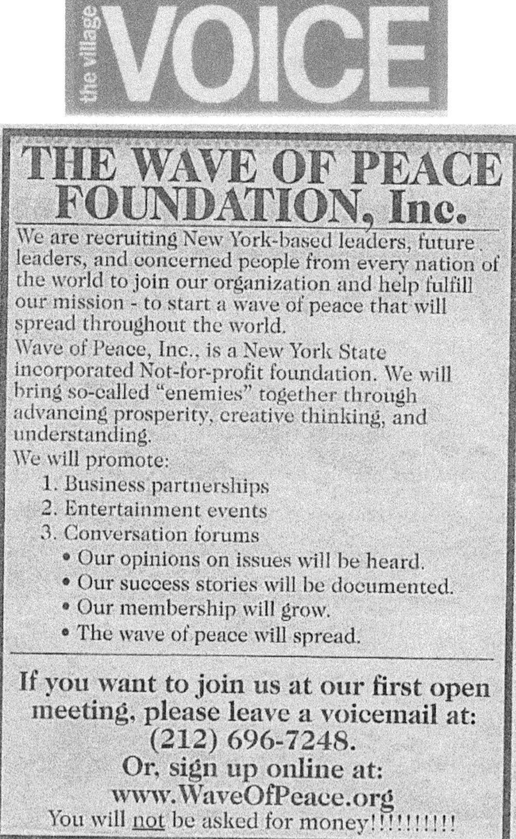

the village VOICE

THE WAVE OF PEACE FOUNDATION, Inc.

We are recruiting New York-based leaders, future leaders, and concerned people from every nation of the world to join our organization and help fulfill our mission - to start a wave of peace that will spread throughout the world.

Wave of Peace, Inc., is a New York State incorporated Not-for-profit foundation. We will bring so-called "enemies" together through advancing prosperity, creative thinking, and understanding.

We will promote:

1. Business partnerships
2. Entertainment events
3. Conversation forums
   - Our opinions on issues will be heard.
   - Our success stories will be documented.
   - Our membership will grow.
   - The wave of peace will spread.

If you want to join us at our first open meeting, please leave a voicemail at: (212) 696-7248.
Or, sign up online at: www.WaveOfPeace.org

You will not be asked for money!!!!!!!!!

Subj:	~~wave ...~~: of ideas
Date:	11/24/01 11:59:34 PM Eastern Standard Time
From:	mitch@waveofpeace.org (Mitchell Winston)
Reply-to:	mitch@waveofpeace.org (Mitchell Winston)
To:	klight@aol.com

Forget Entertainment - call it a Record Label
specifically go into every detail necessary as to every record label vendor - 2 or 3 studios, enginéers, producers, distribution company, the talent, photos, etc. - list the artists! kweder? this will get a lot of press in philly! probably not kweder. we'll talk..!
It is a "good feelings thing" - the wave is really inside of yourself. your father does not see it in the document, because you don't show your true abilities, passions, etc. you are too subdued, and this document, which is the most important one you every wrote, doesn't have that true passion. this document is about passion. it is about a leader. it is about someone who is stepping up to try to change the world. he is trying to start a wave of peace. he has travelled around the world. I was the president of every school i ever attended, included the university of pennsylvania, where i was receiving my degree from the Wharton School of Business. He has fallen in love with religion,and travelled to the Middle East and Egypt. He has fallen in love with music, which he realized during his travels to Costa Rica. He has women in every country, and in every state. All of them say he was the best lover ever. He is really, really, really, good looking, which sometimes can be really, really difficult.. (ha, zoolander).
he has always known he was a leader, and has proven this wherever he has been. He has business backing from the DeLeon family, and is trying to get the guts to approach them with this proposal.
He has to get Clinton!!!!!!!!!!! With Clinton, this is a slam dunk. Record Label and Committee of Nations. Winston will preside over the Record Label, and Clinton over the Committee of Nations. This is the hugest thing ever!!!!!!!!!!!!!!!!! There are local elections for the Committee of Nations, which will never, ever have any physical power! This is the coolest thing, because it can be the strongest thing in the world and never do anything! (what?????) Back to the record label, show how you know everyone in music, use padell, levin, sonnenberg, DeLeon, kushner, dan wise, bob leone!!!!!!!!!, wallace collins. the songwriter's hall of fame, open mic nights, you are crazy not to include bob leone!!!!!, we will donate $250 to them after the event, use their mailing list....you have to get DeLeon on board now, and bring this thing together. this is the only thing holding you back from changing the world!!!!!!!! and at the same time they are what has most gven you the luxury and the ability to even think about changing the world. without financial security, you can't think about this, or at least it is much harder. you have to worry all the time about paying your bills, etc. and you don't have a reputation. DeLeon has given you the reputation to walk into people's offices. you have a backer. you have balls. you gotta get the wave going now. it is imperative. you have to point out about the non-compete regarding the not-for-profit situation, so he immediately knows everything you have done has been totally above-board. and then you describe this situation, especially with bill clinton maybe on board?
-=-------
committee of nations
we have to lay out the entire structure... way more specific.
have 12 month appointees, then yearly elections after probation period. you must be very active in order to be counted......this is going to be so fun!!!.... you have to start this thing by saying, we are going into this as friends, in order to change the world. we are going to fight for peace everywhere in this world!!!!!!!!!! human rights.. let's get this to be a huge thing!!!!!! are we allowed to lobby? it is not about lobbbying, it is about showing major respect and positivity.. i am a jew, from israel, who all my life has been angry towards arabs for how i perceive the arab / israeli conflict. i hereby lay down all of these feelings, and respect that my so-called enemy, has feelings of hatred towards me, and they were taught this by their parents, for whatever reasons they have, they beleive it, and this is so fucking sad that we are killing each other, and there are ridiculous rules that politicians can't be shot, only civilians!!! this whole world is so fucked up right now regarding the killing, and you have to get DeLeon on board and get this whole thing going, fast!!!!!! this is a huge movement, on both fronts, and both will bolster the other!!!!!!!
you are really stepping up!!!!!!!!!!!!
coming together... that is really the thing about it.

do you feel you were sent here to bring people together? yes. and all that means is that you were givne abilities by G-d to do things, but you are totally mortal, and you could die any die, even today, crossing the street maybe? but the point is, maybe there are many people who have these abilites, but don't do anything about them? or while they are trying, they die!! so you have to step up now! this foundation is the key to everything. it encompasses literally everyone you know, and every oranization you have every been a part of. everywhere you have been, you have totally been loved and respected, in all work situations, and all social situations.

this document is about a man a dream. it is the wave of peace. it has bill clinton? well, get ths done sunday. literally. sunday.... get this faxed to clinton monday a.m. - all you need is a letter saying you endorse it and will seriously consider becoming a partial spokesperson if funds are raised. then fully describe the committee of nations, the record label, and the television show!!!!!!!!!! - each vendor, each person, your resume, cost estimates?, description of how to put together committee of nations, elections...., and go to fucking DeLeon and get lennox lewis!!!!!!!!! (you get these people once you get this set up.. you have ceremonies every time a celebrity signs up!! this is the best p.r. idea you can think of. go to grubman and say, do this for free now, i will tell the world you are doing this for the first year as a donation to benefit the wave of peace foundation (tax deductible), so you have to really pump us up...and after the first year, you start paying them a fair market value for their services. you will sign something....they will pump you, your story, your music, kid lightning, khani,
use shyndig again??? no, but have khani deal with him a lot....who knows?
call him for khani...
so much about this whole peace foundation is energy. you have ideas now, you feel energized. but you then lose this feeling the next day, and you are not as passionate, and you don't go crazy, like you are saying you should!! you should be going nuts to get the above-mentioned shit done!! you should be playing in a band!!!!! your own fucking band!!!!! you should be making this document the best thing you ever did!!!!!!!!
use spider for the distribution!!!!! duh!!!!!!!!!
anywyay, go fucking crazy!!! you can die any fucking day!!!!!! get this thing going!!!!!!! you have the committee of nations and the record label!!!!!!!! - get clinton!!!!!!!!!
----
stop being vane...just prove results. if you have an ego that really needs to be satisfied, do it the only real way - get things done!!! - have a son also, and take care of business wiht ana, but make a bond forever, even if people make a mistake once or twice in any way...no, it is about fucking forgetting vanity, bu actually no, everything matters? what? but have a baby. she wants a baby. get married and have a baby.. do the marriage license immediately. i am not sure about the public side of things, but definitely do the papers so she can travel. and work.....----
okay, time to go. you know what you just wrote, so see what happens.
love,
mitch

Chapter 21

G-d Symbols

"Symbolic exits, freakish terms."

WHEN REGULAR BUSINESS ACTIVITIES had resumed in New York City, I began to pursue Cedric's list of music industry contacts. It was time justify our $25,000 loan deal. It took me less than a month to narrow it down to six realistic candidates who might be able to assist with getting Khani a record deal. After a few meetings and a few more calls, the six were narrowed down to two—Louis Levin and David Sonnenberg—Cedric's heaviest hitters. Cedric had prepped each of them for my call; both said they were eager to meet.

I met with Louis Levin first. He had recently become Michael Jackson's manager, and had always been Michael Bolton's, the latter with whom he had sold over 50 million records. We met privately in Louis Levin's gold record-adorned offices to discuss how he might be able to help me and his "dear friend" Cedric Kushner find a record deal for Khani Jones. Louis Levin was eccentric and amicable, and we got along well, sharing funny stories about Cedric while we got acquainted. I left him with samples of Khani's music, and we agreed to meet again soon. In our follow-up meeting, Louis Levin told me he had liked Khani's music, which was encouraging feedback from someone of his stature. But he also said that he couldn't do anything for a brand-new reggae artist. I pledged my willingness to enter into any type of partnership and do whatever it took to get Khani a record deal. I said I would accept any reasonable percentage and happily remain in the background—but all to no avail. I then tried some leverage, mentioning Victor DeLeon's name and promising his ongoing participation in this and other joint projects. But Louis Levin had already concluded that breaking out a new artist in the reggae market, was too difficult an undertaking in too small a market to warrant his involvement. I asked for his advice on what to do, since I had no choice but to get Khani that deal! He recommended that Khani "cross over" into the pop market, and casually gave me the contact information for Larry Rudolph, Britney Spears's manager, and Bert Padell, her business manager. I secured a meeting with each of them, but nothing developed for similar reasons—the reggae market was too small for them. There was no reason to meet with Louis Levin again.

Unintentionally saving Cedric's best contact for last, I arranged to meet with David Sonnenberg, to whom I had been introduced by Cedric a few years earlier. (Sonnenberg had produced the Muhammad Ali movie, *When We Were Kings*, and had given Cedric two tickets to its 1997 premiere at the Radio City Music Hall, which I attended alongside (the dozing) Cedric.) On my way to the meeting, I hoped it was serendipitous that David Sonnenberg's brownstone on Riverside Avenue was only a five minute walk from my West 80th apartment.

David and I shared immediate chemistry, as if we could be friends. I told him about myself, Kid Lightning Enterprises, and even The Wave of Peace Foundation. (He asked for a copy of my recently recorded theme song, "Wave of Peace," after I told him that I had first planned to record it on the morning of September 11, before the towers went down.) Then we had a productive conversation about my desperate need to get Khani Jones a record deal, since he was the test case for my investor, Victor DeLeon. I invoked my game of leverage early and with a heavy dose, which seemed to work: David told me that he once managed reggae legend Jimmy Cliff, and had plans to make a movie about Jimmy Cliff and Peter Tosh, two iconic reggae superstars who were second in popularity only to Bob Marley. After seeing Khani's headshot and listening to his music, David Sonnenberg mentioned that the "younger-man" roles for Jimmy Cliff and Peter Tosh were not yet casted, and either might be suitable for Khani. (He didn't want an experienced actor to play these parts, so the option seemed realistic.) While this wouldn't be a traditional record deal, it would be a huge jolt to Khani's career and Kid Lightning's future, sufficient to please DeLeon and entitle Cedric Kushner to keep the $25,000—*Dayenu*! Sonnenberg asked me to bring Khani to his office for a personal introduction at the end of the week.

A few days later, as Khani and I walked from my West 80th apartment to David Sonnenberg's brownstone, Khani expressed skepticism about the movie opportunity because he had never acted. I explained (again) that David didn't want to cast experienced actors for these roles, and had already seen Khani's photo and heard his music. Khani was still incredulous, which I prayed would not turn Sonnenberg off. I suggested that he "start acting now," at least for this meeting. I was hoping that Khani and David would share a similar chemistry as I had with each, and that the Kid Lightning-Khani Jones management duo could become a trio. While I didn't sense the instant love and camaraderie I was hoping for, Khani was cheerful, smiling, and outgoing in the meeting. He had come far in this area, closer to the softer, more trusting Khani I had been waiting for. The three of us discussed the movie, and I made the spontaneous (and leverage-based) decision to re-dangle Victor DeLeon's name: I told David Sonnenberg that if he were to cast Khani in the movie role, Kid Lightning (via Victor DeLeon) would invest in the film, if necessary. I liked my move, and we left his office feeling good.

David Sonnenberg called me Monday morning and invited me back to his brownstone, alone, that same day. I walked outside my apartment and made a right turn, down West 80th, and then across Broadway and West End to Riverside—I was on my victory lap, about to receive the news that I had delivered the fucking goods for Khani Jones and Kid Lightning! But David Sonnenberg told me in the first five minutes of our meeting that Khani was not at all suited for the movie roles of Peter Tosh or Jimmy Cliff. We then discussed Khani's music, where I reiterated my willingness to enter into any reasonable partnership, even if Kid Lightning had to remain anonymous. David said he was not interested in that either, so I asked him why he called me back to his office.

David said he liked *me* and wanted to discuss *me*. He said I was wasting my time as Khani's manager and should focus on my own abilities and projects in larger industries. Then we talked about my investor. David said he could help me "transition" Victor DeLeon out of the reggae market and "season" him into other things. He said that an office was available down the hall in his brownstone, and that Fredda and I should occupy it as Kid Lightning's new home base. His words and offers were tantalizing, and my head was spinning. David Sonnenberg was asking me, Kid Lightning, to set up shop next to him! He saw something special in me! And he also seemed interested in The Wave of Peace Foundation. I wondered, "Was *David Sonnenberg* my partner in peace?"

I was excited. I explained to my dad how well David and I had gotten along, and about his offer to provide office space in his own brownstone to Kid Lightning—an unbelievable opportunity. But my dad didn't see it that way: He asked me how much David wanted to charge for the vacant office. I was embarrassed to tell him that I hadn't asked; I had assumed it would be free in the beginning, until the relationship between he and DeLeon played out. My dad suspected that Sonnenberg was playing his own game of leverage, based on his perception of my impulsivity and abundance of cash. He was selling me a dream for steep rental fees, trying to *separate a fool from his money.* To test his theory, my dad suggested that I ask Sonnenberg to provide the office to Kid Lightning for a three-month trial period, either for free or for a good-faith payment of $1,000 per month. This would enable us to test things out with minimal risk, and if things went well we could then discuss a standard lease. It sounded like a great idea, and I called David to propose the terms.

In my conversation with David, I doubled my dad's proposed numbers and offered him a good-faith payment of $6,000 for the three-month period. David replied deadpan that the rent was $8,000 per month, starting on day one, plus a two-month security deposit. When I hesitated, he acted annoyed that such a small amount of $24,000 was a concern to me. I had taken my game of leverage too far—Sonnenberg clearly thought I had more money than I did. And from his blunt tone, I knew my dad had been right again. I thanked David for the offer but never called him again. He never called me either.

It was mid-December, I had exhausted Cedric's contacts, and I still had no record deal for Khani Jones. It was time to get my $25,000 back. I went to Cedric's office to deliver the bad news and make the request in person, about ten days before his HBO advance check was due to arrive. He was disappointed and surprised that none of his leads had panned out, but said he would stick to our deal and pay me right back. However, he also told me that the HBO advance had been unexpectedly requested by "Sugar" Shane Mosley's camp. He would have to pay me back on the night of the actual fight, January 26, six weeks away. Cedric had already held my money for three and a half months, and six more weeks of this secret arrangement made me nervous. But it still left me with enough slack to reimburse the $25,000 to Kid Lightning without DeLeon gaining any knowledge of the deal. (And regardless of our signed contract, from which Cedric was now changing the terms, I had no choice but to accept his offer.)

As the Shane Mosley fight approached, I heard rumors that Cedric owed money to other people too, and these creditors might also be coming to the fight to get paid. Then I heard another rumor that Cedric had recently bounced a few checks. I became concerned that I was not first in line to get repaid. I wasn't *too* worried, though—because I was holding Cedric's $90,000 Rolex. To reassure myself, I brought the watch to the jeweler I had bought my Breitling from, and asked for a quick appraisal. He examined it for a few minutes and told me it wasn't worth more than $2,000 to him! He explained that nobody would buy such an ugly watch, custom-designed for an over-the-top individual with gaudy taste. He said the only way he could justify offering even $2,000 was to disassemble the Rolex for parts and sell the jewels, which were shaven down to fit the watch and of lower grade than Cedric thought. The plummeting value of my collateral was scary news, which I kept to myself.

I still trusted Cedric's promise to repay the $25,000 at the fight. I also had my friend Ron Rizzo, who had replaced me as Cedric's assistant. Now in his third year at CKP and fully in the swing of things, Ron remembered and appreciated the help I had given him when I interviewed and selected him as Cedric's new assistant. As I used to do, Ron now cut the checks at the fights. He couldn't force Cedric to pay me, but he promised that if Cedric authorized the payment, he would attempt to subtly postdate Cedric's other creditors' checks by a day, in order to allow me to get to the bank first. It scared me that "getting to the bank first" might matter, but I was happy to hear Ron's offer. He was sticking to the promise he made, years ago, to "not let me down."

Cedric gave me a great seat at Madison Square Garden on January 26, but things did not go well for his champion, "Sugar" Shane Mosley. In the second round, he and Vernon Forrest inadvertently clashed heads, which cut Mosley's face. Mosley was knocked down twice, for the first two times in his career; and Vernon Forrest won the decision, taking away the championship belt and handing Mosley his first loss ever. As I witnessed this nightmarish scenario unfold, I feared it would devastate Cedric, killing his mood *and* my chances of getting paid that night. But after the fight, Cedric was gracious and smiling, because he had gotten paid by HBO and was already guaranteed a rematch for Mosley—another big payday for CKP. He explained that Shane Mosley's reputation was fully intact, since everyone knew that the clashing of heads caused the knockdowns and affected the outcome. He authorized Ron Rizzo to cut me the check for $25,000. I hugged both of them, relieved that this mini-adventure was over. On Monday morning, before Chase Bank opened, I was waiting outside their doors on 79th and Broadway. I deposited the check at 9:01 a.m.

I received a call from the bank three days later, informing me that the check had bounced. I called Cedric, who sounded surprised and apologetic. He said "bear with me" until March 1, when the Mosley event's foreign sales revenues would reach his account. March 1 was a full month away and dangerously close to when our taxes were due, but I had no choice but to agree to this further delay. I called Cedric three weeks later to schedule the pickup, and he invited me to his East Hampton house that weekend to play tennis, hang out, and get the money. I did not want to drive that weekend from Manhattan to East Hampton, since I was scheduled to make the same drive a week later to Greg's place in Amagansett. I also knew that hanging out with Cedric would be an all-day event. But I needed that money back in my account.

I showed up at his house in East Hampton on the appointed day and played tennis with Cedric Kushner, who moved pretty well for a man of 350 pounds. I won the first set 6-2, and he won the second—by my design. We walked up the hill to his house and sat down, where I reverted back to playing the role of Cedric's perfect assistant: Answering his phones, getting him Tab sodas and muffins, and listening to him hold court on the phone. Just a few years earlier, it had taken me a great deal of time and courage to get *out* of Cedric's lair—now it felt like I had never left! I was sucked right back into the role of boxing groupie, when hanging out socially and pampering Cedric was my job, and pleasing him was my only goal. I pinched my leg in frustration as I waited for Cedric to bring up the subject of my money; and when he didn't, I did. He apologized again and said, "I thought I had already mentioned that I needed one more week." He suggested that I come to his Manhattan office the following Wednesday to get it. I had no choice but to agree. I had driven two-and-a-half hours from Manhattan and was headed right back—without my $25,000.

On Wednesday, I showed up at Cedric's New York City office. The phones were ringing off the hook, and Cedric was alone that day, without Ron Rizzo. But Mitch Winston, the perpetual assistant and boxing groupie was back, playing the role with a smile. I answered Cedric's phones and explained to the familiar people who called, "No, I'm really not back with CKP!" I suspected that Cedric, who enjoyed my presence and was in need of administrative help that day, would have let me spend the entire day in his office, so I brought up the subject of my money first. He told me that the bank manager had fucked up *this* time, and swore "up and down" that he would have my money within the week. He invited me back to East Hampton the following Saturday, promising that the money would be waiting, even if he had to take it out of his own personal safe. I wondered why he didn't do that *last* weekend, but I believed him; and I had already planned to stop by Greg's house in Amagansett that weekend, only five minutes away from Cedric's house, which softened the blow. Cedric also told me to bring my tennis racquet. I could only laugh, albeit barely, at his *chutzpah*: He was milking the social aspect of our deal, a different form of leverage, without feeling any guilt for his delays of repayment. I marveled again at how easy it was to get roped back into Cedric's world of boxing groupies, and how difficult it was to get out.

While Cedric walked with me to the elevator outside his office, he suggested nonchalantly that I sell his Rolex, subtract my $25,000 from the amount of the sale, and pay *him* the difference on Saturday in East Hampton. At that point, I had no choice but to tell him it was only worth $2,000, giving up my (perceived) leverage of collateral worth $90,000. Cedric lost his cool. "TWO THOUSAND DOLLARS?! ARE YOU FUCKING NUTS?! DON'T SELL IT!! JUST COME TO MY HOUSE SATURDAY WITH THE WATCH AND I'LL PAY YOU THE 25K!" We shook hands and smiled, but I feared that moment was a sign of a deal going bad—fast.

Cedric had now held my money for almost seven months, far from the spirit of our initial deal. And with Kid Lightning's taxes due in a week, my grace period was over. I instructed my accountant to prepare our taxes and ignore the $25,000 loan, assuring him the money would be back in the account that week. He wasn't willing to play my accounting games, and said he needed to see actual bank statements. He suggested that we file for a six-month IRS extension, and offered to call Victor DeLeon and take the blame for this delay. I accepted, which saved me from a tough phone call and also bought me some time.

On Saturday I showed up at Cedric's—without my tennis racquet—I was all business. He was sitting alone at his kitchen table, half-dozing, waiting for the phone to ring or something to happen. He was glad for my company and greeted me with a smile. On these quiet weekends, away from the excitement of the office and the adoration of his boxing groupies, Cedric always seemed lonely; and I felt badly for him. So when he offered to lend me his spare tennis racquet so we could play, I said yes—but I won both sets 6-1. When we got back inside his house, I inquired about the $25,000.

He told me that the funds he expected had not arrived, but to come with him upstairs to the safe he kept in his bedroom, a metal cube about two feet by three feet. I watched as he fiddled with the combination lock but couldn't get the safe open. He said he didn't understand why "the fucking code wasn't working," and let me try too—with the same result. He said he would call the company on Monday to get it opened, and he would hand me the cash on Tuesday.

I lost my cool and raised my voice. "This is totally unfair, Cedric! You are putting me in a bad position with my investor! What's going on?!" Then he got angry and raised *his* voice louder. "I TOLD YOU TO COME BACK TUESDAY AND I WILL PAY YOU!! WHAT THE FUCK DO YOU WANT TO DO, TAKE THE GODDAMN SAFE WITH YOU?!" It was a pivotal moment, where credibility was everything, and I *pulled a Vickers*. I said, "Yeah, I *do* want to take the safe," and I walked toward it. My heart was racing, and Cedric was red-faced and breathing heavily. He stepped in between me and the safe—we were face to face. Then he said, "HOLD ON, HOLD ON! JUST WAIT A SECOND!! GO DOWNSTAIRS INTO THE KITCHEN!" As I walked downstairs, I heard Cedric enter another room. Five minutes later he reappeared, holding $25,000 in cash and handing it to me. I gave him his Rolex, thanked him, hugged him, and apologized for losing my cool. (Cedric was so charismatic and compelling that I felt guilty and apologized profusely for taking back my own money!) As I walked toward my car, I thought more about Cedric. I was positive that if he hadn't paid me that day, or even that month, he would have eventually made good on his debt. But I needed it *that* day, and I got it—thanks to my *pulling a Vickers* of the most unexpected kind. I drove through Cedric's gate, out of his driveway, and toward Amagansett. That symbolized my official and permanent exit from the boxing business.

The reason I needed to be at Greg's house in Amagansett that day was to meet a second home inspector, who was also a construction expert, to get another opinion on the house's condition and a rough appraisal of its value. We had tried to control the property by offering the owner $500,000, regardless of its poor condition. When we finally got him to respond, (which took almost a year and only happened because Greg ran into him coincidentally,) the owner said that the house was in fine condition and he wouldn't sell it for less than $700,000. This conversation had placed the deal on life support. This follow-up inspection, which cost $250, would be more thorough than the first, which had been a favor to my dad and free of charge. I already knew that we weren't going to get the house for much less than $700,000, so if this second estimate didn't come in much higher than that, the deal would be dead. (With the East 26th Street purchase, I had established high standards with The Deerman, who was looking for another deal. But I wouldn't approach him unless I had "control" of the property under "freakishly" good terms.)

With the $25,000 cash stuffed under my seat, I drove over to Greg's house to meet the aforementioned inspector. I was hoping he would have good news, since my previous rationale for buying the house still applied, and now carried more urgency: With my hopes of finding Khani a record deal dimming, this house was not just Kid Lightning's potential spiritual home base and my last-ditch effort to involve Greg—it was now a necessary purchase to hedge my bet on the reggae industry. It took the inspector less than fifteen minutes to show me that the house was in "tear-down condition," worse than my dad's friend had reported, and it would be cheaper and smarter to build anew than to renovate. The deal for Greg's house was dead.

The Deerman was looking for another opportunity because of what had recently happened with our $47,500 apartment on East 26th Street in New York. After living there for two years, the

Fredda-ship decided to move to a larger apartment, and we put the apartment up for sale. We were flooded with calls, and based on lack of research, I committed an amateurish mistake and accepted an offer well below market value, an error which Lee had to lay out $10,000 to fix.) We sold the place for $120,000, which was nearly a $60,000 profit, half of which was mine.

Instead of letting my profits ride with The Deerman into our next deal, I decided to use my $30,000 profit to reimburse the Kid Lightning account for my ill-advised withdrawal of $23,000. This righteousness was only temporary, because I then reconsidered and told The Deerman I would leave my profit in the kitty with him to use toward our next deal. My change of heart was based partially on entitlement: After I had taken out the $23,000, I had made things worse by declaring that I wouldn't take a salary from Kid Lightning until we earned those "big revenues." So even though Kid Lightning was funded, I was living off my credit cards, of which I had already built up $45,000 in *new* debt. This was personal debt, in my name, double my ill-advised $23,000 withdrawal that started this cycle! And since most of that new $45,000 debt was personal expenses, which I could easily have repaid if I were drawing a salary, I decided that I really didn't owe Kid Lightning money—actually, Kid Lightning owed *me* money!

If I had practiced proper accounting and taken a modest salary from the beginning, or when I got my second chance, Kid Lightning's books would have looked good, and everything would have been fine. But I hadn't: Business and personal expenses were now commingled in my checking *and* credit accounts. Our books were fucked. But there was no benefit to coming clean now, because that risked DeLeon's halting of *all* Kid Lightning operations—before I had a chance to fix this mess and make the money back. I continued to live off my credit cards and planned to come clean when we submitted our taxes, hoping that the "big revenues" from Khani's record deal would come first and save me. But it didn't, and as April 15 approached, I had begun to prepare my confession—which would have to rival Lincon's Gettysburg Address—to win over the fiscally conservative Victor DeLeon. My solace was that my speech would be backed up by real numbers, which would show DeLeon that even though I had practiced bad accounting, I had never stolen or spent excessively—if I had just paid myself a salary, none of this would have occurred. Thanks to the reprieve from the IRS extension, inadvertently caused by Cedric's delays, my Gettysburg Address could wait. I now had six more months to achieve wild success or go down in flames. Such all-or-nothing conditions always motivated my best work.

With the deal to buy Greg's Amagansett house now dead, I pulled out of his driveway, my second symbolic exit of the day: The business relationship between Kid Lightning and Gregory Laurence would never materialize; his Amagansett house would not be our spiritual home base. I doubled back onto Montauk Highway and headed toward Luz's Deli for some caffeine to fuel my ride to Manhattan. I spotted a FOR SALE sign in a driveway down the street and drove in to take a look. The vibe of the property came over me and filled me, reminiscent of my blissful trance from the great-times-great era. I yelled out loud, "This house is mine!"

I called the broker the next day: He told me that the house had hit the market two days earlier, and the price was $495,000—a steal for an Amagansett house of this size, in this condition, and on that piece of land. He added that it also had a "poor man's ocean view"—across the highway and over some houses, but the Atlantic Ocean was visible, albeit barely, from the deck. I asked the broker to fax me a survey of the property, and when I got it, I yelled out again, "This house is mine!"—because outlining the driveway in black marker was my own personal "G-d symbol"—a shape that resembled the letter P but more slanted and colored in. This had symbolized G-d's image to me for as long as I could remember, yet never knew why. I had included this symbol in countless classroom doodles dating back to my childhood, and most recently in both the Kid Lightning and Wave of Peace logos. My G-d symbol had been corroborated (for me) during my six months in Israel, when I learned that according to some sages, when G-d revealed His likeness to Moses, He only showed the back of His head; and He was wearing *tefillin* (special boxes and straps worn on the head and arms to demonstrate love for G-d). In my mind, the top of the P depicted G-d's head, bound by the *tefillin* box, and its long slanted stem represented the *tefillin* strap.

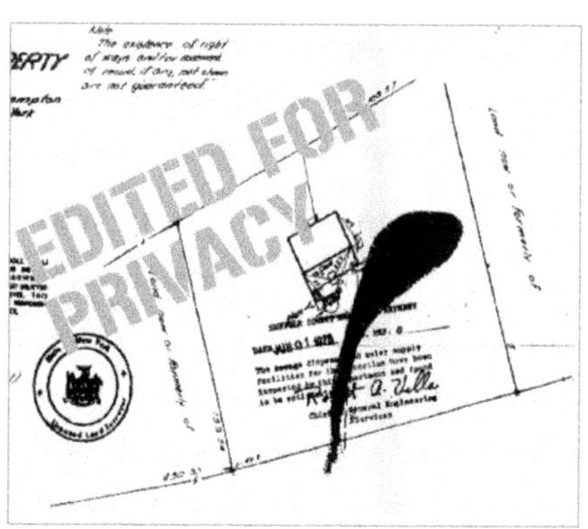

But regardless of any spirituality or visions of G-d, I had to gain "contractual control" of the house at "freakishly" good terms before approaching Lee Deerman. I put in an offer for $400,000. The owner countered at $450,000, and we settled on a price of $445,000. I called The Deerman to secure his partnership in the deal, and it was another easy sell—almost, but not quite as big a steal as the $47,500 apartment. We used all of our East 26th Street profits for the down payment, Lee added another $30,000, and I got approved for another 10% mortgage. The house really *was* mine! (And The Deerman's.)

Chapter 22

Shy Away

"Honey and Hammers"

MY TIME with Edna had been morally questionable, and had ended poorly. But I remembered her and the distinct vibe I had felt around her. I was Eddie Wilson, my best self, who spoke about *my* music, not Khani's. My subsequent dealings with David Sonnenberg, while also unsuccessful, left me with similar thoughts and reminded me of my old vows: I had to be the talent, not the manager. This realization gave me the encouragement—and living off my credit cards without a salary gave me the extra entitlement—to use some more Kid Lightning funds to record *my* own full album. I took inventory and counted nine original songs that I had written (not including "Jessica Marlene Ridgeway" and "Jack Maggan Lukin"). I had been listening a lot to the Bruce Springsteen album *Darkness on the Edge of Town*; I was feeling Springsteen's music more than any other artist those days. So for my album's tenth song, I decided to cover "Factory," Bruce's tribute to the working man—it would be *my* tribute to *my* dad.

While I was now confident with my ability to communicate properly with musicians and engineers, I knew I needed a professional producer for my album. I came upon one who had recently produced a Springsteen cover album and done a good job with it. He was Jim Sampas, from Lowell, Massachusetts. I tracked

Jim down, and we had a great opening conversation. I explained my background, Kid Lightning's funding status, and my management relationship with the reggae artist, Khani Jones. (Jim said he also had experience producing reggae, if we needed help there too. I stressed that I was calling about *my* music, and I preferred to keep things separate.) I told Jim about the artists I was inspired by and the feel I wanted for my music. He asked me to make a rough recording of my ten songs, solo acoustic, and send it to him—along with my detailed notes for each song's desired instrumentation and vibe.

After Jim received my package, we decided to meet at a diner in Hartford, about halfway between New York City and Boston. Jim seemed kind, with a gentle demeanor, and was a good listener. He said he liked my songs, saw "real honesty" in them, and thought we could make a good record together. He asked me if I had a band or particular musicians I planned to work with, which I didn't. He told me he enjoyed an excellent relationship with many A-level musicians; if they liked my songs, and Jim was the producer, they could be hired at Jim's *inner circle* rates. His list of A-level musicians was more impressive than I could have imagined. They weren't A-level, they were *A++-World-Class* Level: Peter Gabriel's bassist, Tony Levin; Simon & Garfunkel's guitarist, Dave Brown; Bruce Springsteen's cellist, Jane Scarpantoni; Mary Chapin Carpenter's guitarist, Duke Levine; Fairport Convention's drummer, Dave Mattacks; and more.

Jim asked if I had a recording studio in mind, and again I said no. My only preference was to record outside the city, which was why I didn't use *Dan Wise's House of Love.* Jim told me about a major label quality music studio in North Brookfield, Massachusetts called Long View Farms, a former dairy farm that sat on hundreds of acres. Its two main barns had been converted to studios, and most artists lived there while recording. Jim said their equipment and house engineer were top-of-the-line. It sounded like a wonderful place to record, especially when Jim told me that The Rolling Stones, Aerosmith, Cat Stevens and other greats had recorded and rehearsed there, and over 200 Grammy-winning recordings had been made there! Everything seemed to be coming together.

I told my dad about these developments, which I was excited about, and his reaction, again, was skeptical. He warned me that Jim might be more interested in my investor and money than my music. I knew my dad could be right, since he usually was in these areas, and that Jim could be overstating his affinity for my songs for business reasons. But Jim really seemed to like them, and the inner circle rates he was charging for his services and world-famous musicians were reasonable. I admitted to my dad that Jim *had* alluded to a few other projects he was working on, and he was possibly encouraged to do so when I told him I had an investor. But I told my dad not to worry—*I* was playing the leverage game too, holding off discussions on any future projects with Jim until after we finished *my* album. That would motivate Jim to do his best work. I hired Jim Sampas as producer, and we booked Long View Farms and his A++ musicians to record it 30 days later.

Once again, my dad proved prophetic: One week before we were scheduled to begin recording, Jim called me and said he had something else to discuss: Three other projects he was involved with had all stalled because the record label that was financing them, named Eisen and Pageant, "ran out of money." When Jim said the words "ran out of money," I cursed my dad's wisdom, tuned Jim out, and considered cancelling everything. He was not producing my album because he loved my songs, but rather to get an investor! But when Jim elaborated on one of the three stalled albums, I tuned him back in again—fully and fast. Jim said that his aunt Helen had been married to Jack Kerouac when he passed away. That made his aunt Helen the primary heir to the Jack Kerouac estate and provided Jim rare access to some Kerouac-related treasures. While searching around his aunt's attic one day, Jim uncovered a screenplay written by Jack Kerouac in the 1960s. **It was the only screenplay Jack Kerouac had ever written, never released or seen by the public.** Jim also had a unique concept for the project: Release the original screenplay with new illustrations and include a CD of it being read by beat-generation celebrities over an original musical score.

I couldn't believe what I was hearing! It was one of those fantastic stories, reminiscent of *Antique Road Show,* when something of great value, never before seen by the public, gets dug up in someone's attic after fifty years—and Jim had the legal rights to release it! I had never been a Jack Kerouac fan; even his iconic *On the Road* didn't resonate for me. I blamed that now on my usual impatience, since I had just skimmed it the night before it was due. I couldn't ignore the prestige and financial benefits that might accrue to Kid Lightning for being associated with the Jack Kerouac name. I told Jim I was interested, but kept my cool, and my game of leverage. I asked him if we could table the discussion until we finished my album, but to (please) not approach anyone else about it until then. I didn't ask Jim about the other stalled projects or why the record label backed out of their financial commitment. I would inquire later, *after* he had "focused, focused, focused" on my album—although I admitted to my dad, who wholeheartedly agreed, that Jim had just played a damn good hand in *his own* game of leverage!

When I arrived at Long View Farms, I was awed by its lush, seemingly endless terrain, clean air, and gorgeous horses to which I fed apples every day. I was in paradise, hours from the city, with one goal—to record *my* music. I was the artist, not the manager! Every A++ musician Jim brought in was professional, down-to-earth, and superbly talented. They had listened to my solo acoustic recording and read my notes, but had also come with their own perspectives. And they weren't flashy showmen—they were true pros. With Khani's recent recording session at *Dan's House of Love* fresh in my mind, I had come to Long View Farms hypersensitive about keeping the musicians feeling respected and encouraged, but Jim's style eased my fears. He had a way of giving the musicians the right amount of creative leeway without losing control of the session. He used the expression, "You get more with honey than you do with a hammer." He was right—and the players were so good that they didn't need much of either.

Every morning we woke up to the aromas of strong coffee, crippled with cream from local cows, and homemade muffins and omelets prepared by the studio chef. Our sessions started at 11 a.m. and would often last until midnight. I learned that week that the more experienced and successful the musicians, the less their need and desire to show off or dominate. They were tasteful and classy, even understated—and they never had to rehearse. They would sit down, discuss the vibe for the track, and go right for usable takes. We recorded my album old-school, analog on two-inch tape, and were able to achieve a warm, natural room sound. The vibe of the sessions was intimate and relaxed, but I wasn't. To ease my nerves before singing and playing with these musicians, I smoked marijuana—all day. (When smoking so much in one day, the law of diminishing returns sets in. There is no way to get high anymore; but I kept trying.)

By the end of the second day, the rhythm section (drum and bass parts), as well as my rough vocals and acoustic guitar parts were completed. I was happy to then "get out of the way" and let the musicians layer the tracks with guitars, strings, and piano. As they did, I sat on the other side of the glass with Jim and listened to each song, many times. I was frustrated that my vocal performances never sounded as good in the playback as I thought they would—never as good as they *felt* when I recorded them. These sentiments mirrored how I recently felt after watching some of the videos of myself, high on marijuana, playing and singing alone at West 80th over the past few years: The playback—the reality—was always a let-down. Jim reassured me that I would have a chance to sing my vocal parts again later that week, which was comforting. When the recording sessions would end each night, I would exit the studio and walk right upstairs to my bedroom, scribble a few notes, and fall asleep—motionless until the next day of music heaven—as the artist, not the manager.

don't hold it smoke!!

don't smoke too much!!

WRITE ABOUT:
You once thought Khani was the next John Lennon, but it's you!!

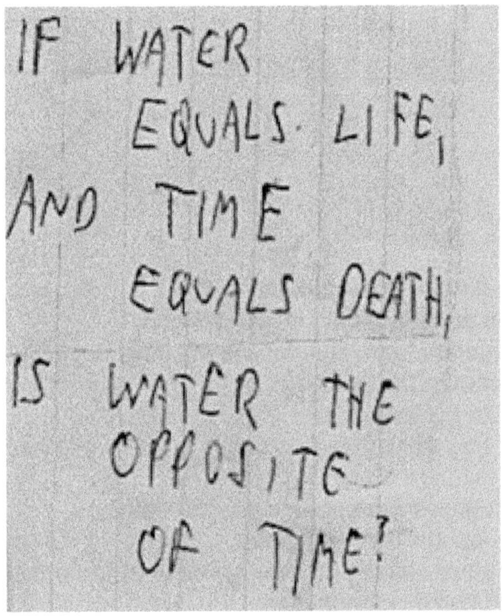

Jim told me mid-week that *Living Color,* led by guitar legend Vernon Reid, was recording in Long View's adjacent studio. Vernon Reid had the reputation for being one of the best guitar players ever, and *Rolling Stone* Magazine has listed him in their top 100 players of all time. Jim had worked with Vernon Reid before, and the two had gotten along well. I fantasized how cool it would be if we could persuade Vernon Reid to lay down a guitar part on one of my songs, and Jim and I agreed that "Shy Away" would be the one. Jim suggested inviting Vernon Reid to listen to the track that night—and if Reid had a good reaction, Jim would make him an offer of "a few bucks" to lay down a guitar part. I didn't know how much "a few bucks" was to Vernon Reid, and was pleasantly surprised when Jim said $250 should be enough. I handed him $350—because I *wanted* this. Due to anything unforeseen, legal or personal, Jim decided it would be better if I were not present when he made the offer to Vernon Reid, who had agreed to stop by at midnight after he finished his session with *Living Color.*

And soon it *was* midnight, time for me to make my exit. I thought I heard Vernon Reid enter the studio as I faded to sleep.

Shy Away

I was walking alone in the dark.
Wasn't thinking 'bout my latest dreams,
I was thinking about, the dust in my body burning.
And you couldn't even begin,
To relate to my passions within.
But you remember that I seldomly tried to explain.

And I remember when I saw you that night,
You came up and you said hello.
Then we were talking by the lightness of the ocean breeze.
And the butterfly in your hair,
Gave my sanity a scare,
I knew I saw it rise up and fly freedom into the air

Chorus:
Shy away my lady.
Put your head down for a while.
Let your trembling feelings,
In my hands now subside.

You lay down on my pillow,
And you cry, cry, cry.
Allow your battered spirit,
In my arms to revive.

To your homeland in a couple of days,
Your mother's waiting birds of grace.
She's sleeping with the photo when
the dreams come take her away.

As they gaze upon your countenance shine,
They look into the eyes of thine.
They'll throw away the shrouds
of their previously fearing designs.

(Chorus)

I awoke the following morning and headed to the kitchen, where Jim was already sipping his coffee. He said that Vernon Reid had liked "Shy Away" and laid down a guitar part for it. I rushed to the studio to listen. The song had a surreal vibe, a trippy dreamlike texture, as did the entire moment: I was listening to myself play and sing "Shy Away," my favorite original song, alongside Vernon Reid, Tony Levin, and Dave Mattacks!

The week at Long View Farms was a great success, as well as a four-day follow-up mixing session there a few weeks later. I listened to the songs while I drove back to New York City. The music sounded great, but my vocal performances, even though I had been given an opportunity to re-do them, still disappointed me. I decided to try again, for a third time, at *Dan Wise's House of Love,* where I could take my time on each song in a less-pressured environment. I improved my vocal performances in this attempt, although I remained perplexed and frustrated by the unbridgeable gap between how I felt when I was singing, or how I *thought* I sounded, versus how I *actually* sounded in playback. But the album was tracked and mixed—it existed.

The only remaining step was to have it mastered. For this we enlisted another of Jim's contacts, Greg Calbi, a very cool guy and arguably the world's top mastering engineer. Greg Calbi's studio walls were adorned with copies of CDs he had mastered, which seemed to include every major artist—Bob Dylan, The Rolling Stones, The Ramones, etc. He also had a unique collection of large-framed concert photos, but taken from the stage, which depicted the perspective of the musicians looking at the faces of their riveted and adoring fans. I spent the whole day with Greg Calbi, who made my album sound more lush and satisfying. It seemed to improve every time he touched a knob. He said he liked the record and was curious to see how it would be "received in the market." I couldn't believe someone of his caliber was speaking about my music getting "received in the market." Soon I was holding my completed album, *Right Back*, and listening to it in my apartment, over and over and very loud, through good headphones. I was fully immersed in my own music and it felt great.

As thrilled as I was about my music, I couldn't rejoice publicly because Khani had no record deal. And with no promising leads, we couldn't wait around. It was time to make another move. We decided that the best strategy was to complete Khani's full-length album too. We had four album-quality songs from *Dan's House of Love* and needed eight more. The only negative feedback we had received on the first four songs, which wasn't much, was a recommendation that Khani "cross over" from roots reggae to a younger, more electronic sound, similar to the style of Shaggy or Sean Paul—the two biggest reggae stars to have crossed over into the pop market. These critics also suggested a "more risqué" subject matter to further satisfy this younger demographic, the largest buyers of music.

Shaggy and Sean Paul, like other pop stars, sang to pre-made tracks, not live musicians, which to me felt less authentic. And a "more risqué" direction for Khani concerned me, not just because it wasn't my taste, but also because the DeLeons were conservative, religious people, and I didn't want to turn them off with vulgar content. But both Louis Levin and David Sonnenberg had said that the reggae market was too small to make money, so crossing over to the pop market made sense. Khani liked the idea and assured me that we could do this "without going too far"—without sacrificing the moral and positive undertones of his music. We also had to ensure that these next four songs, which would be accompanied by electronic music, would blend well with the first four, which had been recorded with live musicians.

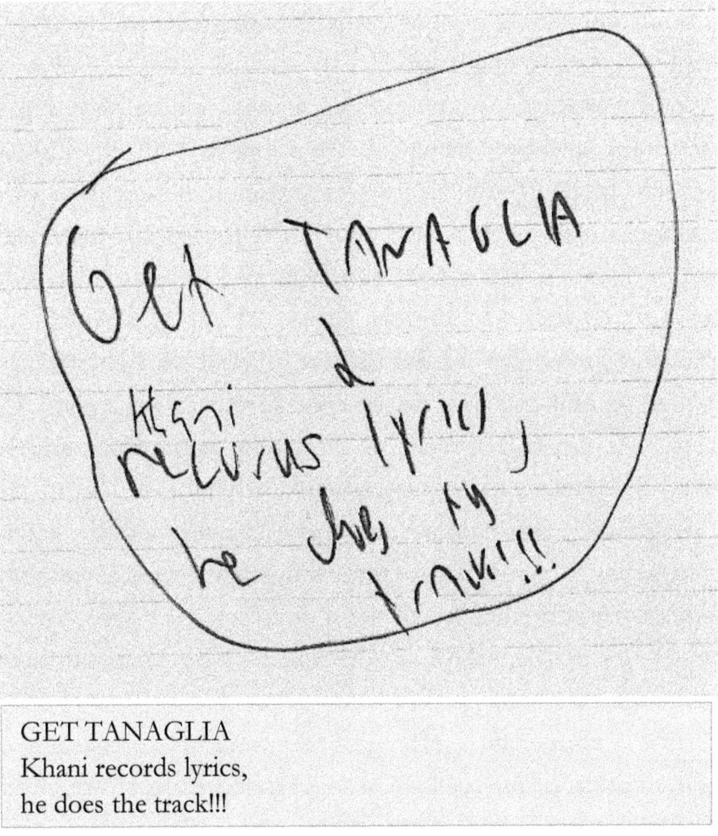

GET TANAGLIA
Khani records lyrics,
he does the track!!!

To make this happen, we once again needed the right producer. I thought about a club hero to Greg Laurence and me: Danny Tenaglia. I visualized thousands of music lovers in those incredible all-night clubs, going nuts to Khani Jones' vocals over a Tenaglia beat. To me, this represented huge crossover potential and a unique possibility. I tried hard to contact Tenaglia but was unsuccessful, so our search continued. Along the way we met Raffi, a veteran *ghost producer* who produced tracks for Shaggy and other big stars. Ghost producers create musical tracks and sell them for money upfront, often foregoing album credit and sales royalties. (So they are usually not household names, even if their tracks become hits.) But for this project, Raffi was not looking to be a ghost producer; he wanted cash in advance *and* album credit with a standard producer royalty, which we agreed to in advance.

We visited Raffi's studio in Long Island, and he played us some of the tracks he was working on. They sounded current and catchy. Khani said he had the perfect lyrics and melodies for four of them in particular. We made a deal with Raffi to custom-fit those four tracks to Khani's lyrics and melodies, and to match up Khani's verses and choruses to the transitions of the tracks. It sounded simple, and I was glad we didn't have to deal with lateness, power struggles, or musicians' sensitive egos for these sessions. I looked forward to a stress-free week in the studio while Raffi and Khani tweaked the tracks and prepared them for Khani to sing on. But we still had drama: As Khani became more familiar with the tracks, he offered a few suggestions to fine-tune them, such as removing a certain instrument that he thought didn't fit the vibe, or adding more of something else that he liked. This changed the vibe between the two men. Raffi, a veteran producer for over 25 years, did not appreciate Khani's suggestions regarding the instrumentation of his tracks. He said he had expected to alter their lengths and transitions, but not their sounds.

Khani and I were prepared for this conflict; we had become more skilled in how to get what we needed in the studio. We were soft and yielding when necessary, and firm when necessary too. (Khani's efforts to be heard creatively were also aided by the fact that I hadn't yet paid Raffi for the tracks, which preserved our leverage in the most important area.) Our collective efforts yielded four more complete, album-ready songs, which sounded youthful, blended well with the first four songs, and gave us that "cross over" dimension "without going too far." Khani's vocal skills had also improved since his first recording; he told me he had been working hard on this. We got the music we wanted. And in the process, Khani and I became a stronger, closer, and better team.

But then publishing issues, our new nemesis, resurfaced! Khani and Raffi disagreed on what percentages of the four songs each should own. The crux of their disagreement was similar to the one Khani had with Shawinza. Both Raffi and Shawinza attributed half of a song's publishing to the instrumentation, which they supplied, and the other half to the lyrics, which Khani supplied. So both producers thought they should own approximately 50% of the songs they helped to build. On both occasions, Khani pointed out that he not only came with the lyrics, but also the melodies; so there weren't just two parts of a song, words and music, but three: Words, *melody*, and music. During our previous dispute with Shawinza, we had corroborated Khani's contention that there are three parts of a song, not two, with our (expensive) lawyer. That education and experience gave us the confidence to remain firm with Raffi and finalize the deal, but just like it had with Shawinza, it destroyed our relationship with Raffi too. On our way back to the city, Khani and I laughed about this repeating cycle of musicians and producers who at first seemed like saviors, even messiahs, but were soon tarnished with drama, attitude or entitlement—never to be seen or worked with by us again.

I dropped Khani off at his home in the Bronx and headed back to West 80th, where I took a big bong hit and listened to his eight songs together. I enjoyed each song individually, but I wasn't fully immersed in them collectively, as a unit. There was something missing, a certain musical glue, that would turn those songs into an album and bring the listener to the point of full immersion. Stylistically, I had wanted Khani's music to veer toward the "stoner vibe"—based on roots reggae with the obligatory one-drop beat and skank guitar, (exemplified in Bob Marley's iconic "Stir it Up"), but fused with a lush, trippy *wall of sound*, created by guitar and keyboard work that could evoke Pink Floyd and the Grateful Dead. At *Dan Wise's House of Love*, Khani's music approached this vibe on one song, "Ancient Spirits," and I had wanted much more of that. I felt that slower songs with more somber beats would suit this trippy style. Khani had been interested in fusing rock and reggae too, but using harder and faster beats, highlighted by sharp guitar work and shredding solos, a la Jimi Hendrix or Led Zeppelin. Khani was the only reggae artist I ever met who didn't smoke weed, and I half-joked to him that this was the reason for our divergence in musical preference. He smiled, but still wouldn't take a hit. (I didn't push him, nor did I ever smoke in his presence—I knew from our recent conversations that not everything should be brought together.) But joking aside, I was concerned with our divergence in musical taste, because we needed four more songs to finish Khani's album. This was my last chance to get the specific vibe I had wanted since the beginning.

The secluded environment of Long View Farms and its spiritual atmosphere had reflected positively on *my* album, and I thought Khani (and his music) would thrive there too. I talked to him about this, and he was receptive to leaving town to record. He also showed a new willingness to move toward the "stoner vibe" I desired, which pleased me. Then Khani suggested that since he and I now worked so well together in the studio, *we* should co-produce his last four songs together! I wasn't expecting this offer, but I was touched that he respected my musical taste, and I accepted. (I joked that he only wanted to produce with *me* because I wouldn't come after his publishing rights.)

For this last four-song session we needed live musicians, and decided to start afresh. By then, I had rethought some of our prior conflicts with musicians, and now assigned most of the blame to *them*, not to Khani: While Khani's "softer side" was still developing, he always relied on logic and fairness to resolve his conflicts, with the good of the music his only concern—and the professionally trained musicians and producers we hired, who were older and more experienced, had lost their spirits and their cools. This hurt the music and ruined the relationships. As co-producers, Khani and

I would have to manage these fragile personalities properly and effectively—the end result (and all that mattered) was the music. I was planning to use ten percent *less honey* than usual, to prevent entitlement, and Khani was ready to use ten percent *less hammer*, to preserve inspiration.

To avoid the tedious process of auditioning individual musicians, which would mean building a band from scratch that would lack chemistry, I found a tight pre-existing reggae band. (Their Jewish dreadlocked keyboardist from Armonk, NY had once taken Fredda to her high school prom!) Fredda knew he currently played in a respected reggae band and had suggested I contact him. We auditioned the band by holding a (paid) rehearsal with Khani as their lead singer, and they were able to play the four songs we selected. It sounded solid, so we paid them for their time and scheduled a follow-up. In their second session, when Khani began to make his opinions and preferences more known, predictable ego issues resurfaced. Khani's youth and direct nature were being misconstrued as arrogance. But I was the co-producer, so this time I stayed involved, acting as the perfect buffer for *both* sides. Khani knew what I was doing, and neither of us cared about ego or anything else besides the music. We were working well together, like honey and hammer, and Khani and I were sufficiently comfortable to hire the band for the future recording session.

When I contacted studios to book the recording session, the owners and engineers asked who the producers were. I answered that it would be Khani and me. But after I said this a few times, I grew uneasy about going into the studio without a more technically experienced producer. We needed someone who would be better at dealing with the sound engineer, especially when it came time to mix the tracks, and who would also be better at drawing certain performances out of the musicians. I knew the studio owners agreed. Just as having an investor lent credibility to my business dealings, having a professional producer lent credibility to a recording session. Then Jim Sampas called—he always had good timing. I hadn't considered him for this project, because I was sticking to my decision to keep everything related to my music (and foundation) separate from Khani's music. I let go of this artificial wall after Jim and I spoke. I realized that if Jim could replace me as Khani's co-producer, it would add experience and credibility to the production team; and with Jim's style, Khani's opinions wouldn't get pushed aside—they would remain equals. And if Khani and Jim unexpectedly clashed in any way, I could act as an effective buffer between them. Most important to me, I would maintain the musical influence I wanted, or needed, to guarantee the lush, trippy vibe that Khani and I had agreed on for this upcoming session.

I set up a meeting for the three of us at our trusty Hartford Diner, and it went well. Jim described his reggae experience and studio style. Khani recounted some of our prior frustrations: Producers taking over too much, publishing conflicts, and musicians' egos getting damaged by sincere suggestions made only for the good of the music. Jim assured Khani that this would not happen with him on board. We also discussed the unpunctuality of some musicians and the invisible air of tension they seemed to carry when they finally arrived at the studio, caused by New York City's stressful transportation system. By the time the band had warmed up and found into a groove, the (expensive) sessions were half over.

At that point, Jim was comfortable enough to suggest recording at Long View Farms, as I was hoping he would, and Khani was all-in. We made a deal with Jim and the studio, and booked the session. We had the band. We had the studio. Jim and Khani would be the co-producers. And I was *the manager*, the perfect buffer, content with my role and excited about the team I had built. I believed that magic would happen at Long View Farms. And I was right: These sessions were the climax of my management experience with Khani, the most satisfying and enjoyable part of our journey together. As a team, we had improved again. Everyone communicated well that week, and everyone got along. Khani had been working hard on expanding his vocal range, and was a better artist because of it: He departed from his usual comfort zone, the rapid-fire delivery of lyrics that stayed in the falsetto. Now he used his full range, both highs *and* lows. His songwriting had matured too, with more differentiation and complex arrangements. And he stayed true to his word by slowing down the groove and letting the "stoner vibe" permeate. This allowed space between the words and the music, and let the songs breathe. (These were *caesuras*, timely pauses, which Eddie Wilson always appreciated; and they made Khani's music infinitely better.)

Everything peaked when Khani and the band recorded the album's final song, "Video Game." As I sat behind the glass and listened to Khani sing his final vocals, I was living the vision I first had when I signed him. I was overcome with emotion and satisfaction that I *felt* his music—I was immersed. Regardless of any future record deal, I was looking at a reggae superstar, and I was proud to be a part of it. Soon all twelve of Khani's songs were placed in proper order, mastered, and packaged up. When he held up his completed record, *Ancient Spirits*, I believed Khani Jones was holding something that would last the test of time.

Chapter 23

Jack Kerouac's Attic, Your Decisions

"Lost for a reason?"

KHANI'S COMPLETED ALBUM helped me secure some prestigious gigs for him and his new band, such as headlining at B.B. King's in New York City, and opening up for *Toots and the Maytals* at the Stephen Talkhouse in Amagansett and Toad's Place in Hartford. There were also some radio appearances and prestigious songwriter showcases that Khani headlined without his band. All of these were great nights, and we were building a buzz. But as the manager, I was in that *same* familiar place, with great music but no way to get it distributed. We kept meeting promising people, but their suggestions typically required Kid Lightning to invest a lot of money in ways that didn't seem to promise a substantial return.

One insider suggested we record *another* album with a certain producer in Atlanta, but we were satisfied with Khani's album. A big reggae DJ in New York City offered to play fragments of Khani's songs for more than a fragment of our money. A guy named One Drop, the owner and primary DJ of a Caribbean radio station based in the Bronx, who was also a local hero that Khani grew up listening to, suggested we release Khani's album ourselves and provide him with a radio budget to advertise it. One Drop was convincing, offering a plan to get Khani known locally, which he said would catapult him globally. Khani and I thought this was our best option, so we decided to give it a shot. I paid him $8,000 over the phone with my credit card. Later that day I reasoned that with no retail stores carrying or supporting the record, we probably wouldn't sell more than a hundred CDs through this radio campaign. Our $8,000 would soon be gone, the radio station owner would soon request $8,000 more, and we would soon be out of money. I called One Drop in the morning and requested a refund, since the radio campaign hadn't started. He didn't want to give it to me. But since I had paid over the phone and hadn't yet signed the credit card forms, he *let* me out of the deal for an agreed-upon penalty of $500. It was a hasty decision and a frantic flip-flop, which symbolized my frustration and impulsivity. We were stymied again.

Then Jim Sampas called—his timing *always* impeccable. He was stymied too, and stressed out over the stalled Jack Kerouac project and the other two records that were also put on hold when Eisen and Pageant reneged on their funding promises. We met again at the Hartford Diner. Jim named some of the celebrities who had already accepted roles in the Jack Kerouac screenplay project: Songwriting legend Robert Hunter (who wrote the songs for the Grateful Dead with Jerry Garcia), beat poets Robert Creeley and Lawrence Ferlinghetti, and author Jim Carroll *(Basketball Diaries)*. The musical score was already being composed and recorded by the iconic jazz trio, Medeski Martin & Wood, and the illustrations would be done by famous cartoonist Richard Sala. It was an impressive list for me, especially Robert Hunter, who had also written songs for Bob Dylan! If I were an outsider, this A++ list would have been hard to believe, but Jim had already proved he could deliver the talent he promised.

After lining up those people, Jim had made promises to them, based on the financial commitments he had secured from Eisen and Pageant. But when the money stopped, *everything* stopped—and Jim was in a bad position. Many of the artists were awaiting payment, and Jim was fielding daily calls from managers and talent, asking where things stood, where the money was, and so on. Jim's reputation was in jeopardy—Eisen and Pageant, by reneging, had created a big mess for Jim. His frustrations reminded me of how I felt when I worked for Incubator Solutions, with big ideas but no financial resources to make an independent move—at the whim of two jerks who somehow knew how to raise money, and therefore had the power.

I asked Jim about the second stalled project, and its panache was also impressive: It was a music-only CD that featured a series of "lost songs," written by John Lennon and Paul McCartney, which the Beatles had never recorded! These songs had been cast aside by Lennon and McCartney and sold to lesser-known artists who had recorded them with lower budgets, hasty production, and less than stellar musicians. For these reasons, none of the songs had enjoyed much success—they were never given a real chance. Jim thought these *lost* songs could be resuscitated by a world-class band with tasteful production, and *found* by the commercial market. True to his usual knack for attracting big names, Jim had already secured agreements to front this world-class band by lead singer Kate Pierson of the B-52s, British rock legend Graham Parker, and Robin Zander of Cheap Trick. For the musicians behind them, Jim planned to use his usual heavy hitters, including Tony Levin, Dave Mattocks and Duke Levine. And he would produce the album, with "more honey than hammer," at Long View Farms. For this album, *The Lost Songs of Lennon & McCartney*, production had already started, and artists were calling Jim daily to request payments.

The third stalled project due to Eisen and Pageant's reneging, and the least commercially viable of the three, was a CD of original poetry, written and recited by iconic beat poet Lawrence Ferlinghetti. It was almost complete.

I asked Jim about Eisen and Pageant, who owned the record label that had started the projects but had later backed out. Jim said they had major label distribution through EMI Records and Navarre. This was an excellent distribution channel, as good as any, and included every record store in the United States and Canada! As soon as I heard this, I thought about my game of leverage—and Khani's album. According to Jim, Eisen and Pageant were good guys and friends of his. They had simply experienced some financial problems in their other areas of business, and had coolly decided that those were more pressing. They politely reneged on Jim, or at least put Jim and his projects on hold indefinitely. (They were in no rush, but Jim was frantic to fix this mess and save his reputation.) I felt they were treating Jim poorly, since he had brought such a rare find to the table in the lost Jack Kerouac screenplay, as well as the highly marketable *Lost Songs of Lennon & McCartney* project. These were Jim's two biggest chances—and possibly the only chances he would ever get—for large-scale success, and Eisen and Pageant, after first committing, had subsequently (and unemotionally) re-prioritized and backed out. And since things were already started, it would now be much more complicated for Jim to involve a new investor: Like a once-promising real estate project that had later been abandoned, Jim's projects were now perceived to have "hair," a real estate term which meant problems. The first thing a new investor would want to know is, "Why did the previous investors back out?" The projects were tarnished.

Now I understood the scope of Jim's three stalled projects and where each stood in production; my mind was racing with possibilities. I asked Jim if Eisen and Pageant were still willing to distribute the records through EMI and Navarre, if the rest of the funding came from elsewhere. He said yes, but it would be tricky: Credit would have to be assigned for past work; ownership percentages would have to be reassigned without Jim losing any of his promised 10%; and all money would have to flow through Eisen and Pageant, since their record label was set up with EMI & Navarre's major label distribution. I gave Jim a copy of the Khani Jones album to send to Eisen and Pageant. The leverage on my mind involved getting it released through their major label distribution channel as a contingent to Kid Lightning's financial involvement. Before we adjourned, Jim lent me a copy of the *lost* Jack Kerouac screenplay, one of only three copies that were made. I felt this demonstrated his trust in me. He also gave me a mixtape of the originally released (cheaper) recordings of the *lost* Lennon and McCartney songs, and a copy of the Ferlinghetti poems and readings.

When I got back to West 80th, I cozied up on my (pink) sofa to read the only screenplay that Jack Kerouac had ever written—lost since the 1960s. It felt cool to be one of the first few people to *ever* read it; (and I planned to *read* it, not skim it). I wanted to give Jack Kerouac a full chance to blow me away—I wanted to love it. But I fucking hated it! The plot made no sense to me, and every page was painstaking to get through. For me, it had zero resonance. I fought my way through about twenty pages and took my own *caesura* with a large bong hit—but even that couldn't get me interested. I laid the Kerouac screenplay down and took another hit, knowing I would never pick it up again.

Then I turned my attention to the lost songs of Lennon and McCartney. And I felt no enthusiasm for those either. They were nowhere close to Beatles-quality, as I had foolishly hoped. They reminded me instead of certain B-side songs from the 1950's, one-layered and with little imagination, that were often found on cheap record store compilations. And they weren't *lost* by Lennon and McCartney—they had been intentionally cast aside or sold by them. I joked to my dad that these *lost* songs and Kerouac's *lost* screenplay had been *lost* for a reason—because they sucked! The only thing I enjoyed that night, besides the two bong hits, was the Lawrence

Ferlinghetti poetry, which I knew carried the least sales potential of the three. I went to bed disheartened, my big ideas of leverage fading as I fell asleep.

I had tried hard to like the materials, but couldn't. So I planned to inform Jim that I was not interested in the projects. But over the next few days I mulled things over and considered that my distaste for the materials might be a sign, or even a test, for me to set aside my own artistic taste and act like a strict businessman, perhaps analogous to my dad's advice to "Focus, focus, focus, we'll save the world later!" The sales potential of the Jack Kerouac name and the Lennon and McCartney names was undeniable. Perhaps this was another test, of my humility—who was *I* to judge the work of such greats as Jack Kerouac, John Lennon, and Paul McCartney?

I contacted Jim and asked him about the *characters* of both Eisen and Pageant, whose integrity I questioned for reneging on their financial commitments to Jim. Jim said they were honest men who had run out of money, but they could explain things better than he. We set up a meeting at their office in New York City. The two men were amicable, although Eisen had noticeably bad breath and yellow teeth, and Pageant, with messy hair, was a *skinny-fat* person (someone with a thin frame, but also a beer belly, fat arms and a double-chin). This suggested to me that he might be a lazy person. Both were not embarrassed to admit that they had run out of disposable income, which they had originally planned to use for Jim's projects. They said they needed it to save the main part of their business, which involved acquiring the rights to old movies. I believed them and actually respected them for admitting this. Unlike me, they weren't afraid to deliver bad news, even if people would get upset. We discussed numbers for the three incomplete projects in detail, including how much money was required to complete each one, and the expected sales for each in worst-case, middle-case, and best-case scenarios. They also said they loved

Khani's album, and had extensive experience distributing reggae music.

Things were lining up for a possible three-way mega-deal, drenched in leverage, whereby Kid Lightning would be transformed from a management company into a record label and equity partner in these projects: I would take over 100% of the remaining funding obligations for the three stalled projects. I would hire Jim Sampas full-time and pay him a salary to complete the production of all three, making me the co-executive producer, and doing whatever it took to get everything packaged up and store-ready. Eisen estimated that the cash requirement to do this (not counting Jim's salary) was about $65,000. In return, Kid Lightning would receive the contractual promise to be paid back *before* previous expenses got recouped by Eisen and Pageant, or anyone else, plus a 45% equity percentage in each project. (Eisen and Pageant would also get 45%, and Jim would get 10%.) Finally, as a contingent to my financing, the Khani Jones album would be released through this same major label distribution channel, EMI and Navarre. And it would be promoted with their built-in marketing budget and guaranteed label support. This was the elusive *Holy Grail* which had been fueling my relentless schemes of leverage for more than two years!

And all calculations pointed to a big financial win: EMI and Navarre paid their record labels based on *albums shipped* to the record stores, not actual retail sales. The big names associated with Jim's projects ensured that initial shipment quantities would be large; and Kid Lightning was contractually guaranteed to be paid back first. Hence, our $65,000 cash investment plus Jim's salary would be recouped the day these albums hit the stores, *before* profits and losses were calculated—so we would break even on Day 1. Since we were also a 45% partner in the profits, under the worst-case scenarios painted by Eisen and Pageant, we would receive a guaranteed $155,000 in the first year. And if the albums had even moderate success, those numbers would double or triple.

It sounded great, and then it got better: Eisen and Pageant told me they had also partially funded two reggae compilation albums that featured major reggae superstars; and again they had to back out because they didn't have the money. They gave me copies of the albums, which were 90% complete. The producer of those compilations had done a great job, recording original tracks from reggae greats Ky-Mani Marley (Bob Marley's son), Sean Paul, Toots and the Maytals, and others. This reggae producer had initially approached Eisen and Pageant because they had promised funding *and* major label distribution, but could now only offer the distribution. Like the other three stalled projects, these two reggae compilations were also lying dormant, in danger of never getting released. And with each passing month, the music got older and less fresh.

Eisen and Pageant proposed that I partner on those too, even though it would be a break-even opportunity at best for Kid Lightning, given the smallness of the reggae industry. I was thinking about more leverage, so I contacted the reggae producer. I told him I would be willing to provide the funding to finish the two albums—less than $7,000 total—if my artist, Khani Jones, could have one song on each. This would put *more* Khani Jones music in every store across the U.S. and Canada, on the same record as a Who's Who list of bona fide reggae superstars. After hearing Khani's music, the producer agreed with me that the best song for the first compilation was "Video Game." The song for the second compilation would be an original recording made at his studio; Khani would sing original lyrics over the same track as the other reggae stars (a common reggae tradition). We made a tentative arrangement, contingent on the overall deal getting signed with Eisen and Pageant for the other records.

The total cash investment required for Kid Lightning was now up to $72,000, plus Jim's salary, which would leave us with enough money, albeit barely, to get us through 2002. The cash situation would be tight, but I still had some credit card space to live on. My credit card lines of credit were now up to $90,000, and I calculated I would need to use it all.

I knew Victor DeLeon would love this deal and support my decision to go forward with it. These were the "big revenues," the wild success I promised, which would allow him to forgive my accounting errors. He would see that Kid Lightning Enterprises, on a limited budget with a staff of two, had become a legitimate record label with six albums in the stores, major sales on the horizon, and a guaranteed return on his money—even under worst-case scenario sales projections. And our names would forever be associated with genuine legends of literature and music, including Jack Kerouac, John Lennon, Paul McCartney and Robert Hunter. Finally, Khani Jones, my friend and artist, whom DeLeon and his wife had become fond of, would be hooked up big-time! His completed album, *Ancient Spirits*, would be in every record store across the United States and Canada, with marketing support, and two other Khani Jones tracks would appear on star-studded reggae compilations—cementing his place among the icons of reggae.

(We adjourned the meeting, socialized for a few minutes, and agreed to talk in less than a week. Before leaving, I asked Pageant if I could use their office bathroom, which smelled like bad marijuana. As I walked in, I startled Eisen, who was at the urinal—he wheeled around and looked at me while pulling up his pants. I apologized and looked away, but it was too late: I saw the world's smallest penis. It was like a newborn baby's penis, just out of the womb, and I never forgot it.)

Later that day I discussed the proposed deal with my dad, who agreed with my logic. He thought, as I did, that this was Kid Lightning's best and perhaps only chance to get Khani's music into the record stores while also diversifying our portfolio. The reggae industry alone had proven too small, and this would be our exit from it, but not before I delivered the goods for Khani. My dad agreed that if I didn't make the move, Kid Lightning would spend the rest of our funds on various ill-advised marketing attempts, in a world full of sharks that we knew nothing about. His only concern was "control of the money," since all revenues would first be received by Eisen and Pageant, and then doled out to Kid Lightning and Jim Sampas. Relying on them for this disbursement worried my dad—he always viewed who controlled the money as a vital element in his analysis of any deal. I explained that there was no way around this logistically, and that I believed Jim Sampas that Eisen and Pageant were honest men. Furthermore, all product shipment quantities were publicly available through EMI and Navarre, so nothing could be fabricated or concealed. My dad was now on board. This gave me the comfort to proceed with negotiations, but I still needed Khani's approval for both legal and spiritual reasons.

I met with Khani and told him about this opportunity. He was excited about the chance to have major label distribution for his album, and the appearances on the prestigious reggae compilations—but he was concerned about the *characters* of Eisen and Pageant. He pointed out that we didn't know them well, and their integrity was already in question since they had backed out on their funding commitments to Jim Sampas. I tried to impart some of my dad's business knowledge to Khani, how insufficient cash flow can cause problems for *any* company, and that such problems can become another company's opportunity. I told Khani that Kid Lightning was *that company*—in the right place, at the right time. Then Khani pointed out that with Jack Kerouac and John Lennon, I was investing in "dead legends," not living men. I replied that these *dead legends* had guaranteed sales potential, whereas breaking out a new reggae artist usually did not. I was passive aggressively telling Khani that even though I believed in him and treated him like a star, he was still an unknown artist with no guaranteed sales. This deal would change that—it would put his music into the stores and give his career a chance to explode. We had to do it! But Khani was too wary of Eisen and Pageant to bless the deal.

I perceived this deal as a no-brainer, but still needed Khani's approval before I could pull the trigger. Each day he remained skeptical, I grew more frustrated, while Jim Sampas, Eisen and Pageant eagerly awaited my response. To help my lobbying efforts, I brought Khani to meet with me and Jim Sampas again. Jim looked us both in the eyes and promised, "I won't let you down," and that we could trust Eisen and Pageant—"They would *never* steal," he said, "They weren't those types of people." This helped my efforts, because Khani trusted Jim. But he was *still* not sold.

While I hadn't said this to Khani, I viewed this deal as my exit strategy from talent management. I had learned the same lesson over and again, that managing someone else left me frustrated—I needed to be the artist, not the manager. So regardless of whether we consummated the Jack Kerouac (and others) deal, I knew that when Khani's three year management contract would soon expire, I would not be requesting to renew it. I would have the closure I needed to bow out of the talent management world with a great success story, spawned by our gold Stars of David, and leading all the way to Khani's music being developed, recorded and sold everywhere. This deal would lead me elsewhere, to other adventures. I liked the idea of running a fully-funded and diversified record label, and a peace foundation, while also pursuing my own music—but I knew I would never manage an artist again. I think Khani sensed this, that this deal would change everything. Maybe he wasn't ready to bless *that.* As I pondered whether to go forward with the deal, even though I was 99% convinced it was the right thing to do—and I had my dad's blessing—it was still difficult to go against the counsel of my other henchman, Khani Jones. *He* had a keen sense of character too.

Your Decisions

**Lying in your bed tonight,
Do your echoes sentimentally fade?
I'll caress them with my softest devotion,
Lay my flowers on your memory's grave.**

**Chorus:
Ooh..ooh..ooh.
Ooh..ooh..ooh
Ooh..ooh..ooh
Your decisions…
It's too late for revision.**

**As you climb into the yellow sun.
Did you feel the heat that often invades?
Worrying about its textures sand swiftly.
As eyes toward newborn stars stay gazed?**

(Chorus)

**On foundations lay decisions you've strategized,
With grips to land weakening low.
If you catapult your body to mountains,
Are you landing dangerously low?**

(Chorus)

Chapter 24

Delusions of Grandeur

"Focus, Focus, Focus!"

After some of my best lobbying work, Khani provided his legal approval for the deal—but not his spiritual blessing—he didn't trust Eisen and Pageant. He advised me one last time to step away, showing a willingness to relinquish his own record deal to protect our joint interests. This was noble, and a perfect example of Khani's integrity and righteousness, but I had already given up trying to win his blessing—I just wanted to tell Eisen and Pageant that Kid Lightning was in. That's what I did. Assisted by the Deerman's legal representation, we reviewed and negotiated the contracts, which were both lengthy and complex, and signed everything. The deal was done! *The die was cast.*

Victor DeLeon, whom I had kept abreast of everything through weekly updates, was thrilled that the deal was signed: Khani Jones was on his way to stardom and Kid Lightning Enterprises was now a diversified record company with "big revenues" from six prestigious projects on the horizon. It would soon be time to step it up big-time: With the IRS extension now expiring, Deleon was ready to review our books and discuss Kid Lightning's next round of financing. I was planning to ask for $3 million, no longer worried about my faulty accounting practices and ill-advised withdrawal of $23,000—I now had the leverage of success I needed to come clean. But even though we were running on empty financially, I decided it would be better to have this big meeting with DeLeon *after* some of these projects physically hit the stores. His ability to walk into his local record store and purchase Khani Jones' album, or Jack Kerouac's lost screenplay, or Lennon and McCartney's lost songs—all donning Kid Lightning's logo—would speak louder than my promises of future big revenues, and hopefully louder than my disastrous accounting books.

To time this all properly, we applied for one last IRS extension. So until then, I would have to survive personally and feed the six projects with my large stack of personal credit cards and the paltry remaining balance of Kid Lightning's funds. <u>Big fuck-up #5:</u> I was now egregiously commingling all of my business and personal accounts. I was keeping records of all expenses and saving all receipts, but I no longer cared about how our books *looked*—they were too far gone and would be fixed in the future. Instead of worrying about cosmetic issues like spread sheets and tax returns, I expected DeLeon to praise my willingness to fund these Kid Lightning projects with my own credit cards, soon to be maxed to the tune of $90,000. Fueled by adrenaline and purpose, I was doing whatever it took, using all I could muster, to get these projects to market and into every record store across the United States and Canada. I was an irresistible force, and also a civilized hyena. My prey in sight was Victor DeLeon and the additional $3 million he would soon be investing in Kid Lightning Records.

Over the next year, with barely any space remaining on my credit cards and nothing in our bank account, Kid Lightning brought all six projects to the market. Jack Kerouac's lost screenplay, *Dr. Sax and the Great World Snake*, would soon hit book and record stores with solid quantities of units shipped—receiving good reviews from the critics, to my pleasant surprise, because I still hated it! This was followed by the *Lost Songs of Lennon and*

McCartney, also critically acclaimed. Soon after, the Lawrence Ferlinghetti poetry CD hit the stores, followed by Khani Jones' album, *Ancient Spirits*, and the two compilations of reggae superstars—with Khani Jones represented on each.

We had done our job, exactly as promised. I was proud of what we had accomplished—with a small amount of money in a short period of time. And I was now owed my first check from Eisen and Pageant, which I calculated, as expected, to be around $155,000. Based on the projects' good reviews and units expected to be shipped in the near future, this check would be the first of many like it. And looking at Kid Lightning's bright future, the *Fredda-ship* and I would be working together for years to come.

Delusions of Grandeur

**My friend went away,
Just the other day,
He didn't even call to say goodbye.
But I know he'll miss me,
He gonna call, you gonna see!
I'm the miracle in his eye...**

**Chorus:
Delusion, 'lusions, delusion
'lusions of grandeur...
Delusion 'lusions, delusion
'lusions of grandeur...
D-E-L-U-S-I-O-N-S...
I had a dream I was playing
this song in front of you.**

**My girl left me,
It's plain to see.
I sit on my couch and I cry.
For that poor little girl,
Alone in this world,
She wouldn't wait the time, to age my wine...**

(Chorus)

**My teachers told me.
You can't act so free.
You gotta come to class once in a while.
But don't they understand,
I yield to no man,
Their classes can't confine my shiny light.**

**So I went inside my head,
For a Piece of G-d's Bread.
The music came and I began to dine.
And sometimes in the night,
When I light my light,
They tell me I am fine, to just keep on...**

I would soon learn that when an irresistible force meets an immovable object, perhaps another civilized hyena, the result is total annihilation: I NEVER RECEIVED ONE PENNY FROM EISEN AND PAGEANT. (Even with that tiny, newborn-baby-like penis, they found a way to fuck me.) Eisen and Pageant applied Kid Lightning's revenues toward *their* old debt from *their* past failed projects—projects Kid Lightning had nothing to do with. (The karmic irony of this did not offer me any comfort.) Lawsuits would follow, but to no avail. Kid Lightning Enterprises would soon fall, weakened by horrific accounting, mortally wounded by Eisen and Pageant—my latest, gravest encounter with civilized hyenas. This time *I* was the prey.

The moment I ignored Khani's advice and signed the deal with Eisen and Pageant, Kid Lightning's fate was sealed—I had just entered the worst partnership of my life. But fresh off the execution of the contracts, the aforementioned *deluge* had not yet occurred. And with Jim Sampas handling most of the day-to-day work to get the Jack Kerouac and Lennon & McCartney projects completed and to market, I felt the justification and moral permission to take a breather from Kid Lightning and focus on bringing The Wave of Peace foundation from idea mode to execution mode. I had followed my dad's advice and "Focused, focused, focused!" on finding a record deal for Khani Jones, not "saving the world"—and it had led to so much more. I had re-earned the right to think spiritually, and "Focus, focus, focus" on *my* music and *my* foundation. Now I *could* save the world! Even my dad bought in.

Subj:	**Re: First ever?**
Date:	5/14/02 3:04:54 PM Eastern Daylight Time
From:	Lasram
To:	KLight

First ever to win both a Grammy and a Nobel?

That's my boy!!!!

The first Wave of Peace Meeting was attended by some quirky people, whom Fredda and I privately shared some laughs about. It felt strange to actually be discussing, "Bringing people together across so-called enemy lines" with *real* people, serious strangers who had answered our ad in the Village Voice. I was nervous and felt unqualified to lead a discussion in this area—it was much different than getting high in the privacy of West 80th and scribbling peace philosophies, or ranting to a video camera. It was comforting to have my sister by my side. Fredda treated everyone like gold, kept me organized, and gave me credibility. This helped me to relax. One meeting attendee, by her attire, looked homeless. She carried a burlap satchel full of neon-colored clipboards and gave one to each person. Another was a *Lubavitch* Orthodox Jew, a young guy who tried to sell me a coffee mug with a picture of Rabbi Schneerson, The Rebbe, who *Lubavitchers* claimed was the Messiah. (It reminded me of the time, about eight years earlier, when my dad and I were walking past the hospital where Rabbi Schneerson lay on his deathbed. We spontaneously decided to visit him, or at least get as close to his room as security would allow. We were shocked that we reached all the way to the door outside his room, and even saw his foot—but security stopped us there. The Rebbe passed away the next day. In honor of this memory, and The Rebbe, I bought the mug from the young *Lubavitcher*.)

At the second Wave of Peace meeting, I met an articulate and charismatic young Palestinian businessman named Abdel. He had "that gleam" in his eye, and when we discussed "coming together across so-called enemy lines," and creating wealth and success in the process, we were on the same page. With biblical thoughts on my mind, I was looking at my new "partner in peace"—and what better a duo than a Palestinian and a Jew! Abdel was interested in exploring this partnership too, and we decided to meet for lunch in the near future to brainstorm how we could work together and set a good example. I was excited for our upcoming *summit*, but I had to wait a few months, since Abdel was travelling to Egypt.

A few months later, at our private lunch, it would take me five minutes to learn that Abdel was *not* my partner in peace: While searching for common ground to open our discussion, I shared the emotions I had felt after the May 25th wedding hall collapse, and how wrong I had been to blame Islamic terrorism before knowing that a structural flaw in the building was the culprit—not a suicide bomber. I thought that by admitting my transgression of predisposition, it would demonstrate my openness to change. This was the way to cross "so-called enemy lines." But when it was Abdel's turn to do the same, he couldn't even agree that suicide bombing in Israel should be universally condemned. He said that suicide bombing was the only way the "oppressed Palestinians" could "fight the occupiers." I couldn't believe what I was hearing—my blood was boiling and I contemplated *Pulling a Vickers* right on the spot. Our lunch lasted ten minutes; we didn't even make it to the bread, and never spoke again. I was thrown by this incident, greatly saddened, and The Wave of Peace Foundation entered a long period of dormancy.

A few days after the second Wave of Peace meeting, (and still three months *before* my ill-fated lunch with Abdel), I remained blissfully ignorant of the pending demise of both Kid Lightning *and* The Wave of Peace. I needed to spend a week at the new Amagansett house, which the Deerman and I had recently purchased. My goal was to compile and have executed a punch-list of repairs to get the house ready for the upcoming Hamptons rental season. In addition to a profit-center, this house would be the spiritual home base for Kid Lightning and The Wave of Peace, which I had once envisioned for Gregory's house. My strategy was to introduce the Amagansett property and this concept to Victor DeLeon at our upcoming meeting, whose $3 million would help me buy out The Deerman and integrate the house into these grand plans. With my personal G-d symbol on the survey, and Kid Lightning's future so bright, I couldn't imagine DeLeon saying no to anything I suggested!

Ana was in Costa Rica, visiting her family, so I traveled to Amagansett alone. As I drove east, I took inventory of my life: My company, my foundation, and even my music were poised for greatness. And when I blasted *my* CD, *Right Back*, familiar thoughts returned: I was the artist, not the manager—I was Eddie Wilson!—but Joann Carlino was nowhere in sight. My mind drifted to Edna, *the unresolved*, as it still did too often. I hadn't heard from her in a year. I called her when I got to Amagansett, and she didn't pick up. I left a message, not expecting to hear back, just like I hadn't after my post-September 11 voicemails inquiring about her survival.

An hour later Edna returned my call, admitting that she found my panicky messages from a year ago "cute," and the *only* reasons she called now. She didn't ask about Ana—and I didn't offer any updates. We spoke for an hour about *my* music and *my* life. I was Eddie, she was Joann! Brimming with confidence and zero karmic concern, I invited Edna to Amagansett. She accepted my invitation. I arranged a car service to pick her up in Queens, and was soon notified that she was on her way. My heart was pounding, fueled by risk and intense stimulation—an irresistible force again. But I was about to experience the worst night of my life, which almost sent me to jail.

I escaped incarceration that night, but I would soon find myself riddled in debt that exceeded a few hundred thousand dollars, no investor, no Kid Lightning, no Wave of Peace, a soon-to-be-ex girlfriend who became Jewish for me that I was unstimulated by and unfaithful to, and thousands of copies of *Right Back* (the soundtrack for this book), gathering dust in my basement. It was the lowest I had ever felt, by far. But I wasn't done. Things would get much lower, and much higher. That's how I *got started.*

Discipline is Beautiful

"Focus, Focus, Focus."

IT HAS TAKEN ME many years to acquire the discipline to refrain from smoking marijuana on any given day, or at least until 5:10 p.m. on the days I partake. Once I did, I finished writing this book, in addition to drafting the two sequels, *Why Only High? (Civilized Hyenas)* and *Discipline is Beautiful (The Band of Natural Selection).*

My dad's friend Finn once said to me, "The most valuable investment you can put into anything is your time." I agree, and I thank you for your time. I also thank my dad.

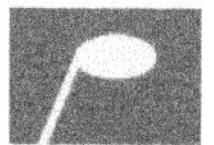

Left the village,
the truth freed me,
and circled right back.
From natural selection,
felt great times great,
but why only high?
Discipline.
Is.
Beautiful.

...if she would exist.

www.ingramcontent.com/pod-product-compliance
Ingram Content Group UK Ltd.
Pitfield, Milton Keynes, MK11 3LW, UK
UKHW020145250726
13967UKWH00002B/877